DALIT MIDDLE CLASS

DALIT MIDDLE CLASS

Mobility, Identity and Politics of Caste

Gurram Srinivas

RAWAT PUBLICATIONS

Jaipur • New Delhi • Bangalore • Guwahati • Kolkata

ISBN 978-81-316-0688-9

Published by
Prem Rawat for **Rawat Publications**
Satyam Apts, Sector 3, Jawahar Nagar, Jaipur 302 004 (India)
Phone: 0141 265 1748 / 7006 Fax: 0141 265 1748
E-mail: info@rawatbooks.com
Website: www.rawatbooks.com

New Delhi Office
4858/24, Ansari Road, Daryaganj, New Delhi 110 002
Phone: 011 2326 3290

Also at *Bangalore, Guwahati* and *Kolkata*

Typeset by Rawat Computers, Jaipur
Printed at Chaman Enterprises, New Delhi

Contents

Acknowledgements

This book has benefited from comments and suggestions of many friends and colleagues at the Centre for the Study of Social Systems, JNU. Prof. Surinder Singh Jodhka offered suggestions on many drafts of this work. I have immensely benefited from the comments of Prof. Nandu Ram in preparation of the manuscript. Prof. Vivek Kumar constantly encouraged me to publish this work.

I place on record my gratitude and thanks to Dr K.J. Vijayatilakam, Dr V. Janardhan, Prof. Sasheej Hegde of University of Hyderabad for guidance, encouragement and kind help at various stages of collection of empirical data this work is based on.

My friends Ramesh Bairy (IIT, Mumbai), Tarakeshwar (EFLU, Hyderabad), Sudarshan (CUG, Gandhinagar), Satyanarayana (EFLU, Hyderabad) and Narsaiah (JNU) offered assistance at various times.

My gratitude lies towards my parents for their constant encouragement to complete this work. My wife Parvathi (CUG, Gandhinagar) played a crucial role in refining the arguments and analysis.

Preface

This book on Dalit Middle Class is a result of my doctoral work carried out during 1999-2004. It primarily concerns itself with providing empirical evidence to the emergent ideological trends and patterns of identities among the middle class Dalits in India, specifically in Hyderabad city. By focusing on the emergence, growth and consolidation of Dalit middle class in the city of Hyderabad, this body of work, attempts to understand the trends and patterns in ideology and identity among the Dalit middle class.

The identity consciousness long ignited among the Dalits has enabled them to utilize all opportunities to overcome their 'untouchable', 'marginalized' and deprived status towards assertion of contemporary Dalit identity and also paved way for the formation of a notable middle class with community consciousness among them. Dalit middle class is perceived as new and distinct from the general middle class in India not merely due to its distinctive origin, formation process, composition but its ethnocentric identity and ideology. Emergence of this class is mainly attributed to the post-independence period. The reservation policy plays a prominent role in directing and sustaining the contemporary Dalit movement, defining and redefining Dalit identity and formulating and reformulating Dalit ideology.

In the backdrop of changing socio-economic and political milieu, internationalization of Dalit movement and irreversible impacts of globalization on Indian society, it is important to closely examine the socio-economic background, lifestyle and world view (including interpersonal relationships, work life, neighbourhood, etc.) of middle class Dalits. In a changing context of Dalit assertion and the caste-Hindu opposition to Dalit mobility, it is essential to understand the rapid changes occurring not only in their economic status, but also in their own perceptions of their socio-political status, especially by focusing on their ideology and identity. This would help us in understanding the socio-economic, political changes and the mobility process the Dalits are undergoing in the last two centuries, which also enables us to understand the general process of social change in India.

The book is organized into six chapters, of which three chapters deal with empirical data and analysis thereof. The first chapter is a general introduction to the book. The second chapter discusses the theoretical framework and review of literature. The third chapter profiles the middle class Dalits included in the study; the fourth chapter focuses on identity and ideology of the Dalit middle class; fifth chapter deals with few case histories of middle class Dalits. Finally, the sixth chapter outlines the sociology of Dalit middle class.

CHAPTER 1

Introduction

The growing social awareness and assertion of identity among Dalits is a result of the process of social change, certain historical developments and various attempts by the Dalits themselves to overcome their 'untouchable', 'marginalized' and deprived status and instead acquire a contemporary Dalit identity[1] The various factors that contributed towards this transformation include the religious movements during the Bhakti period, the social reform movements in the nineteenth and twentieth centuries, the anti-caste movements led by Jyotiba Phule and Periyar, the Dalit movement initiated by Dr B.R. Ambedkar and, in the post-independence period, a number of Dalit movements in various states asserting Dalit ideology and identity.[2]

In the last 200 years, Dalits have availed the limited opportunity within their reach and tried to rise from the subjugation, marginalization and various other exclusions imposed upon them by the Hindu caste system. This modern awakening began with the utilization of the nominal representative provisions under the British rule and the various constitutional safeguards made available to them later in the post-independence period. Since then, resisting the increasing opposition to their social mobility and the growing number of atrocities being committed upon them by the 'upper castes', the Dalits have come together as a distinctive group with a collective identity.[3]

The social consciousness engendered by various forces and factors such as the Dalit movements, government welfare programmes, modern education and contact with wider society has resulted in rising aspirations among the Dalits. In their quest to realize their rights, the Dalits now participate in almost all the important spheres of national life. The last few generations of the Dalits have been consciously nurturing democratic values and a secular outlook, those in turn have accorded them a distinct identity – the Dalit identity.[4] Since then, the Dalits have been incessantly taking to modern education, as it is a means of attaining increased economic and social status.

Dalits today are not mere 'passive participants' – they now have a systematic programme. Their aspirations for social, economic and political equality have led them to adopt various strategies and the means necessary for their realization. They have not restricted themselves merely to government jobs; they have also entered various other occupations and professions as well and achieved a considerable level of success and improvement in their socio-economic status. They are also nurturing aspirations equal to that of caste-Hindus in educational, occupational, political and cultural fields. Their entry into the modern occupations, especially in the post-independence period, was unsuccessful compared to the caste-Hindus.

SOCIAL STRATIFICATION AND MOBILITY IN INDIA

According to Aiyappan (1965: 37), the term 'untouchability' denotes 'the socio-religious practice by which the Hindus keep a large number of lower castes from touching or coming near persons, houses, temples, tanks and sometimes even public roads'. About the theories regarding the origin of 'untouchables', Mukherjee (1988: 12–13) states that 'there are a number of hypotheses explaining how it had come into existence'. The first one and most popular is that of the Tribal origin, which is supported by Oppert, Fick, Bose and Sharma and by Ambedkar who called them 'broken men'. The second one says untouchables originated from the family and village slaves.[5] The third hypothesis is of *Varna Sankara* theory based on *anuloma* and *pratiloma* marriages.

Throughout the Indian caste history, those social groups who controlled economic resources and wielded political power became the privileged upper castes while others were treated as social outcastes. Without access to the ritual and economic resources and bargaining power, the Dalits became the most exploited peripheral groups in the Indian society.[6] According to Ghurye (1969: 180), the idea of untouchability and 'unapproachability' arose out of the ideas of ceremonial purity, first applied to the aboriginal Shudras in connection with the sacrificial ritual, and then expanded to other groups because of the theoretical impurity of certain occupations. Further, Gokhale (1993: 17) observes 'the domination of *varna* ideology applies both to caste and class relationships'. As Ambedkar observes:

> The outcaste is a by-product of the caste-system. There will be outcastes as there are castes. Nothing can emancipate the outcaste except the destruction of the caste-system. Nothing can help to save Hindus and ensure their survival in the coming struggle except the purging of this odious and vicious dogma. (as cited in Nagaraj, 1993: 12)

The earlier nomenclatures of Dalits, namely, *Untouchables, Outcastes, Panchamas, Atishudras, Avarnas, Antyajas, Namasudras, Pariahs* – as *un-seeables* and *un-approachables* – were in use during different phases of Indian history and in different parts of the country.[7] As an effect of being made *untouchable,* Dalits have suffered socio-cultural, economic and political sanctions imposed upon them by the caste system. It was during the British period, the first concerted efforts by state to end their apathy had begun. The British used the terms *Depressed Classes* and *Exterior Class* to notify Dalits, meaning they were kept away from the Hindu Society (Singh, 1987: 2).

Gandhi preferred to call them *Harijans,* which he borrowed from a Gujarati Brahmin, Narasinh Mehta.[8] Many leaders of these caste groups, including Ambedkar, had objections against calling them *Harijans* because they found it derogatory and insulting to be called fatherless. Ambedkar demanded a change of nomenclature at the first Round Table Conference in London. He proposed referring to them as 'protestant Hindus' or 'non-conformist Hindus'. However, it was the term 'Scheduled Castes' (coined by the Simon Commission in the year of 1935) that was officially recognized by both pre- and post-Independence states. Until recently, the term 'Harijan' was also widely employed in common usage.

Traditionally, the caste system was non-competitive in its character,[9] which meant that each caste had its own occupation, and distinct lifestyle and none of them were allowed to trespass into the other's arena. However, some degree of social mobility was allowed for the non-Dalit castes, it was virtually impossible for the ex-untouchables to move up in the caste hierarchy.[10] Values of caste hierarchy, purity, pollution and untouchability segregated the Dalits in all spheres of life, with respect to physical touch or social contact with others for centuries together.[11] However, as observed by many scholars,[12] in the recent past, there has been a shift from ritual status to secular status in patterns of social stratification at most levels in the Indian society. At present, different castes aim at the same goals such as education, employment and various kinds of mobility, including occupational and socio-economic status. Consequently, individuals belonging to different castes compete for similar kinds of positions.[13] Many studies dealing with mobility among the Scheduled Castes suggest that the Dalits today are a changed lot.[14] Their ritual status in the caste hierarchy does not bind them any more to their traditional occupations.

SOCIAL MOBILITY: THEORIES AND PERSPECTIVES

Pimpley (1990) opines that the movements (c. nineteenth century) aimed at the 'improvement of the "untouchables" did not succeed and would not have succeeded' because they were directed towards changing the 'superstructure' of the caste system (the bundle of attitudes and beliefs), instead of correcting the system, with the appropriate cognitive restructuring of caste. He observes:

> The practice of untouchability and the various disabilities imposed upon many castes has an economic function ... No reform movement till date has attempted to link cognitive restructuring with economic restructuring. (Pimpley, 1990: 161)

The struggle against the caste system goes back to the Buddha. Muslim culture gave rise to Bhakti movement, which preached egalitarianism and rejected the caste system and the practice of untouchability. British rule gave rise to social reform movements (Pimpley, 1990: 162). The doing away with untouchability and the social disabilities of the untouchables in the recent past sprang up because of the contact with British liberalism. The hold of ritualism lessened with these movements to some extent and the latter were successful in that they created some level of sensitization in the case of untouchability. However, Hinduism again lapsed into ritualism and exclusiveness after some time. With the entry of the British in the eighteenth century, Hinduism once again woke up to resist the British stronghold and Christian expansionism. He feels:

> This was a threat to the Hindu elite as the latter's status position could only be maintained vis-à-vis the lower castes. And if the lower castes and untouchables get out of Hindu social system, elite can no longer be elite; their position would further slide down the ladder of the social system. (Pimpley, 1990: 162)

Again, the artisan castes among the untouchables such as carpenters (*Barahi*) and Blacksmith (*Lohars*) have raised their material position vis-à-vis the same upper castes because of the new technology. The untouchables rose from the lower caste status creating dissonance and inconsistency in social relations. He explains further:

> As a result of these changes, the Hindu elite to retain its position at the apex was forced to widen its base and recreate a myth on equal footing. The socio-religious reform movements of the 18th and 19th century were probably a consequence of this struggle for power between the British and the Hindu elite. (Pimpley, 1990: 162)

The programmes of the *Brahmo Samaj* such as the congregational form of worship, the *Prithi Bhojans* and inter-caste marriages, though not successful, were far ahead of the times. The general criticism against *Brahmo Samaj* was the acceptance of European culture. The caste-Hindus did not accept social reforms as they were too daring an act for those times. Similarly, *Arya Samaj* took up *shuddhi* – reconverting those who converted to Christianity back into Hinduism and purifying the lower castes by offering them *dvija* status within the Hindu social system as the main programme.[15] The *Arya Samaj* opened schools and colleges for the education of outcastes, mainly providing technical know-how to complement their traditional occupations such as weaving, tailoring and carpentry according to their traditional occupations. However, the *Arya Samaj* mainly concentrated on the artisan castes rather than on untouchables. Hence, it could provide neither a better social status nor educational facilities and thereby better occupational status to the untouchables.

Since most of these movements were initiated by the educated high caste-Hindus, they were not expected to disrupt their own power positions within the caste system. Therefore, none seemed to really attack the legitimized 'ascriptive hierarchy' of the Indian caste system. Among the many precepts, untouchability was one, which remained in the background as liberal education and addressing of the social evils within the upper castes were driven to the foreground and manifested as a problem. Most reforms failed to touch the core of the problem of untouchability and address the social oppression of the outcastes, which was perpetuated under the guise of the religious sanctions of untouchability, and continues even today in the Hindu society.[16]

The concern for the outcastes was more nominal than real (Pimpley, 1990: 165–166). He further observes:

> The main contribution of the missionaries lies in their indirect contribution in spurring up socio-religious reform, and reforms in the field of education. For them both conversions and spread of education were means to political power and the continuance of untouchability helped them to broaden their base for such a claim. It seems to me that there was a struggle for power between the higher Hindu castes and the British. Socio-religious reform movements and the Christian missionary conversions were means through which they tried to establish their supremacy. (Pimpley, 1990: 166)

While advocating the importance of education to the Scheduled Castes in achieving social mobility, Vishwanathan and Reddy (1985) state that 'historically speaking, they (Scheduled Castes) have not monopolized any economically profitable and socially valued skills' and suggest that they utilize education as the means to economic independence, through entry into modern profit-making occupations.

DALITS AND SOCIAL STRATIFICATION IN INDIA

The various disadvantages faced by the Dalits in the caste system and the various social mobility options that were available to them have led to the generation of many ideologies against inequality in the caste system and identity processes of Dalits. The process of social mobility has been an opportunity for the Dalits in reinterpreting their past as well as visualizing a future with self-respect and dignity as the main components. The various attempts at understanding the past had democratic and egalitarian goals as the axis.

Nagaraj opines, 'The caste system in India is not only a structure of cultural values, but also a certain pattern of inequitable distribution of power and wealth of different kinds along the lines of caste hierarchy' (1993: 6). Similarly, Pimpley argues that the inequalities within the caste system are not merely religiously ordained, but are a consequence of the unequal distribution of power and privileges in the society. Accordingly, higher castes have a monopoly over scarce goods or have relatively greater access to power and privileges (Pimpley, 1990: 167).

Raj (1998: xv) argues that the opposition to globalization is manifold, asserting peoples' right over economic and political systems, safeguarding of local cultural identity, self-assertion of indigenous and marginalized people and various environmental, Dalit, Women and Peasant movements, etc. He observes that the Dalit community, despite having been 'subjugated' for 3,000 years, continues to be distinct and vibrant to pose challenges to the forces of globalization and 'objugation' (objectivity and subjugation).[17]

In the context of Dalit identity formation, Raj (1998) also lists out the following identities to be found in an individual in multiple degrees at different points of time:

> (1) personal/emotional identity, (2) gender identity, (3) religious-cultural-spiritual identity, (4) primary group identity, (5) community identity, (6) institutional identity, (7) social identity, (8) knowledge identity, (9) skills identity, (10) professional or occupational identity and (11) physical identity.

Khare (1984: x) proposes that the 'untouchable' possesses a distinct ideology, identity and pragmatism from the 'Hindu'. He states that the untouchable discovers a ground from which to consolidate his positive self-definition. A positive cultural ideology and identity are always very precious gains for the socially deprived. The more pronounced the deprivation, the more socially sensitive, coveted and contested are these gains generally. Above all, for identifying the untouchable's ideological categories, it is crucial that a distinction be maintained between 'the Hindu' and the earlier 'pre-Hindu' roots of civilization. Throughout the history of the caste system, the various attempts made by the untouchables to regain a respectable social position for themselves in the society, both through submission and opposition, have made them more rebellious and have made the caste-Hindus more aggressive towards the untouchables.

The urban Chamar reformers, leaders and ordinary persons as studied by Khare (1984) articulate their distinctive cultural perspectives, as well as a serious awareness of their changing role in the Indian society. The knowledge passed on by the ancestors and their own day-to-day experiences guides them to formulate their opinions about the society. The untouchable is expressing himself through a distinctive culture, which negates the Hindu order, in order to claim spiritual as well as material equality.

Khare (1984: 143–144) sums up the following four strands taking place in Dalit asceticism:

1. *Ideologically explicate* rests on a transcendent, ultimate order of Indic equality and justice, aiming at absolute spiritual equality and gathers support from spiritual ascetics and heroes to reform the social. This is to demonstrate the superiority of spiritual over worldly morality.
2. The prospect of social reform, often slow and sporadically inspired. It is marked by the *ascetic's and the hero's efforts to reform.*
3. Shaped by the changing politico-economic character of the Indian society during this century, *organized political protests and their culmination in a pragmatic pursuit of legal and economic claims* (and its contests). Ambedkar is obviously the fountainhead.
4. In the context of a decline in cultural innovation and a rise in the free play of pragmatic evaluations and accountabilities. The *claims of moral, legal, and economic equality start a pervasive*

politics for equal social rights. The fourth strand represents a step toward the routinization of the politics of social equality.

Khare, visualizing these four strands as woven together – 'in different patterns and under different regional lights' – asserts that there emerges 'a thumbnail sketch of what engages the Untouchable's mind'. For Khare, the 'untouchable ascetic' is 'partly resigned, partly protesting, partly rhetorical, but largely politicized'. Further, 'the Untouchable, as a true civilizational member, continuously totalizes the ideal and the practical to conform to a non-dichotomous view of knowledge and reality' (1984: 143).

K.N. Sharma (1986: 172) observes that the system of 'protective discrimination' has granted free education facilities and reservation of a certain percentage of jobs in various government organizations and public undertakings to the Scheduled Castes and the Scheduled Tribes. It appears that the assumption behind this policy is that, through free education and job reservation, their social mobility in the class system may be enhanced. Thus, either caste status would become irrelevant for their life chances and social intercourse, or through an improvement in their class status, a change in caste status would also be achieved. By and large, the members of the Scheduled Castes are rejecting birth as the criterion of social status in general and caste status in particular. A process of de-structuration has begun. Referring to Ram's study, he observes that 82.9 per cent of respondents acquired middle-class status, while 7.5 per cent of respondents reached an upper-class status based on objective criteria.[18] In addition, their perception is more or less on the same lines, that is, 77 per cent and 5.5 per cent respectively. Sharma further elaborates:

> In terms of the evaluation of their caste status, he accepted the interactional approach, because ... the status of a person based on his birth is possible only at the 'theoretical' level. But in reality (empirical situation) change in the status of a person is possible in the caste system though such a change may not completely alter his status based on his birth in a particular caste. (Sharma, 1986: 182)

Then he continues

> Although a vast majority of Indians and probably many Scheduled Castes insist on birth as the sole criterion of caste

> status, and the attributional theory also asserts it, the growing number of educated castes do not seem to accept this theory. They have acquired education and better jobs, as a result of which they have improved their class status as well as interaction with higher castes. They, therefore, perceive a change in the caste status at the individual level without bothering about the corporate rank of their caste. As has been stated earlier, this is a process which is the reverse of the process which led to a replacement of the varna system based on dharma, karma and guna by the jati system based on birth. (Sharma, 1986: 182)

For, it is through an improvement in class status that the Scheduled Castes are succeeding in acquiring the desired social status. Moreover, the reverse is occurring in three stages: (1) birth as the sole criterion, (2) a section of SCs rejects birth as a criterion for social status and insists on education, employment, and interaction as criteria for caste status. At this stage there is a divergence between the theory and practice and (3) rejection of birth totally, where divergence is removed (K.N. Sharma, 1986: 108).

Social mobility is mainly intergenerational occupational mobility, which involves movement of individuals or groups in the society in a particular direction. In any given society, persons and groups are never stable in the same position forever, but engage in some or the other sort of movement or undergo mobility, in their economic and social status.[19]

Roy and Singh (1987) observe that in a society like ours where inequitable distribution of resources follows more or less the hierarchical order of the caste system, even acquired attributes (elite position) are monopolized by a section of society, which is already placed high on ascribed statuses. Prasad (1970: i) describes that 'social mobility':

> Is usually taken for flow of people, events, and ideas. It, therefore, refers to two important social phenomena: movement and change. 'Movement' is the transition between lower and higher positions ('vertical mobility') and one group to another group at same level ('horizontal mobility'). Change is the extent of invention and innovation, which takes place in the institutions, ideas and cultural forms of a society. Mobility in the caste system was possible through individual movement

(mostly downward mobility) and mobility through entire caste changing its status (into equal plane due to essential/necessary circumstances).

The mobility of individuals and castes in the Indian society is not a new phenomenon. The mobility of intermediary castes, *per se*, from one occupation to another occupation and taking on the name of another caste was permitted in the past. M.N. Srinivas named this process as 'Sanskritization'.[20] Upward mobility of the lowest castes or 'outcastes' was tabooed in the traditional caste order, with several restrictions imposed to curtail changes in their occupations and lifestyles. There were no changes in the positions of the two polars – the topmost and the bottom one in the caste hierarchy. The Dalits located at the bottom of the hierarchy could not raise their social status until the caste system was attacked from outside by the British and modern social reformers. Under the British rule, Dalits were employed in secular jobs and, for the first time, were brought into continuous contact with caste-Hindus. The social reformers mainly tried to educate the Dalits and instil 'awareness' among them, in addition to attacking the caste hierarchy.

The process and the fruits of modernization were initially not accessible to all castes. Even among caste-Hindus, the degree of mobility, to a great extent, depended on their location in the caste hierarchy. Those who enjoyed a better social and economic status traditionally, by virtue of their caste, moved up more easily than those who were placed 'below' them in the caste hierarchy. In all, the process of modernization largely reflected the traditional status system rather than any other criteria. In a way, the modern social order is superimposed on the traditional social order. Caste plays a significant role in one's access to education, particularly with regard to one's attitudes, consciousness and participation in social relations.

Roy and Singh (1987: 125) observe that the impact of modernization created spaces for the Scheduled Castes to become elites. The world view acquired from the British period transformed their 'status of passive subjects to active citizens', and it sets up a new goal to be achieved, that is, 'equality democratically'. Raj (1998: xiv) suggests that the awareness and assertion among the Dalits and their consequent transformative struggle continues to make a fundamental difference to the caste based, hierarchically divided society of India. He further adds that the awareness 'converts itself' into the act of community and then on to rebellion, to shake the very foundations of the system.

UNDERSTANDING DYNAMICS AND PROCESSES OF SOCIAL MOBILITY IN INDIA

Under the British rule, though the Dalits were to some extent encouraged in the fields of education and employment, their socio-economic development was systematized only after India's Independence in 1947. Reservations were provided to Dalits according to their proportion in the population (15%) in education and employment under Articles 15 and 16 of the Indian Constitution. They were also provided with reservation of seats in state and central legislatures under Articles 332 and 334 of the Constitution of India. Further, Article 17 abolished untouchability in any form and declared its practice an offence. The policy of 'protective discrimination' thus chosen by the Indian government provides developmental measures for Scheduled Castes and Tribes. They are broadly classified by Nandu Ram (1988: 8) as: (1) protective measures such as prohibition of discrimination, of forced labour, and of untouchability; (2) welfare measures, guaranteeing representation in various categories of public services, in state assemblies and in parliament and (3) developmental measures providing grants-in-aid and other facilities for social and economic development.[21]

Various developments and social justice policies initiated by the British, and continued by the independent Indian government, helped the Dalits to become upwardly mobile/move up in the economic and political ladder, but at the same time, led to increased instances of atrocities being committed upon them. Consequent to their economic development and social mobility, Dalits had to face many threats, atrocities and massacres.[22] Wherever Dalits asserted their rights and fought for equality, they faced social boycotts, forestalling of social interaction, denial of work and other threats. These kinds of repressive activities, singling out the Dalits, are in response to the increasing socio-political organization of Dalits in cities as well as in rural areas. The caste-Hindu response to Dalit socio-economic development and mobility is very aggressive and violent most of the time. Often, it demonstrates weakness and fear of caste-Hindus of losing their privileges, especially with regard to economic development; Dalits try to gain social respect and equality on an equal footing with others. Consequently, the 'upper' castes not only lose free labourers, but also feel hurt and 'reduced' vis-à-vis Dalits. Often caste-Hindus who grew anxious that these hitherto inarticulate and politically subordinated sections were posing a threat to them economically and politically; resorted to atrocities and massacres on Dalits (Chunduru, Karamchedu, Vempenta, etc. are examples from Andhra Pradesh). Incidents like these have been occurring all over the country, though the oppressors hail either from middle castes (land owning) or upper castes. This variation rather depends on the geographical area and the castes affected by the Dalits' economic and social mobility.

However, though the rising aspirations of Dalits somctimes result in social conflict and atrocities being perpetuated upon them, without such aspirations nonetheless Dalits cannot climb the socio-economic ladder. They have always remained backward in all walks of life for no fault of theirs. In spite of the many protective and development measures in their favour, all the spheres of modern life are under caste-Hindu control; nevertheless, the Dalits have to take part in all these spheres of the smooth functioning of the nation.

Now Dalits have entered new occupations to which they did not have access earlier, occupations and new arenas such as entrepreneurship, sales, business, contracts, medicine, law, engineering and government jobs. However, such mobility has not been without its problems. They have had to face many obstacles in the form of social conflict, resistance from the upper castes, non-implementation of reservation in employment, in promotions, continued caste discrimination in their workplace, residential area and so on. In the face of these socio-economic disabilities, their numerical strength, better economic opportunities, urban contact, better communication, better exposure to mass media, assistance from external leadership and increased participation in political processes have helped them in the process of development by way of greater resources to engage in political action.[23]

Accordingly, the trajectory of Dalit consciousness suggests that Dalits have come a long way in inventing, rediscovering, defining, redefining, shaping and sustaining an ideology that is emancipatory in nature. The process that has shaped this ideology would be examined later in this book.

As we have noted earlier, the questioning of caste and its hierarchical system from the very bottom and fighting against its various inequalities and injustices existed in the pre-independence period too, but these attempts were within religious contexts and the value framework of the Great Tradition of Hinduism. None of them had any meaningful impact on the political system. Hence, those attempts did not bring about any structural changes (Singh, 1986: 193). Yogendra Singh further observes:

> The rapidity in the emergence of new social aspirations of people is such that it could not wait for development of appropriate institutional-mechanisms as it did in the West. In India, traditional institutions like caste, ethnic and linguistic groups, therefore, offer natural arenas for articulations of new values and aspirations and spheres of activities. (Singh, 1986: 169)

In contemporary times, the situation of caste has undergone few external changes. Caste as a socio-religious system, concerning mainly with caste endogamy and clan exogamy, combining hypergamy and hierarchy, has become visibly weak. It has now *turned into a politico-economic formation*. It has thus acquired those dimensions that were traditionally considered outside its scope. Ritual power is substituted with economic and political power, organic and segmentary relations, the closed and open nature of the caste system and its cultural and structural aspects not only imply one-sidedness of these devices, but they also undervalue caste as a dynamic and resilient formation (Singh, 1986: 171–173). This transition or development has been due to the various forces and factors discussed below.

The constitutional provisions of equal rights and concessions and reservations to the unprivileged sections of society give them heightened confidence in articulating, estimating and questioning the injustices meted out to them, while, at the same time, a reverse trend began to manifest itself. M.N. Srinivas (1989: 20) and

Ghanshyam Shah (2002a: 399) observe that there is a keen competition among castes for backward status in order to gain protective discrimination. The articulations opposing the notion of *Sanskritization*[24] are *Backwardization* and Dalitization.[25] The process of *Backwardization* can be seen among traditional middle castes or present 'dominant' castes, which are economically well off, land owning and politically dominant. Their political domination helps them in getting into the backward classes, for example, Vokkaliga and Lingayat of Karnataka, and Kamma and Kapu of Andhra Pradesh.

Similarly, the process of *Dalitization* as opined by Raj (1998: xv) challenges the status attached to caste. Being at the bottom of the caste system, Dalits negate both hierarchy and the process of *Sanskritization* by not being Sanskritized and thus not being assimilated into the Hindu society, opting instead for alternative cultures, along with the exhibition of an interest in their cultural past. *Dalitization* thus involves taking pride in and upholding their own traditional cultural past and highlighting it as an alternative to the dominant Hindu lifestyle and culture. Sachidananda (1974: 282) observes that 'nowadays the Scheduled Castes are turning more and more to the alternative symbols of prestige and values, which the modern secular order provides rather than to Sanskritization'.[26] To this extent, Dalit ideology and identity differ from Sanskritization, in that they are anti-Sanskritized and secular in nature. Both the processes of *Dalitization* and *Backwardization* are political in origin and aim at economic benefits.

Social change in India facilitated social and economic mobility among the large sections of society including the Dalits. The emergence of and access to new 'secular' occupations and policies of protective discrimination helped some Dalits gain in terms of social and economic status. This development also reflects a general shift from the caste-based social stratification to the one based on class in the Indian society. The emerging social structure, in a sense, is independent of the caste system. The new occupational structure stresses more on values of achievement and much less on those of ascription.

DALIT IDENTITY

Evaluating the various facets of the Dalit identity, Kananaikil (1993: 401) observes that the Indian society has witnessed the 'emergence of a new consciousness and a new identity among the "untouchables" in the last two hundred years'. 'Today the Dalits – the new name they have coined for themselves – demand aggressively their share in the shaping of the destiny of the nation'. Further, he observes, 'The term Dalit is no more another name for "untouchables". It connotes dignity, pride and self-identity of a people'.[27] Similarly, K.L. Sharma, delineating on the implications of Dalit identity, observes:

> The notion of Dalit is not the same as those of 'Harijan' and 'Scheduled Castes'. The terms 'Harijan' and 'Scheduled Castes' connote 'socio-cultural' and 'legal' meanings, respectively. The word 'Dalit' symbolises 'knowledge' and 'power' of the oppressed people, particularly belonging to the untouchable caste/communities. It refers to the genesis and expression of their consciousness. 'Identity' of the 'oppressed people' is central to the term 'dalit'. Thus, the emergence of the identity of the dalit has created a new social language, a language of protest and struggle, of deconstruction and reconstruction of meanings of social situations, contexts and status parameters. It is an 'oppositional' side in creation of new cognitive structures. (2001: 98)

Webster (1999: 68) traces the origin of the term Dalit historically and argues, 'Dalit (meaning "oppressed" or "broken") is not a new word. Apparently, it was used in the 1930s as a Hindi and Marathi translation of the "Depressed Classes", the term used by the British for what are now called the Scheduled Castes'. The term 'Dalit' is a politically loaded term. Zelliot (1992: 267) explicates Dalits as 'those who have been broken, ground down by those above them in a deliberate and active way. There is in the word itself an inherent denial of pollution, Karma and justified caste hierarchy'.

Providing an alternative perspective to the conscious, programmatic approach of the term Dalit as defined by others, K.L. Sharma (2001: 100) opines:

> The notion of 'dalit' is a new arrival; it is an ad hoc concept; it is a culture-bound construction; it is a reactive and not a generative 'concept'. Squeezing between caste and class reduces its 'atomistic' existence as a concept. It has more emotional and effectual appeal than rational and logical message. Lastly, it is a concept in making.

There are many studies on Dalits, which dealt with their social mobility, economic development, socio-economic and political status; atrocities; ideology and identity, and so on. However, various scholars have paid much attention to the process of social and economic mobility among the Scheduled Castes. The focus of such studies ranges from their socio-economic status and mobility (Prakash, 1989; Selvanathan, 1989) to Dalit movements (Omvedt, 1994; Zelliot, 1992), to Dalit ideology (Gore, 1993) and identity (Shah, 1985; Oommen, 1968), both during the pre-independence and post-independence period. Such studies focused on either socio-economic status or mobility. In a changing context of Dalit assertion and the caste-Hindu opposition to Dalit mobility, it is essential to understand the rapid changes occurring not only in their economic status, but also in their own perceptions of their socio-political status, along with their ideology and identity. This would help in not only estimating the socio-economic and political changes and the mobility process that the Dalits are undergoing but also in enabling us to understand the general process of social change in India.

EVOLUTION OF DALIT IDENTITY AND IDEOLOGY: AN HISTORICAL OVERVIEW

In different phases of the Indian caste history, the Dalits were addressed differently in relation to the then Hindu religious and societal conservatism. However, at the pan-Indian level, the Dalits had not faced the same degree of untouchability or the other forms of oppression uniformly; they were called by different names in different parts of the country and were assigned different economic roles.[28] To trace historically, the different phases of untouchability and the nomenclatures used to refer to them helps in understanding their socio-economic position in those times. Quoting

Bougle, Prasad (1970: 121) observes, 'the untouchable is not hated primarily; he is feared for his power to defy any class of men with whom he may come into contact'.

As a result of the continuous efforts to search for a self-identity and for the articulation of a collective political interest, the term *Dalit*, for the first time, was used in a cultural context in Marathi literature by the followers of Babasaheb Ambedkar or the neo-Buddhist writers, and the Dalit Panthers of Maharashtra in 1972, with the inspiration taken from the American Black Panthers. Since then the term has gained popularity and is being widely used.[29] Zelliot observes that today:

> Dalit is not a caste. He is a man exploited by the social and economic traditions of this country. He does not believe in God, Rebirth, Soul, Holy Books teaching separatism, Fate and Heaven because they have made him a slave. He does believe in Humanism. Dalit is a symbol of change and revolution. (Gangadhar Pantwane, as quoted in Zelliot, 1992: 172)

This definition gives an account of who and what a Dalit is. The emerging identity, that is, Dalit, negates the past impressions and positions given to them and denotes the aspirations to evolve as a new political force with a distinct identity. According to Shah (1994: 1133), 'identity' is concerned with the self-esteem and self-image of a community. Seeking political power is the crucial significance of Dalit identity, argues Oommen (1994). He further adds that this identity is the product of a long historical process rooted in a collective conscience specific to them. It is a consolidating identity.

Webster (1999: 77) states in definite terms thus:

> Caste alone has determined who is a Dalit, not class or religion. Social stigma and a variety of disabilities were based on caste; these were and, to a significant degree, still are the defining characteristics of a Dalit, even if a Dalit moves up in social class or changes religion.

Locating the origin of the category Dalit, Zelliot (1992: 170) points out that – in the 1970s – some writers from the 'untouchable' castes compared Indian untouchables with the Blacks of

America took inspiration from the Black Panthers movement and called themselves 'Dalit Panthers'. It soon became a dominant trend in Marathi literature and later inspired Dalit politics. According to her, the term 'Dalit' seems to be more secular and self-respect oriented than other categories such as the Scheduled Castes or Harijans. However, Zelliot feels that the term Dalit overemphasizes aspects of culture and fails to explain the changing trends among them, that is, social status, political identities and economic aspirations.

Dalit identity arose because of exposure to modern education, social reform movements, Bhakti movements and finally Ambedkar's Mahar movement for social equality. The followers of Ambedkar spread his ideology not only in Maharashtra, but also in states such as Karnataka, Gujarat, Andhra Pradesh and Tamil Nadu. Politically conscious of the untouchables position in society resulted in searching for a solution in determining a political identity such as Dalit identity, which is more secular and self-respecting than the other names used for the Scheduled Castes, which do not explain the changing trend among them, that is, social status, political identity and economic aspirations under the cultural identity of Dalit.

Nagaraj (1993: 4) observes 'the Dalit movement was a product of the mental state that believed in the firm rejection of the Gandhian model of tackling the problems of untouchables, and that has shaped the contours of its themes and patterns'. Dr Siddalingaiah[30] in his play 'Panchama' (The Fifth-one) portrayed Dalit identity at two different levels: (1) the upwardly mobile Dalits are those who present different faces of the making of modern Dalit identity in all its unauthentic forms, who lie and are caught in the act and show an attitude of wilful amnesia towards their past and (2) the new Dalit, who not only refuses to forget his past, but also remembers it deliberately. The first category, according to him, needs 'a radical atmosphere which will accept and respect their Dalit identity, which only a strong movement could provide. The entire Dalit movement at one level starts from the assumption that the first four will be eventually transformed as Panchama'.[31]

Dalit movement does not refer to a single movement, but it includes several different movements says Shah (1990: 108). He further argues that different movements highlight different aspects of caste oppression and use different ideological frameworks for articulating their politics. However, 'all of them overtly or covertly assert a Dalit identity, though its meaning is not identical and precise for everyone'. 'Identity', he says, 'is concerned with the self-esteem and self image of a community'. He identifies the weakness of the Dalit movements as internal social hierarchy, economic differentiations and dispersed populations. He argues that the ideology of Hinduism, that is, hierarchy, plays a major role against a unified Dalit identity.

K.L. Sharma argues that Dalit movements have a class character. He further elaborates:

> Dalit Movements may be seen in terms of (1) the sociology of knowledge and communication paradigms, and (2) neo-Marxist view emphasising the class-caste approach. In the first case, the social context of Ambedkarian is highlighted, whereas in the second approach emphasis is on the understanding of the broad situation of the underdog mainly in class terms without losing the sight of the specific caste situation in India. As such, dalit movement is an anti-systemic movement. Both manifest and latent consequences of the dalit movement are observable in the socioeconomic spheres of life. (Sharma, 2001: 99)

For the first time, the Bhakti movement facilitated the Dalits to raise their voice against religious restrictions on worship. During the British rule, the grip of Karma ideology loosened with the changes in economic and political structures and during the freedom movement, a struggle for social equality was launched. Shah (2002b: 36) suggests that gradually a middle class has developed among the Dalits. For these middle class Dalits, the question of a new social and religious identity and reservations are more important than the problems of poverty and exploitation. For the poor Dalits, poverty and exploitation are more important problems than the search for a new identity.

Oommen (1994) deals with questions of Dalit identity and its contexts and contents. He identifies five phases in which the collective identity was made up through the ages, with different contexts and contents, and through the dichotomy of the self and the other. In the first phase, the pre-Aryan categories were caught up in the process of assimilation in and exclusion from Aryan/Hindu identity. The non-assimilation and loss of identity led to their entry into Hinduism with a stigmatized status as untouchables or *Panchamas*. In the second phase, Bhakti tradition tried to enhance Dalits by professing human equality and rejecting the authority of the Vedas, Brahmin priesthood and ritual practices. In the third phase, the nineteenth-century British rule began recognizing Dalit problems, and the terms 'depressed classes' and 'exterior castes' were coined during this period. This was the time of social reforms in India. Status mobility was initiated in this period. Sanskritization and conversion to Christianity and Buddhism were the distinct features of this phase. The term 'Scheduled Castes' was also coined in this period to group them together for legal purpose and give them some specific benefits.

The fourth phase involved Gandhi and Ambedkar. Gandhi called them Harijans. He wanted to absorb Harijans into the Hindu fold to fuse their identity with Hinduism. Ambedkar opted for alternatives other than Hinduism to renounce caste status. Gandhi aimed at a change '*in*' caste system, whereas Ambedkar aimed at a change '*of*' caste system. In this context, Gandhi was a reformer and Ambedkar, a revolutionary. The final phase starts with a new self-definition as 'Dalits' from within, with the formation of Dalit Panthers in Maharashtra in the 1970s. The content of contemporary Dalit identity is primarily political and its orientation is militant and rebellious. Seeking political power is of crucial significance in the concept of Dalit identity.

AMBEDKAR AND DALIT IDEOLOGY

Ambedkar is the most prominent articulator of Dalit rights. He caused a paradigm shift in the Dalits' social vision, ideology, identity and political action. He propagated 'social revolution' as the solution to Dalit development; the annihilation of caste system and the creation of a new society based on social, economic and political equality. He was multifaceted: he was a professor, lawyer, journalist, educationalist, social reformist, the great economist and visionary, the architect of the Indian Constitution and leader of downtrodden classes in India. He, being one of the few highly educated among the depressed classes, led the movement among them for 'social reform and political education' (Desai, 2000: 184).

For the first time, Ambedkar planned a systematic approach for the economic as well as the social development of Dalits. Combining these two, Ambedkar visualized that only the socially and politically developed Dalits could destroy the caste system. 'Ambedkar', in his new ideology of integration, 'provided a totally different perspective on an autonomous social and cultural space for the Dalits, markedly different from the one they had in Brahminical Hindu society' (Singh, 1995: 114). Ambedkar is also seen as a 'dynamic and charismatic (but fettered) leader in life, who posthumously became a cultural hero, a demigod for "untouchables" having led them through the processes of counter-caste demarcation, competition, confrontation, and routinization of politics' (Khare, 1984: 143).

Emphasizing on equal importance of 'liberty, equality and fraternity' as basis for an ideal society, Ambedkar (1946: 30) observes:

> An ideal society should be mobile, should be full of channels for conveying a change taking place in one part to other parts. In an ideal society there should be many interests consciously communicated and shared. There should be varied and free points of contact with other modes of association. In other words there must be social endosmosis.

By envisioning 'annihilation of caste' Dr B.R. Ambedkar transformed the Dalit vision. He prepared the untouchables to fight the caste system and its discrimination. He led the Dalits with a vision, creating an ideology to educate Dalits politically. He not only fought for the economic development of Dalits, but also argued for the formation of an alternate identity as against the Hindu identity, which kept them low and degraded. Ambedkar's vision and initiatives continue to inspire and guide the contemporary Dalit movement.

For the first time, Dalits fought the caste system in a systematic manner, with a supreme ideology under the leadership of Ambedkar. He organized the untouchables, the Mahars of

Maharashtra, to fight the caste system. The programmes, he took up in his anti-caste movement include the following:

1. Mahad water tank movement in 1927;
2. Burning Manusmriti on 25 December 1927;
3. Formation of Samaj Samata Sangh in 1928 for caste-Hindu and untouchable unity;
4. Formation of Samata Sainik Dal in 1929 to fight the caste oppression;
5. Temple entry movement in Nasik in 1930;
6. The decision to quit Hinduism in 1936; and
7. Mass conversion into Buddhism in 1956.

Ambedkar believed that as long as the Dalits remained within the fold of the Hindu religion they could not escape the caste system and, therefore, doing away with Hindu religion was the solution to limit caste discrimination. During the nationalist movement, he fought for Dalit rights, and he made a number of representations to the British Government to take steps to develop Dalits and to award separate electorates for Dalits (which resulted in the Communal Award 1932). The Congressmen refused to accept that the problem of untouchables was a political matter; they always dubbed it as social. Nevertheless, in changing India, the untouchables were also assuming a political force (Vakil, 1985: 7).

Ambedkar realized the importance of education for Dalits, and he opened schools and hostels for them. While he was a practising barrister, he helped the poor Dalits with legal aid. As early as 1919, he made a representation to the South Borough Election Reforms Committee on Dalit political rights. He started weeklies, fortnightlies, journals and so on to voice Dalit issues. He started *Mook Nayak* a fortnightly in 1920; *Bahishkrit Bharat* in 1927 and the weekly *Janata* in 1930. Ambedkar worked in state and central ministries before and after independence. Though Dalit politics remained his main concern, he utilized all the positions he attained to benefit Dalits. He demanded separate electorates, gave a call for a separate state for Dalits', *Dalitstan*, and finally, as the chairman of the Constitution Drafting Committee, he took care to provide concessions and development programmes for the Dalits' economic development, along with reservations in education and employment. He also took measures regarding the abolition of untouchability, action against caste discriminations and political reservations for Dalits. Ambedkar largely influenced all the clauses in the Constitution of India relating to the Scheduled Castes and Scheduled Tribes. In many of his speeches and writings, he made it clear that education, employment and economically stable life are the preconditions of social reform.

The other major contributions of Ambedkar to the Indian society include (1) the Economics of Flexible Socialism in the early 1920s and his 'problem of the rupee'; (2) the cultural revolutionary theory of Indian history; (3) crucial questions posed related to the identity of Dalits, Shudras and other high castes; (4) examining the relevance of 'Hinduism'; (5) the attempts to understand 'Hindu India' and 'Buddhist India';[32] (6) the reinvented Buddhism – a Rational and Social Religion and (7) the Strategy of Fighting Brahminism and Capitalism.

The importance of Ambedkar in framing the Dalit movement and ideology is well captured by Omvedt (1994). She compares the models of class revolution (Marxism) and social revolution (caste annihilation of Ambedkar) in addition to assessing how both models influenced and were successfully utilized by Ambedkar. The caste system, Brahminical superiority and the significance of 'Hinduism' – particularly the way it had developed and had been made sacred – were questioned by Ambedkar. Alternatives were offered, to benefit not only the Dalits but also others, mainly those who were inside the caste system. Towards realizing this goal, Ambedkar adopted a few specific measures such as the Dalit movement, mass conversion of the Dalits to Buddhism and the theory of 'indigenousity' (in Ambedkar's words Indian nation or Indian people).

The rejection of the idea of the nationalist school of thought, the 'Hindu India' and, in its stead, the identification of three Indias in Indian history, that is (i) Brahminism (the Aryans); (ii) Buddhism (rise of civilization and human equality) and (iii) Hinduism (reactionary/counterrevolution to Buddhist discourse and subordination of women and Shudras), formed Ambedkar's understanding of the relevance of 'Hinduism'. In his struggle to secure equality for the Dalits, Ambedkar had to face many obstacles such as Gandhi's integration policy and the Nehruvian approach to development along the mode of Socialist heavy industry, which could neither address Dalits problems directly nor contribute to their development. For Gandhi, 'Hinduism' is the religious – cultural identity and for Nehru, 'secularism' is 'exalted modernity'; both appear to be promoting a 'nation' contrary to Ambedkar's demand of 'Dalitstan', a separate nation for Dalits. In this context, Dalit movement under Ambedkar's leadership could be only a passive observer, with limited influence to achieve a few gains and concessions. The Dalit democratic liberation movement was led by Ambedkar in colonial India in the face of the secularist and nationalist discourses, which claimed to be broad based in including all Hindus, Muslims and backward classes, and Dalits. Even though it is against the very basic idea of segmentary interests and promotes nationalism, secularism without taking the interests of the weaker sections into consideration. Omvedt (1994: 223) observes that 'Ambedkarism' is a living force today as much as Marxism. It defines the ideology of the Dalit movement, and largely, an even broader anti-caste movement. The main significance of Ambedkarism is equality, fraternity and social justice – in a way, Ambedkarism is general movement ideology.

Dalit movement has had a political thrust. A share in power is a precondition for Dalit liberation and reservations should not be limited to economic gains, but should lead to access to power and a rejection of the politics of patronage. Thus, Ambedkar insisted, 'we (Dalits) must become a ruling community'. He further reiterated that 'Brahminism'/Hinduism and 'Capitalism' are their enemies; Dalits as the 'super oppressed' must maintain their autonomy with the alliance of the other oppressed (sometimes Shudras and minorities, and sometimes the working class).

In forging political alliances, during the 1930s Ambedkar allied with the *Samyukta Maharashtra Samiti*. As for forming a separate political forum for Dalits, he formed the Independent Labour Party (ILP), his first political party – a worker and peasant party with a red flag with Dalit leadership. However, it was limited to only Marathi-speaking districts. He wound up the ILP and turned it into the Scheduled Castes Federation in 1942, which sought the alliance of the Shudras and Muslims. Finally, the

Scheduled Castes Federation wound up into the Republican Party of India, which aimed to be a party of all the oppressed and exploited. He was converted to Buddhism in 1956, along with hundreds of thousands of untouchable masses, to gain a new identity other than Hinduism (which he opposed in each aspect). He thus took the ultimate political step in giving Dalits a new social and political identity.

Thus Omvedt's (1994) comparison of class revolution (Marxism) and social revolution (caste annihilation) clearly shows how B.R. Ambedkar effectively utilized both and how Ambedkar's ideas on issues such as social equality and national integration or development were different from Gandhian and Nehruvian approaches.

Zelliot (1992) charted out the contributions of various Dalit movements, in a social space provided by one movement to another. Religious protest (*Bhakti* mode) to social revolution (Mahar movement) was constructed in a form of social history. The religious reformers from Scheduled Castes who created a liberal social space, the non-Brahmin movement against Brahmin ideology by Jyotiba Phule, the Mahar movement led by Ambedkar and finally the Dalit Panther movement of Maharashtra are the issues she dealt with. In Maharashtra, because of *Bhakti* mode of consciousness, non-Brahman movement and Ambedkar's Mahar movement, Dalit consciousness emerged in the 1960s and derived inspiration from the Black Panthers, which laid the path to Dalit identity, and initiated a trend in Marathi literature and inspired Dalit politics.

DALIT IDENTITY AND SOCIAL MOBILITY

The conscious, collective attempts of the Dalits to acquire social mobility started in the nineteenth century, during the British rule. In the pre-British period, the social mobility attempts made by Dalits were not significant, for they were often lacking in 'consciousness' and often not fruitful; though in the medieval period, the *Bhakti* movement created some saints (*Bhaktas*) even from among the *untouchables* such as Ravidas and Chokhamela. This kind of mobility had several limitations. It was largely confined to the upward mobility of very few individuals,[33] who were not accepted by caste-Hindus, and thereby their influence on the society was limited only to spiritualism. Though these individuals broke caste restrictions imposed upon the Dalit communities to become *Bhaktas,* they could only preach human equality and criticize caste practices. However, their impact on caste-Hindu society is very limited with regard to the confidence they nurtured among the Dalits. Given their limitations, these saints from the Dalit communities referred to *Moksha* as the salvation for the Dalits' socio-economic and political subordination. However, the Bhakti mode was not sufficient for the emancipation of the Dalits' socio-economic problems, as it searched for emancipation more on a spiritual plane. It's important contribution was in recognizing these problems and thereby instilling hope among the Dalits. The concerns raised by the Bhakti movement were addressed by the socio-religious movements in the colonial period to some extent. Thus, social change and transformation in the nineteenth century brought about an overall change in the social structure and created new social groups.

Dalits have used various means of mobility to enhance their social and economic status since the nineteenth century. Reddy (1984: 68–71) identified these as (1) social reformation, (2) religious conversions, (3) Sanskritization, (4) protective discrimination and constitutional guarantees and (5) political action.

The ideology of *social reformation,* for which the leadership was external (the reformists), mainly addressed the ritual degradation and cultural repression. The thrust on education and economic betterment motivated this mobility. Cleanliness and purification were preached among the untouchables to bring them into the Hindu fold. However, this model could only make a partial progress in gaining caste-Hindus' acceptance of Dalits. To some extent, a new kind of identification as a clean caste with new status was made possible within this mobility, but overall this mobility was not successful because of the prejudices of the upper castes.

The *religious conversions,* 'another mode of mobility for Dalits', had change of religion as its ideology. In this model, external as well as internal reformists, priests and holy men offered leadership. The ritual degradation and access to resources such as education and economic betterment in the society motivated conversions among the Dalits. Conversions into religions such as Buddhism, Islam and Christianity were attempted and encouraged. With conversions, often, a new religion and a new culture were achieved, but discrimination based on caste continued. This model was mainly followed by only the lowest among the Dalits and was partly successful.

The third model *Sanskritization* has Sanskritic and Brahmanization ideology. Internal (caste) reformists, attempting cultural change, and high and new social positions mainly led to this mobility. It involved imitation of the higher castes and/or the Brahmin lifestyle. Mostly individuals or groups belonging to the elite sections among Dalits adopted this model and were separated from the Dalit masses in the process. However, this mode was also not successful due to the attitudes of the upper castes; they closed all channels for Dalits in this mobility process.

Social security, equality and justice as ideology orient protective discrimination and constitutional guarantees. Political leadership, administration and judiciary carried out this task. The thrust for social equality, numerical strength and politicization motivated this mobility. The Anti-Untouchability Act, seats in legislatures, employment and education along with other welfare measures are the issues involved in this mobility. The beneficiaries of such programmes, who became elites, came to be alienated from Dalit masses. This mobility was also partly successful, because it was not a collective mobility, but a person centred one, while the lackadaisical attitudes of administrative and judicial systems are the limits in this kind of mobility.

Finally, *political action* – militant and mass political participation and action – was the ideology behind this mobility. The politicians and social activists, both external and internal to the caste, led this mobility. The motivations for this mobility are the destruction of the traditional order, perception of relative deprivation and quest for power. This mobility proceeded through organizing protests, *dharnas* and mobilizing people on sectarian lines. It involved radicalization of caste; it responded to new ideologies and political actions, while ignoring caste solidarity. This mobility was relatively successful. Conflicts, however, increased due to a high degree of resentment by the upper castes.

These five modes of mobility explained by Reddy (1984: 68–71) can be classified into three different phases, and these are different approaches to social mobility in so far as the Dalits are concerned. They are (1) social reformations and religious conversions as reformatory which aimed at improvement in the Dalits' social status, (2) Sanskritization, protective discrimination and constitutional guarantees as improvement and development, oriented at Dalits' economic as well as social status and (3) political action for securing an alternative identity, aimed at Dalits' political identity as a solution to their subordination. Thus, it can be stated that the attempts of Dalits towards social, economic and political mobility employed diverse means and strategies.

All castes follow the caste system irrespective of their ritual rank; untouchables also practice the caste system as practised by caste-Hindus. This does not mean that caste ranks are, as a whole, accepted and practised without questioning. There have been individual attempts to change one's social status ascribed by birth, as well as some attempts questioning the validity of the caste system (such as Buddhism, which propagated equality from the beginning).[34]

Whenever the Hindu culture encountered a foreign/distinct culture, it underwent some changes. Each time it encountered a different culture and it was faced with a situation of needing to account for its unequal structure, Hinduism made some cosmetic changes within it without altering the larger normative framework. In the medieval period, the contact with Muslim culture had given rise to the Bhakti movement, and in the eighteenth century, the contact with British culture gave rise to the socio-religious reform movement by the high-caste Hindus. These movements implemented some reforms, which were not wholehearted, yet prevented the threat to Hindu religion. The Bhakti movement did not question the existing *Varna* order adequately; instead, it tried to resolve the problems of the lower castes (socio-economic and political) by offering *Bhakti* or salvation. The Bhakti movement at first gave signs of a burgeoning new social order based on brotherhood. The adherents of Bhakti, however, did not abandon the *Varna* model of society. Within that model, they were prepared to grant some semblance of equality to the lower classes (Augustine,

1991: 198). Similarly, socio-religious movements in the nineteenth and twentieth centuries mainly aimed at the prevention of conversions of the lower castes to Christianity; they did not try to resolve untouchability in its entirety, except through the preaching of equality.

In the eighteenth and nineteenth centuries, under the British rule, Indian society, especially the Hindu caste system, experienced attacks from outside in the form of state-initiated social reforms – abolition of *sati*, child marriages and encouragement of widow remarriage – though these were not aiming for a change in it. The British, in order to legitimize their rule in India and further strengthen it, introduced a new land revenue system, which gave rise to tax collectors, who, in turn, exploited the peasants, grabbed their lands and formed a new landed class. In addition, the group of middlemen, the mediators between the British and the people, the interpreters, small businessmen, etc. formed a middle class.[35]

Singh (1986: 89) observes that 'the result of educational changes was two-fold: first, the interjection of the Western values and ideologies among the members of the new educated class, and secondly, the rise of social and cultural reformation movements'. Pimpley (1990: 166) opines that the conversions of the lower and untouchable castes by the Christian missionaries also indirectly contributed to the 'socio-religious reform and reforms in the field of education'. According to him, the missionaries' main aim was to spread the Western culture and the spread of Christianity. Thus, the 'conversions and the spread of education helped the missionaries in their attempts'.

The attempts of the Christian missionaries to convert the lower castes and untouchables were facilitated by two factors, namely: (1) continuance of untouchability and (2) essence of liberal education. There were some significant changes, which took place in traditional occupations under the British rule. They were as follows:

1. The introduction of liberal education, which attracted mostly upper-caste Hindus to government jobs, leaving their traditional occupations;
2. New technology, which caused alterations in caste occupations and which enabled the artisan castes to enter industries and migrate to urban areas and

3. The expansion of Western culture and Christianity, the conversions to Christianity mostly from the lower castes and untouchables whose low ritual status made them turn to Christianity, while materially benefiting from education and modern occupations.

These primary changes resulted in many social movements, which can be broadly classified into: (1) socio-religious reform movements; (2) anti-Brahmin or Non-Brahmin movements and (3) untouchables' movements.

Regarding socio-religious movements, Pimpley (1990: 162) opines that as a result of the changes that took place in the British period:

> The Hindu elite to retain its position at the apex was forced to widen its base and recreate a myth on equal footing. The socio-religious reform movements of the 18th and 19th century were probably a consequence of this struggle for power between the British and the Hindu elite.

Most of the social reformers received a liberal education and were high-caste Hindus. Desai (2000: 253–254) feels that the social reformers, who attacked the caste system, stood for equality and national progress. However, Pimpley (1990: 165–166) observes that they could not attack the caste system wholeheartedly, since they were enjoying positions of power in the caste system. They only addressed the issue of 'liberal education and social evils within the upper castes' and did not heed the problem of untouchability, he complains.

The socio-religious reformers and movements that took up issues of social reform (reform in caste system) and reform in Hindu religion (the mode of worship, the belief systems, etc.) strived for equality in the social as well as in the religious system. Samaj such as the Brahmo Samaj, the Prarthana Samaj and the Arya Samaj carried out this movement. Matto (1991: 31) classifies these Samajs based on their programmes and priorities: Brahmo Samaj stands for a middle path (secular education with Hindu religion); Prarthana Samaj for eradicating social evils; Arya Samaj for the upsurge of Nationalism and Ramakrishna mission for Neo-Hinduism.

To some extent, these liberal ideologues from upper castes did facilitate a ground for the lower castes and untouchables to raise their voice against the caste system in the future. The material help provided by these socio-religious reformers and movements created some space for educational and occupational development of the untouchables. Their various activities and spread of new values of equality and humanitarianism in the long run helped the untouchables. Pimpley analyses:

> the efforts of these movements were merely adjustive to the changes being introduced in the society in keeping with the new values of equality and egalitarianism. They were humanitarian in nature, which was in keeping with the Hindu philosophy of Karma, as well as in maintaining the *status quo* as far as the power structure of the society was concerned. Such an approach leads to conceptions like Brahminization and Sanskritization. But this does lead to upgrading of the entire stratification scale. It does not lead to structural changes in terms of power relations of the different elements of the social structure. As promised, the low status of the Scheduled Castes is a result of deprivation of power and privilege and not in their low ritual status, so the efforts of the socio-religious reform movements which maintained the *status quo* of the society were bound to fail. (Pimpley, 1990: 167)

Unlike many scholars who had a laudatory approach to the socio-religious reform movements, Pimpley adopts a critical view and he concludes:

> Yet one cannot totally negate the efforts of the socio-religious reform movements. In all fairness, they did manage to stir the traditional social system. Although the inhuman caste injustices were substantially mellowed down but when it came to larger issues like removal of untouchability, they inadvertently helped to preserve the existing structure of the society. (1990: 165)

On the other hand, Heimsath (1964: 5) compares social reform in India and in the West as:

> In India, social reform did not ordinarily mean a reorganization of the structure of society, as it did in the West, for the benefit

> of underprivileged social, economic classes. Instead it meant the infusion into the existing social structure of new ways of life and thought: the society would be preserved, while its members would be transformed.

When it was necessary, the members of different castes mingled with other castes, but broadly, they remained loyal to their own castes.

The emergence of the non-Brahmin movement is understood best in the context of the attempts of the British Government to create a clerical class to serve their needs, the liberal education and modern outlook provided towards this end and the consequent social equality brought forth by the socio-religious reform movement, urbanization, etc. which facilitated the middle castes to become economically dominant. Their urge for better economic position and for a social status equal to that of Brahmins and the twice born castes resulted in the non-Brahmin movement. Though it is considered a South Indian phenomenon, in reality it occurred in other parts of the country as well, even when not taking the proportions of a movement, as it did in Tamil Nadu and Maharashtra. The Yadav upsurge in Bihar and Uttar Pradesh are examples to prove its pan-Indian nature.

Some of the factors that contributed to the emergence of such movements were (1) the politics of colonial intervention; (2) the British policy of elite recruitment; (3) the desire for upward mobility among the lower castes and (4) the urge to fight the hegemony of Brahmins in government jobs and to secure proportionate jobs for every caste (Nagaraj, 1993: 5). He describes the non-Brahmin movement as:

> a deliberate, organized and conscious effort on the part of the lower castes and social groups. They chose to fight the hegemony of superior castes through gradualist and constitutionalist methods that they had learnt from their white masters.

While it primarily involved the middle castes and lower castes fighting the Brahmin hegemony in education and jobs, it also took anti-Brahmin, anti-Hindi and anti-Sanskrit issues in Tamil Nadu.

On the other hand, the untouchables' movements before Ambedkar, in which the untouchables fought the caste system since its inception, were not organized at a striking level, nor were they ideologically driven. The medieval period's individual untouchable saints such as Ravidas and Chokhamela broke their traditional occupations and sought *Moksha* as a solution to end the troubles of untouchables. Though breaking up of the traditional occupational structure and the pace to become an ascetic might have been radical developments in so far as that period is concerned, but their urge or call for equality was mostly spiritual in nature than materialistic. However, it is largely understood in a context that, the advent of Muslim rule, the threat of Muslim culture and religious conversions facilitated the *Bhakti* movement in the medieval period and similarly the British rule and expansion of Christianity gave rise to socio-religious reform movements of the eighteenth and nineteenth centuries.

With the weakening of caste rigidities in the nineteenth and twentieth centuries and social change in favour of modernization of the society, a few untouchable castes tried to elevate their caste status wherever they improved their economic condition, for example, the Nadars and Ezhavas of Kerala, the Shanars of Tamil Nadu, the Jatavs of (Agra) Uttar Pradesh, and the Mahars of Maharashtra.[36] While identifying themselves as being on an equal footing with high-caste Hindus, these castes spread *Sanskritic* norms among their castes to raise their caste status in the social hierarchy. Another model that was followed was through identification with alternative religions and culture – *Adi Dharm,* the indigenous or native religion – through which the Dalits tried to improve their social status by distancing themselves from the dominant Hindu social order. In addition, conversions to other religions also played a crucial role such as conversions to Islam and Christianity, in their attempts to achieve social mobility. Mahatma Jyotiba Phule's *Satyashodhak Samaj* too brought some untouchables within its fold even though it primarily attracted the land owning non-Brahmin castes to fight the Brahmin ideology. *Satyashodhak Samaj* falls under the anti-untouchability or anti-caste movements.

The movements in which the Dalits took part in colonial India, prior to the leadership of Ambedkar, adopted methods and ideologies that by and large failed to better their socio-economic status in the caste hierarchy. Until the Dalits came under the leadership of Ambedkar, all the attempts they made lacked a particular ideology of their own that could be called 'Dalit ideology', which rejected the model of 'self-purification' and adhered to a model of 'self-respect'.

DALIT MIDDLE CLASS

The existence of the Dalit middle class is mainly attributed to the 'reservation policy', which aimed at uplifting individual Dalits to raise from the disadvantaged positions of their earlier generations to be a part of an egalitarian society, built on principles of equality. In post-independent India, the Dalit individuals who witnessed mobility as compared to their parents' social and economic class are forming 'a new Dalit middle class'.[37] This Dalit middle class is markedly distinct from the general middle class. Middle class Dalits largely remain a closely-knit community with a certain political temperament, in the absence of a full-fledged assimilation and integration process. They arrange their lives around each other, heavily confining their social relations, especially at the family level to other fellow Dalits.[38]

The social change and transformation processes being experienced by the Indian society have led to the emergence of new social categories, with new aspirations and sense of identity. In India, the very emergence of the middle class has its foundations in 'a new modern India'. Prior to reservation policy, equality of opportunity was available to all but Dalits, for they were considered outcastes or untouchables. It is only during the last 100 years that the Dalits have gained entry into the sphere of 'modernization', principally due to 'protective discrimination' or reservation policy. In this context, Ram (1988: 7–11) identifies the areas where the Scheduled Castes have progressed due to constitutional measures, namely, access to religious and other public places, and lessening of ritual and social distances; growing integration of different caste groups including Scheduled Castes, in schools, colleges and universities; and growing share in political power and occupational mobility.

Regarding upwardly mobile Dalits, Kulke (1976: 253) argues that the middle class Dalits' social environment is different from their community of origin, and they have not as yet been fully integrated into the 'mainstream' middle class culture that is largely dominated by upper castes. In addition, the specific problems faced by the middle class Dalits are due to their newly acquired economic status.

In the case of Dalits, social mobility is not parallel to mobility in economic status. Ram (1995: 207–208) observes: 'Those who are socially and economically mobilized are not fully accepted and assimilated into the social and cultural realms of others, especially caste-Hindus'. Richardson (1977), analysing mobility in England, holds that many of those upwardly mobile had been unable to shake off an attachment to the working class and that 'rather than becoming "core" members of the middle class, their upward mobility is mediated by a peripheral status group'. He further observes that 'translating economic mobility into social mobility' is more difficult. In analysing social mobility, he feels that, the following questions need to be addressed: Whether social mobility leads to changes in the nature of social relationships? Are the socially mobile able to adopt the standards and outlook, typical of their 'new' social class?

Dalits traditionally do not belong to the middle class category; they are newly recruited into the middle class and considered a 'new middle class' (Ram, 1995: 190). Occupationally, the bulk of the Indian middle classes is mainly from 'the educated professionals, such as government servants, lawyers, college teachers and doctors' (Misra, 1961: 12). The Dalits have also mainly opted for the above middle class occupations. In the case of Dalits, reservations helped them enter new spheres of national life and occupations hitherto controlled by caste-Hindus. A small fraction of the Dalit population is represented in almost all modern occupations. Adhering to the trend in the Indian middle class, Dalit entrants into the middle class have also shown more inclination towards white-collar jobs or 'middle class occupations'. At the same time, there is also a growing aspiration among them to become entrepreneurs, businessmen and independent professionals.

Further, upwardly mobile Dalits are faced with the question of identity at both self and collective levels. Their reference points regarding mobility – individual as well as family aspirations – intersect with their perceptions of Dalit ideology and identity – the agenda of Dalit empowerment – and hence, make them identify with both. Historically, Dalits' identity pattern was influenced by the social reality, in relation to their level of resistance to withstand the restrictions imposed on them in the caste system over generations.

Ilaiah opines that in spite of exclusion and marginalization, the *Dalitwadas* (Dalit localities) possess 'creativity, productivity and humanness' called 'Dalitism' (Raj, 1998: xvi). To quote Raj:[39]

> If a Dalit as an individual comes to know about his/her rights, the act of knowing does not remain confined to an individual. It slowly converts itself into an act of community because the relationship between the individual and the community is very strongly tied up through the twofold structure of caste and ethnicity. Secondly, such an act of knowing – becoming conscious – unlike many other acts of Dalits is a 'revolutionary transformative act'.

Similarly, K.L. Sharma (2001: 99) explains that Dalitism implies an 'ideology of protest', but of varying degrees and intensities:

> Dalitism is a historical phenomenon. Dalits as a class can be seen only in terms of human relationships, and not as a category, a thing or as a fixed 'structure' at a given point of time. Dalitism implies ideological and political militancy of the Dalits. They could be referred as 'consciousness community'. Acquisition and control of knowledge and power is treated as the most potent resource by the Dalits. Thus, Ambedkarian discourse on Dalits and untouchability is said to be an alternative perspective to the Gandhian view about Harijans ... Dalitism sets a new agenda for an equalitarian social order, new distributive just processes. 'Equality of outcome/result' is the most concrete and measurable yardstick of the envisaged new social order ... Finally, 'caste' is the central phenomenon in the discourse on 'dalitism', but 'class' is also inherently presenting it. Caste is used as an idiom for waging a 'class war' against the established and entrenched hierarchies of power and domination. However, Dalits are not just a constellation of untouchable castes, they are seen also as actual exploited workers, peasants and agricultural labourers in all parts of

India. Emphasis is laid on their emancipation from economic bondage by bringing about 'economic radicalism' (socialism).

In other words, Dalit middle class is both a vehicle and stabilizer of Dalit ideology and identity. Middle class Dalits play a major role in the modernization among Dalits because, as catalysts, they inspire and assist Dalits in emerging as self-asserting individuals with community consciousness.[40]

The formation of attitudes, a process of identity and perceptions of empowerment among the educated and economically upwardly mobile Dalits, who joined the ranks of the middle class in lifestyle and outlook, are central to Dalit ideology and identity. The articulation of Dalit consciousness and the process of Dalit empowerment are centred on the Dalit middle class, which plays a crucial, catalyst's role in the development of Dalits. The Dalit middle class produces ideas and sets the agenda for the social and political activities of the Dalit movement.[41] Their access to power and resources accords them due importance, both with respect to the state and the Dalit masses on issues pertaining to Dalit development. They, as socially and politically conscious Dalits, represent Dalit interests. The members of the Dalit middle class mediate between the state policies and the Dalit masses' economic needs when they assume the role of a catalyst.

Omvedt (2004)[42] summarizes this development, as follows:

> Dalits are fighting back. In the villages, increasing efforts to claim simple human rights – to walk the same roads and drink from the same teacups that upper-caste Hindus use – have often led to violent rioting. The efforts of young people to break away from caste-defined marriages have resulted in brutal murders. Dalits have formed political parties, fighting elections with notable success in some cases but also coming up against refusals to allow them to vote. They have fought for land, tried small income-generating projects, joined – and where possible, set up – their own NGOs. And finally, the new, small and still insecure dalit middle class that the system of 'reservation' – or positive discrimination – in education and public sector employment has helped to foster, is attempting to move beyond its limitations.

Thus, Dalits need no longer be viewed as a marginalized category of 'underprivileged' people. Owing to various social movements against untouchability and the state policy of positive discrimination, at least a section of Dalits has come to experience the privileges of modern life. Thus, a uniform *developmentalist* or a *welfarist* perspective cannot provide a comprehensive sociological picture, of the social and cultural status of all Dalits. It is in this context that the study of social and economic mobility and formation of new social classes among the Dalits assumes importance.

Unlike in the past – today, the formulation and implementation of socio-economic and political strategies for development of Dalits require the consent of Dalits. In order to understand the status of Dalits today, we need to understand the very authors of Dalit ideology and identity who influence, inspire and motivate the Dalit masses today. Thus, the study of Dalits, especially the educated and economically upwardly mobile Dalits or 'middle class Dalits', calls for an enquiry into the processes of adaptation, assimilation and acculturation in reference to their newly acquired middle-class status, where improving their social status is a major concern. Their mobility in economic status 'reinstalled' their struggle for social and political rights in a new plane. Dalits have come a long way to reclaim their lost status, of social, economic and political equality.

EMERGENCE AND SIGNIFICANCE OF THE DALIT MIDDLE CLASS

Historically, the upper castes dominated all spheres of social, economic and political fields due to the 'higher' status accorded to them, by their 'ritual purity' in the traditional social structure. Also in Modern India, they rendered their positions secure by monopolizing education, and thereby extended their hold in the upper and middle classes. In both the cases, the majority of the society remained dispossessed as 'lower castes' in the caste structure and as wage labouring 'lower classes' in the class structure.

In the post-independence period, the Dalits have gradually made an entry into the modern occupations and professions, with the help of socio-political changes enabling social and economic mobility in general and the state-provided reservations in education and employment in particular. Reservations have supported the Dalits, like other disadvantaged sections of the society, to enhance their social and economic status to reach middle class positions, which were hitherto the monopoly of the upper castes.

The long periods of 'social reform' (pre-independence period) and 'social justice' (post-independence period) enabled at least few Dalits to take to education and thereby enter a class structure that is amenable to their social and economic aspirations. In the post-independence period, Dalits have been able to enter into the middle class. Now they are represented in all modern occupations, but such presence over a period is not proportionate to their population, and they are unequally distributed across various occupations and the positions that exist within them. According to estimates, only 5–10 per cent of Dalits became middle and upper classes in the process.[43]

Amidst many contradictory claims and analyses – surrounding their representation in modern occupations, social and economic mobility, and as having made it into the middle class strata by 'forfeiting' their roots, etc. – the Dalit middle class requires to be put through a thorough enquiry to assess their presence in these fields, vis-à-vis their priorities and politics. The very nature and extent of their shifting of grounds and whether their entry itself is an achievement or trouncing of social and economic mobility needs to be examined. Many Dalits who are represented in these modern occupations are those of the first generation in their respective families and their level of achievement is significant in terms of 'grandeur' and 'noteworthiness'. In such a context, the Dalit middle class is largely constituted of persons who achieved social and economic mobility.

The Dalit middle class is also caught between non-recognition of their achievement by the society on the one hand and the 'jealousy' and 'expectations' from the other Dalits on the other hand.[44] The middle class Dalits are in a sense untouchable to the society and 'outcastes' for other Dalits.[45]

It is in this context that the Dalits who are engaged in modern occupations and professions are classified as middle class. The focus is on middle class Dalits, their life experiences and priorities, and the ideology and identity. With engagement in modern occupations and professions, the Dalits are latently initiated, socialized and stabilized in the course of arriving at and staying in the middle class way of life, within that broader spectrum of social and economic mobility. In the process of becoming middle class, the Dalits have carved out a distinctive identity for themselves. Notwithstanding the fact that technically all the modern occupations and professions are open to Dalits; in practical terms, only few occupations and professions are easily accessible to Dalits. Thus, the majority of the mobile Dalits are congregated in few occupations and professions.

Thus, the formation of attitudes, a process of identity and perceptions of Dalit empowerment among the educated and economically mobile Dalits, who joined the ranks of the middle class in lifestyle and outlook, are central to Dalit ideology and identity. For they lead Dalit movement and only they formulate and implement strategies to empower Dalits economically, socially and politically.

MIDDLE CLASS DALITS IN HYDERABAD

Amidst many interpretations and varied analyses of emergence, status and characteristics of Dalit middle class in various parts of India, the study seeks to map the emerging Dalit middle class in Hyderabad and examine its special identity patterns as well as its ideological position and articulations. The study attempts to understand – to what extent this emerging Dalit middle class in Hyderabad as a group, and individually, manifest in practice – the Dalit identity and ideology that could be considered as examples for emulation by the larger Dalit milieu elsewhere.

The preceding question also assumes importance because many previous studies[46] on this subject have established a clear correlation between Dalits' upward social mobility and its identity-ideological orientation that has been considered as a successful instance in promoting Dalit emancipation. Here, reference is solicited to studies conducted by Eckeharde Kulke (1976, 1983) and Nandu Ram (1988), which established the following:

1. Middle class Dalits' social environment was different from the community of their origin and they were not fully integrated into 'main stream' middle class culture that is largely dominated by upper castes.
2. Middle class Dalits generally lived in Dalit neighbourhoods. Caste continued to be an important factor in assessing their social status.
3. However, with upward economic mobility, they could avail services from others and neither did they feel the need of *sanskritizing* their ritual life.
4. In contrast to the most of the illiterate Dalits who identified themselves with Gandhian ideology, the middle class Dalits identified more with Ambedkar.
5. The identification of mobile Scheduled Castes varies with their education level and social status.
6. Their employment in white-collar jobs meant upward mobility in the class structure.
7. While they were forging new patterns of social relationships with people in their workplace and elsewhere, irrespective of caste and community considerations, the degree and direction of their mobility was not clear.
8. The middle class among Scheduled Castes is different from the old middle class.
9. Since the economic mobility of Scheduled Castes does not necessitate an equal social mobility, there is an incongruity between their social and economic mobility.

At the same time, the previous studies have also noted certain existential dilemmas among the Dalit middle class with which the members of this class live.[47] So, how do members of this class understand these dilemmas and attempt to resolve them in practice? The present study essentially is in the tracks of the previous endeavours, attempting to study similar concerns of the previous studies in a specific urban context, that is, Hyderabad city. An attempt has been made to find out as to how far its conclusions correspond to earlier studies, and its divergence and reasons for the same. Herein lies its essential significance. The latter ought to be considered yet another empirical contribution to the studies on Dalits' upward social mobility, identity and ideology.

In earlier studies, dealing with socially and economically mobile Dalits, for example, Sachidananda (1974: 12) used 'web technique' in which the respondents were selected largely by informal contacts of respondents interviewed to further locate and interview new respondents. Such studies, ranging from 29 to 300 respondents, largely composed of interviews of educated persons, terming them elite (e.g. Issacs interviewed 50 persons, Saberwal 58, Sachidananda 200, Deshpande 29, Roy and Singh 55 elites),[48] and middle class (Ram 240 SCs and Kulke 300 SCs and non-SCs).[49]

On the lines of earlier studies,[50] focusing on the various middle class occupations the Dalits have entered into, the middle class Dalits' ideology and identity in Hyderabad are identified with the aid of a structured interview schedule. It tries to profile the Dalit middle class in Hyderabad, by focusing on 105 middle class Dalits and eight detailed case histories from among them. Thus, few additional parameters have been included in the study to traverse beyond and capture the ideology and identity of middle class Dalits by way of juxtaposition against their socio-economic status. The research tools used for the study include the following:

- Administering interview schedule to a stratified sample;
- Representative case studies of individuals from the sample and
- Recourse to secondary sources to bring out a historical profile of the Dalit middle class.

The study undertakes to explore following questions listed in the context of the absence of any latest empirical evidence to establish the status of Dalit middle class and varied contradictory assumptions about the middle class Dalits. The broad questions dealt within the study are related to:

- The phenomenon of Dalit middle class, its origin and context;
- Characteristics of Dalit middle class, differences between Dalit middle class and non-Dalit middle class;
- Economic and social status of Dalit middle class;
- Religious trends among the Dalit middle class;

- Experiences of untouchability and other forms of caste discrimination ;
- Membership in Dalit, political and voluntary organizations;
- Dalit middle class members' views on women's liberation;
- Their perceptions on various issues such as caste politics, communalism and casteism;
- World view (understanding of larger society) of the Dalit middle class;
- Dalit middle class' perceptions of social change;
- Dalit middle class' perceptions on the question of Dalit liberation and
- Identity patterns among the members of the Dalit middle class.

STUDYING DALITS AS MIDDLE CLASS

In order to understand the nature of emerging Dalit middle class in Hyderabad and to examine its ideology and identity patterns, this enquiry, involves identifying the changes brought about by the social and economic mobility among the Scheduled Castes with special reference to those who have joined 'white-collar' jobs and other independent professions such as law, medicine and journalism. Therefore, it is important to discern the process of changing social identities of these individuals. Thus, the category 'Dalit middle class' is used to grasp the changing social identities of individual Dalits who have been able to enter into the realms of modern life. Further, looking at how caste and class contexts intersect in the articulations of their self-definition and politics is also important. The role of the Dalit middle class in the construction of Dalit identity and ideology on the one hand and to comprehend their influence on the Dalit movement and the larger Dalit social life itself on the other hand is attempted here. The specific questions addressed thus are:

- Social background of the middle class Dalits, educational level, occupation, economic status and rural/urban background of the family of their origin.

- Their understanding of the problem of their community; their opinion on the ways and means to solve them.
- Their preferences for self-identification as Dalits and/or middle class.
- Their new attitudes towards education and occupation.
- Their lifestyle, consumption patterns, assets and debts.
- Their interaction patterns with the members of their own community and other caste groups.
- Their perceptions on reservations as a means of Dalit upliftment.

The study divides the middle class Dalits into two categories: 'government employees' and 'independent professionals'. The fieldwork was carried out in Hyderabad[51] where it was possible to find a good number of middle class Dalits employed in government offices and independent professions. Inquiring about the ideology and identity formation among the Dalit middle class is feasible only through profiling of the Dalit middle class with all its general and specific characteristics in relation to the general middle class in India. Then juxtapose the same, with its priorities and politics, to enquire into the formation process of ideology and identity.

The spectrum of middle class occupations and professions are ever proliferating, whereas information regarding this ever-expanding universe and occupations more or less is non-existent. Given this limitation, the question one had to confront was 'How to locate the middle class Dalits in a city like Hyderabad? At the same time, there were problems such as non-availability of official and reliable records regarding the population of the middle class, occupations and professions they inhabit and the number of Dalits employed in these occupations and professions. In this context, it became difficult to ascertain the total universe to employ any regular sampling methods and thus *web technique* was employed to locate the middle class Dalits. Therefore, an attempt was made to identify and include respondents from all major occupations and professions that the Dalits have ever entered into the sample. However, it was realized during the pilot study that a greater number of middle class Dalits who are employed in modern occupations are largely in government service.

In order to have intra-occupational comparability and to diverge from having any bias to any particular occupation, care was taken to include an equal number of respondents from each category in the sample, except in the case of two occupations, namely, doctors and journalists, as it was difficult to find more number of Dalits in these professions. It was realized in due course that in the case of the remaining categories, they were largely employed in government service and a negligible number of Dalits have entered into the categories of doctors and journalists. It is in this context that more number of employed persons had to be included in the sample compared to independent professionals. Accordingly, 105 middle class Dalits were interviewed for the study with the help of a structured interview schedule and eight representative case studies from among the sample were carried out.

The nature of the questions raised being qualitative in nature, a structured interview schedule was used for collection of data, which was filled in by the researcher in person. Web technique was used to identify the respondents. While most of the interviews were conducted at their work places during working hours, a few interviews were conducted at their residences. However, the family involvement in the interview process was limited only to mutual introductions. Except a handful of middle class Dalits from among those identified for the purpose of the interviews, the rest readily agreed to be interviewed. Those who refused to be interviewed ranged from the officer cadre in government service to a government pleader, as they felt that only those among the Dalits who put in hard work had come up in life, their individual mobility had nothing to do with being a Dalit, and they saw no reason for Dalit consciousness either.

NOTES

1. See Tewari (1998: 180–181) for an account on the formation of Dalit consciousness and its driving force.
2. See Shah (1990: 108–116).

3. See Zelliot (1992: 267).
4. See Tewari (1998: 170–171) for evolution of the Dalit identity from the earlier 'untouchable' identity.
5. See Ruben (1957: 98).
6. See Kananaikil (1983: 79).
7. Dalits in the Indian society suffered socio-cultural, economic and political disabilities and were not allowed to take part in any religious, social or political activities at par with the caste-Hindus. Dalits were treated as 'untouchables', Dalits (broken men), Outcastes, Panchamas, Atishudras, Avarnas, Antyajas, Namasudras and Pariahs – basically as un-seeables and un-approachables (Shah, 1990: 107).
8. Mehta used it to denote 'the fatherless children', see Zelliot (1992).
9. For a more detailed discussion see Bose as cited in Sinha (1974: 237) and Damle and Nair (1982: 6).
10. See Kulke (1976: 254).
11. Tripathy (1994) describes, 'Dalits are discriminated against with references to living wage, sharecropping, money-lending, drawing water from public wells, entry into the temples, service of tea and snacks in the hotels, service in the grocery shops, services of the barbermen, washermen, cow herdsmen, priest community, feasts and marriages with caste-Hindus'.
12. Damle and Nair (1982: 6–7), for example, discuss this process taking a manifest shape forcefully after framing of the Constitution.
13. Damle and Nair (1982: 6–7) observe this because of the replacement of the non-competitive caste society with a partially competitive caste society.
14. Charsley and Karanth (1998) provide a depiction of changing social environment of Dalits in Karnataka with reference to their growing ability to 'challenging untouchability' and other forms of caste discriminations.
15. Rao (1972: 139) observes that 'Arya Samaj movement helped sanskritisation of many castes including the Harijans'.
16. Charsley (1996) discusses elaborately how 'untouchable' as a category has evolved during colonial rule.
17. Ibid.: xi.
18. See K.N. Sharma (1986: 179).
19. Sorokin defines social mobility as 'any transmission of an individual or social object or value, anything that has been created or modified

by human activity from one social position to another' (as quoted in Mathew, 1986: 5).

20. Srinivas (1966: 1–45) provides an elaboration on the concept of Sanskritization, as a tool for status mobility among the 'lower castes'.
21. Ram (1988: 8) analyses the social and economic mobility among the Dalits broadly under these three themes in his study.
22. Venkateswarlu (1987) analyses the context and patterns of conflict between Dalits and caste-Hindus in Andhra Pradesh.
23. Tripathy (1994) treats this as a natural progression or a historical outcome given the adverse circumstances the Dalits have been subjected to.
24. Sheth (1999) observes 'both rituality and sanskritisation have virtually lost their relevance in the formation of the "new" middle class'.
25. Lal (1995: 87–88) reports of a process of downward mobility of 'upper castes' to acquire Dalit identity, precisely Bhangi identity, calling it 'Bhangiization' and 'asprashyeekaran' in Rajasthan. He opines it is not confined only to Rajasthan and it is an all India phenomenon. Guru (1984: 32) observes reservations for Scheduled Castes counteracts the process of Sanskritization among them as reservation policy requires them to prove their eligibility for such benefits.
26. See Kulke (1976: 249) for a similar conclusion.
27. See Kananaikil (1993: 410). Further, referring to the coming together of all Dalit Parliamentarians in 1992, and its significance to Dalits, he opines that 'in recent years, they have become a people in their own right. This is but the beginning of the emergence of a new identity … (and it has) … to find a new meaning in the identity of the Dalit as dignified'.
28. Sachidananda (1977) observes 'the Scheduled Castes in different parts of India do not form any solid mass. They are split up into hundreds of castes and sub-castes. There are about eleven hundred such groups spread all over India. In different regions of India, some of them retain and share a common identity and sometimes a common name. Each group in this Scheduled Caste population has a name, a separate occupation, its own set of rules and, more often than not, its own mechanism of social control. These groups are not equal in social status. They are arranged in strictly hierarchical order as caste sub-units and they practice untouchability among themselves. Endogamy is widely practised among them'.

29. See Zelliot (1992: 170).
30. Dr Siddalingaiah is a famous Dalit writer from Karnataka. Quoted in Nagaraj (1993: 8).
31. Ibid.
32. Ambedkar's writings on Indian history begin with the construction of an 'Indian nation' or 'Indian people' contrary to 'Hindu identity'.
33. Dube (1988: viii) observes these as 'rare exceptions', which had not facilitated the 'entire untouchable groups' to achieve 'upward mobility' mainly due to 'ritual hierarchy of Hinduism'.
34. Pimpley (1990: 162) proclaims that 'the struggle against inequality within the caste system goes back to Buddha'.
35. The features of this class can be noted as:

    (a) Its social composition differed from region to region, (b) The members of this class served as middlemen for the European traders, (c) They generally had a lower class origin and (d) They varied from petty clerks, interpreters, cashiers, to petty contractors (Singh, 1986: 88).
36. All these instances are extensively studied under Sanskritization model that facilitated mobility process.
37. As emphatically articulated by Ram (1988).
38. See Kulke (1976: 248).
39. Ibid.: xv.
40. Sachidananda (1974) feels that Dalit elites are 'torchbearers' of social change, for they are most active and powerful agents of social transformation among Dalits. According to him, they are the catalysts of change.
41. Guru (1993: 570–573) emphasizes on a realistic and critical assessment while analysing Dalit movements as they represent diverse approaches and aspirations.
42. See Omvedt (2004).
43. See Guru (2002: 141) and Saavala (2001: 195).
44. Jogdand (1999: 131) observes that the emergence of Dalit middle class is an unintended consequence of reservation policy and therefore their 'autonomy is curtailed'.
45. See Ram (1988: 120).
46. See Kulke (1976) and Ram (1988).
47. All these aspects have been dealt with in detail in appropriate chapters.

48. See Saberwal (1972), Sachidananda (1974), Deshpande (2003) and Roy and Singh (1987: 29).
49. See Ram (1988) and Kulke (1976).
50. These studies include the present researcher's MPhil study earlier (1994–1996) entitled 'Intersecting Identities: A Study of the Dalit Middle Class'.
51. The fieldwork was carried out during the years 2003–2004 and again in 2007 in Hyderabad city, which today is the common capital of two states, Telangana and Andhra Pradesh.

CHAPTER 2

Dalit Middle Class or Dalit Elite?

The majority of studies conducted on the social mobility of Dalits focused on measuring socio-economic mobility or Dalit as a political category. The studies on social mobility among Dalits were largely confined to changes in their lifestyle, patterns of consumption and perceptions on ongoing economic and social changes, ignoring the need to relate the Dalits with their political leanings, formation of ideology and, more importantly, their direct and/or indirect contribution to the shaping of larger Dalit politics. It is in this context that the need for looking at the economic mobility as well as political, ideological formations among the Dalits arises even if it is in the form and level of individual and seemingly unconnected. The process of induction of individuals from non-middle class families in a class that is considered to have achieved much that is otherwise not possible for many other Dalits is important to understand the transformation and progress among the Dalits. It is very useful to analyse the ideology and identity formation processes among the middle class Dalits who are reportedly having been removed from the Dalit reality of suffering, subjugation and thereby not eligible to represent the Dalit masses, as held by both Dalits and the caste-Hindus, are significant in many ways. While the Dalit masses observe (to some extent of their experience) that the middle class Dalits have been separated from their roots and do not feel for their community any longer, the caste-Hindus, on the other hand, perceive a threat in the mobility of Dalits in general and the existence of the Dalit middle class in particular. The Dalit middle class, thus, faces opposition from the caste-Hindus for closely networking among them and growing independent, advantaged and well placed unlike the poor Dalits. This animosity gets further aggravated when the Dalit middle class organizes itself for its own cause or for Dalits in general.

In practicality, middle class Dalits as individuals are vulnerable like the Dalit masses in villages under the imbroglio of the caste system. They have to either surrender to the authority of caste-Hindus or face harassment meted out to the Dalits in villages. Thus, the individuals belonging to the Dalit middle class are either appropriated by others or engaged in self-surrender to avoid inevitable threats or are tempted by the lure of individual gains attached to such an action. If this does not occur, the caste-Hindus sense the potential threat in the form of organized Dalit middle class. The social change in India facilitated social and economic mobility among large sections of society. Introduction of new 'secular' occupations and policies of protective discrimination helped some Dalits move up in the society. This also reflects a shift from caste-based social stratification to the one based on class. The emerging social structure, in a sense, is independent of the caste system. The new occupational structure stresses more on values of achievement and much lesser on those of ascription.

The Dalits are traditionally not part of the middle class. For centuries together, they remained in subjugation, serving the caste-Hindus. Various streams of socio-religious and political mobilizations in the twentieth century paved the way for Dalits to take to education and employment in non-traditional occupations. In the post-independence period, the Indian state has adopted 'social justice' as its goal, as part of which it has been supporting the Dalits' socio-economic mobility through the policy of 'protective discrimination' or the policy of reservations. Thus, the emergence of the Dalit middle class is largely attributed to the reservation system.

There is an upward mobility in occupational structure among the middle class Dalits in comparison to their previous generations. This 'mobility' is primarily facilitated by the reservation system that aimed at 'development of the community through individual mobility'. However, it burdens such 'mobile' individuals, on the one hand, with the economic responsibility of members of their ancestral family and hence reduces the extent of their economic mobility. On the other hand, they are still struggling to achieve social mobility. Thus far, studies have proved that their economic mobility is not leading them towards social mobility as well. In terms of mobility, whatever Dalits achieved so far was not without resistance from the 'upper' castes. Dalits have had to struggle a lot to make a little improvement in their socio-economic position wherever their mobility was directly involved with upper castes' interests. They faced insults and humiliation all through their history due to untouchability. In a changing state of affairs, they continue to face the same situation because they are looked down upon as a reserved category.

However, Oommen (1977: 189) striking a critical note on positive discrimination observes: 'although the developmental benefits are extended to Scheduled Castes and Scheduled Tribes as social categories, the beneficiaries are specific persons and families. This means, the unit of mobility is an individual and not a group in the context of developmental benefits'. In the post-independence period, the number of Dalits who have benefited from the reservation policy is growing. Nevertheless, the number of Dalits who attained a higher level of social and economic status is small, in comparison to the overall Dalit population. Over the years, the reservation policy encouraged education among Dalits; likewise reservations in employment allowed the possibility of their reaching highest positions in various occupations, resulting in a nominal Dalit representation in various kinds of occupations that can be described as middle class. However, at the same time, it is evident that this policy alone cannot elevate the status of all Dalits. It has elevated only a small section that is considered as middle class or elites among the Dalits. However, for the overall development of Dalits, the crucial assertion and commitment should come from the Dalits themselves. More decisively, their political realization alone decides their future.

Though the reservations were made available to Dalits, in various categories of government sector, on a proportional basis to their population, they were not implemented properly. Only in the case of low cadre jobs – Group III and IV government jobs – the reservations are being implemented adequately. Posts in the categories of Group I and II are not filled even though eligible candidates are available. In technical fields, such as engineering, science, and other technical jobs, there are very limited number of aspirants. This has been principally due to their economic backwardness in the past, but now there is increased aspiration for entry into these fields too.

The enormous volume of literature on Dalits is largely engaged with the socio-economic development of the Dalits. However, studies that deviated from such a traditional trend have focused on Dalit movement, ideology and the identity of the upwardly mobile Dalits, that is, those availing the benefits of the government policies of protective discrimination. These studies tend to show how the process of upward mobility among the ex-untouchables is giving rise to new questions of identity and ideology. However, the literature on the Dalit middle class is still very meagre. Here an attempt is made to provide a theoretical framework for the study encompassing the following concepts: *middle class*, *Dalit middle class* and *Dalit elite*. Literature on these themes has been reviewed thematically under each concept.

THEORIZING AND CONCEPTUALIZING 'MIDDLE CLASS': GLOBAL EXPERIENCE

When we examine the middle class in general, the relevant issues here are: Who are the middle class? What do they consist of and how are they different from others in the Indian situation, where caste is the primary stratification criteria? It is very difficult to trace the origins of the concept 'middle class', which is differently perceived by different scholars. It is generally believed that Lederer and Marschak (1926) are the first to analyse the middle class.[1] In addition, later on, many others developed the concept by offering different interpretations of 'middle class'. The middle class is referred to differently by various scholars, Whyte (1956) called a middle class individual as a 'man of the organizations'; Mills (1956) called them as 'man of corporation'; Lockwood (1958) called them as 'black-coated worker' and Dahrendorf (1967: 94) points out that Renner (1924) preferred to call the middle class, the 'service class'; later on they also came to be known as 'salaried class', 'white-collared worker' and other such names.

While Marxism uses the terms strata, fractions and categories to designate particular ensembles, it remains true that these strata, fractions and categories always belong to a class (Singh, 1985: 6). Mayer (1963: 468) views middle class as Marx's classless society of the modern industrial economy. Marx himself predicted the possibility of 'middle class' and its expansion in his theories of surplus value, in which, referring to Ricardo, he emphasizes 'the constant increase of the middle classes, who stand in the middle between workers on one side and the capitalist and landed proprietors on the other side, who are for the most part supported directly by Revenue, who rest as a burden on the labouring foundation and who increased the social security and the power of the upper 10,000' (Bottomore, 1964).

Holger Stub (1972: 104) hypothesizes 'the variation in lifestyle characterized by various groups in consumption patterns, social values, and political ideologies will increasingly promote the retention and formation of a wide variety of status communities in the middle levels of modern societies'. As Knowles (2006: 228) observes that in the case of Germany, the reason behind the origin of the middle class professions in the nineteenth century was due to more number of workers had freed themselves from land work and became class free labourers, at liberty to barter their services to the best bidder.

'OLD' AND 'NEW' MIDDLE CLASSES

Braverman (1979: 402) writes that 'The old middle class' occupied that position by virtue of its place outside the polar class structure, it possessed the attributes of neither capitalist nor worker, it played no part in the capital accumulation process whether on one side or the other. This 'new middle class' by contrast occupies its intermediate position not because it is outside the process of increasing capital, but because as a part of this process it takes its characteristics from both sides.[2]

There are two theories arguing about the nature of the new middle class – (1) an extension of the old, capitalist or ruling class [Croner (1954), Bendix (1956) and Renner (1952) are with this opinion] and (2) an extension of the proletariat or the one closer to the working class. Moreover, Dahrendorf (1959)[3] opines differently:

'the ruling class theory applies without exception to the social position of Bureaucrats, and the working class theory equally generally to the social position of white-collar workers'. Further, in England, Cole (1955) points out that two characteristic developments brought out the emergence of the new middle class. The public schools increased in number and over the same period the spread of the joint stock system, which greatly fostered large-scale enterprise, brought into existence a new large class of salaried managers and administrators, not only in mining and manufacture but also in banking, insurance and commerce.[4]

Prasad (1968: 6) quoting Lewis and Maude regarding the criteria to determine the characteristics of middle class, 'to which class an individual belongs to', avers that it depends upon a series of factors, 'including income, occupation, accent, spending habits, residence, culture, leisure pursuits, clothes, education, moral attitudes and relationships with other individuals'.

Singh defines the new middle class in India generally as:

> group of white collar-workers as we call it new middle class is constituted by various types of clerks, assistants, civil servants, executives, managers, professionals (such as doctors and engineers, and lawyers), working as salaried employees in organizations, supervisors, teachers and other educationists, employees working in various departments of Government, Banks and commercial firms, and salaried employees other than manual workers, in tertiary industries, viz., hotels, cinema, restaurants, advertising firms, travelling agencies, and insurance companies, etc. They all constitute the new middle class. All enjoy a salaried status, job security, old age benefits, medical facilities, and other perks. The underlying assumption of vital significance is that they work in organizations, big or small, doing non-manual work. (Singh, 1985: 72)

Providing a similar picture of Black middle class in the United States of America, Pinkney (1984) opines that though racism in the United States is less pronounced and racists are less vocal, race continues to be an ever-present part of the American way of life. He argues that the progress of Blacks in America remains a myth. Further, there is a trend by social scientists of either exaggerating the progress of the Afro-Americans or blaming them for their lack of progress, instead of blaming the forces in the society that serve to maintain their oppression.

Generally, education, income and occupation are considered as the three variables by which one's social class may be measured. The three variables are interrelated, although it is possible to use anyone as an indicator of social class. Pinkney (1984: 100) maintains that in the case of middle class Blacks, style of life is as important as income. Whenever middle class needs to be defined, the policy makers consider only the economic class and not the social class. This has resulted in many Blacks being counted as middle class in America by policy makers, though they do not possess the required characteristics of a middle class. It is often alleged that if the Blacks did not rise up to the middle class, the middle class was lowered to include more Blacks in order to show them as middle class.

However, of late many Blacks are taking to education, thereby entering occupations that placed them in a more comfortable social and economic position in comparison with the other Black masses. Here, they face the identity dilemma of either emulating middle class Whites' behaviour or associating with other middle class Blacks, as a fallout of rejection by the middle class Whites. Another significant aspect is that the middle class Blacks provide assistance to those remaining in the slums, if not to a large number, then at least to their immediate and extended families. Middle-class Blacks sponsor fundraising events for Black education, civil rights and community organizations.

LOCATING THE MIDDLE CLASS EMPIRICALLY

Daniel Bell (1974) argues that 'Now within the enterprise, in the position between employers and workers was a new stratum'. Lederer and Marschak (1926) called it a 'new middle class', less for its function than for its social evolution, which was based on their 'own self-esteem and the esteem of others'. Ghanshyam Shah (1990: 161) observes:

> The middle class is placed between labour and capital ... this class consists of the petty bourgeoisie and the white-collar workers. The former are either self employed or involved in the

> distribution of commodities and the latter are non-manual office workers, supervisors and professionals. Thus, in terms of occupations shopkeepers, salesmen, brokers, government and non-government office workers, writers, teachers and self-employed professionals such as engineers, pleaders, doctors, etc. constitute the middle class ... most of these occupations required at least some degree of formal education.

According to Dahrendorf (1967: 52), 'Presumably, a "middle class" is located somewhere between at least two other classes, one above it and one below it. Yet the "new middle class" has stubbornly resisted all attempts to define its upper and lower limits.' Similarly Cole's classification of the middle class as summed up by Prasad (1968: 9–10) includes 'salaried persons, including administrators, managers, social workers, shop assistants, clerks, etc. persons engaged in independent vocations as medical practitioners, lawyers, consultants, persons engaged in entrepreneurial or business activity; and retired persons'.

As the complexity in various fields grew, the need for a 'middle class' increased, so are supervisors, managers and administrators, both scientific and technical. Negating the theories of class, both Marxist and Warner's schemes of six classes – middle classes grew in number and have stabilized themselves as a category. Both the conceptualization of economic class and social class could not predict the emergence and growth of the middle classes. Whyte (1956) gave the 'organization man' thesis and argued that the replacement of the small enterprise by large-scale organizations has led to the rise of the 'salaried' employee leaving back the 'self-employed' man. This growth of large-scale organizations increased white-collar workers and lay down a distinct lifestyle and attitudes of that group.

Even, it is believed that the origin of the middle class has a context, that is, the Industrial Revolution. Earlier, it was mostly the working class who constituted the 'middle' class. In Europe, 'historically, the bourgeoisie has been called the "middle class" because it stood between the landowning class and the working class' (Singh, 1985: 18). After the decline of the gentry, the grand bourgeoisie became the ruling class, then 'petty bourgeoisie' became the 'middle class' – that is, the small traders, independent small businessmen, the self-employed professional and the independent artisan. 'The white-collar people have clean-bowled

Warner's scheme (Warner, 1957) of six classes. Leaving the upper-upper and the lower-lower class, they penetrated inhibitantly and walked in freely in the other four' (Singh, 1985: 3).

As many scholars expected, the middle class has not disappeared, but in fact has expanded and, with increasing modernization, has multiplied numerically along with industrial growth. The 'middle mass', which is not a ruling class, at the same time, neither a pure working class, played its role in the growth and development of the industrial economy. Joseph Mathew (1986: 71) quoting Goldthorpe et al. (1968: 52) observes that even when manual workers earned very high wages, they did not take up middle class attitudes. They saw their work as a means of getting money rather than as a career. They did not mix with middle class people. Krausz (1969: 167) notes, 'Occupation ... has been accepted as the most important single criterion and most useful index of social status'.

The origin of the middle class and its characteristics are thus explained variedly: 'In Great Britain occupation is probably the most important single criterion of status' (Glass and Hall, 1967: 178), and 'Vertical mobility is often inferred from occupational mobility and the inference is generally justified because the position of the individual in the total pattern of inequality largely depends on the occupation' (Broom and Selznick, 1970: 178). Further, Singh (1985: 1–2) notes: 'In the process of growing, middle class has become a different type of social formation. More and more the bulk of white-collar positions open up to competition through achievement and ability. New stratum of the white-collar employee, clerical, technical, administrative and professional emerged'.

The next interesting argument about the 'middle class' is that, as the nature of the class and the members of the class varied from time to time, the feature of the 'middle class' consequently changed, and hence one can distinguish between the old middle class and the new middle class. The old middle class is the one that includes peasants, petty bourgeoisie, traders, artisans, etc. which is located externally to the capitalist relationship of production, in a sense that capitalist production relations dominated them without been integrated into the capitalist class structure. 'However the so called new middle class are structurally ambiguous class situations – draw their ambiguous class character directly from the structure of capitalist relations of production' (Crompton and Gubbay, 1977), that is to point towards the white-collar employees, clerical, technical and administrative professionals.

The emergence of the new middle class is a striking development of this century. The new middle class now stands for no particular criteria compared to earlier definitions. Now, the new middle class has lost its middle class character, 'as painted by Lewis and Mande, i.e. to practice a particular type of occupation white-collar; to enjoy a particular level of income-above average; to have received a particular level of education – at school or university; and to live in a good comfortable house in a good responsible area, has faded' (Singh, 1985: 1).

When everybody else is being drawn under the (rather broad) category of middle class, the imminent question that arises is, 'and then who is not a middle class'? For which, Bendix and Lipset (1966: 22) offer that 'those men whose fate is not determined by the chance of using goods or services for themselves on the market, for e.g. slaves, are not, however, a "class" in the technical sense of the term. They are, rather, a "status group"'.

MIDDLE CLASS IN INDIA: EMERGENCE AND CHARACTERISTICS

The origin and expansion of the middle classes in India have been widely studied. Such studies attempted to locate, analyse and interpret those classes in various social, economic and political contexts. The first and foremost important study till date being, B.B. Misra's *Indian Middle Classes*, that is a singular attempt in terms of its magnitude and nature. Later, studies by Bhagwan Prasad (1968),[5] Y.P. Chibbar (1968)[6] and Gurchain Singh (1985)[7] also focused on analysing the characteristics of the Indian middle classes. During the British period, the British introduced a new land revenue system, which gave rise to tax collectors who in turn exploited the peasants and grabbed the lands, forming a new landed class. The mediators between the British and the people, the interpreters, small businessmen and others formed a middle class (Matto, 1991).

Given the circumstances, the middle class has greater opportunities to address and to lead us to a better understanding of the Dalits, their disabilities, sufferings and their day-to-day struggles through the ages: to overcome poverty, untouchability and participate in the rapidly changing Indian socio-economic and political scenario. Their ambition and their plans for the future are effectively communicated through the middle class. The rich class mainly identifies with the community's past, its dream of a better future for the entire community, unless it is trapped by, and confined to its self-interest.

The self-perception of belonging to the middle class is another crucial aspect that needs to be looked into in a study of the middle class. Prasad (1968: 7) observes:

> Some sociologists are inclined to say that an individual must feel that he belongs to a certain group. It is doubtful whether this criterion will help us. Persons having an air of superiority may very well claim to belong to an upper class, whereas persons having a humbler outlook may derive pleasure in associating themselves with a lower group. It is, therefore, not enough that a man has a feeling of belonging to a certain class. This concept will have the problem of over-estimation as it is a class in which many prefer to remain even when they do not belong to this group.

Further, emphasizing on the importance of self-perception of class he notes that 'many persons earning four digited salaries and enjoying most of the conveniences of life prefer to call themselves as middle class people' (Prasad, 1968: 7). Similarly, S.M. Dubey (1972: 145–146) accepts the self-perception of class status of professionals[8] and reports that they have identified themselves upper class, upper middle, lower middle and lower classes.

Quoting a national-level survey conducted in 1994–1996 by the Centre for the Study of Developing Societies (CSDS), Sheth (1999: 2510) observes that the new criteria evolved for identifying the middle class is as follows:

> The survey conceived the category middle class in terms of subjective and objective variables. The subjective variable pertained to respondent's own identification as 'middle class'

> and an explicit rejection of 'working class' identity for himself/herself. Using self-identity as a precondition, certain objective criteria were applied for inclusion of a respondent in the 'middle class' category. Thus, from among those with middle class self-identification, respondents possessing two of the following four characteristics were included in the middle class category: (i) 10 years or more of schooling, (ii) ownership of at least three assets out of four, i.e. motor vehicle, TV, electric pumping-set and non-agricultural land, (iii) residence in a pucca house – built of brick and cement, (iv) white-collar job. Accordingly, 20 per cent of the sample population was identified as belonging to the middle class.

Further studies carried out in India have revealed that the middle class has certain 'white-collar' attitudes, namely: (1) a 'Babu' mentality, (2) preference for non-manual and non-agricultural work and (3) a largely urban concentration. And,

> [T]here is considerable truth in the belief that the middle class is engaged in non-manual, non-agricultural operations. Prior to independence, it included people belonging mostly to the clerical cadre. After independence there are decidedly more avenues open to this group and we can include people engaged in more varied occupations. A middle earning member includes persons of medium income like teachers, medical practitioners, traders, junior executives, public servants, small entrepreneurs, lawyers, planners, architects, engineers and so on. (Prasad, 1968: 8)

The lifestyle (basically the expenditure pattern) of the middle class differs from the strata above them (i.e. rich or aristocratic class), who spend on luxurious items such as parties, entertainments, maintaining a car and going to clubs, and at the same time the strata below them (the working class). Middle-class families also have to go 'upward' or 'downward' according to the individuals' profession and income (Prasad, 1968: 8–9).

Class and social mobility among the three classes shows that the higher the class, the greater the probability of upward mobility. 'There is a considerable drop in the proportion of upward mobility immediately after the middle classes. The differential between proportions of the middle and lower classes is 33.9 per cent as against a differential of 27.1 per cent in the case of upper and middle classes. The upper class is almost three times more upwardly mobile than the lower class. This rather clearly stresses the deterministic role of class. The circulation of positions is confined to upper and middle classes and the lower classes have only limited access' (Philips, 1990: 68).

Indicating a change in such a situation in the context of formation of a new middle class in India, Sheth (1999: 2510) provides a broad profile of the 'new middle class in India' based on the findings of a latest empirical study on the middle class in India by the Centre for the Study of Developing Societies (CSDS):

> The survey analysis revealed that even today, the upper and the rich farmer castes together dominate the Indian 'middle class'. While members of the two upper categories, the dwija upper castes and the non-dwija dominant castes, account for about a quarter of the sample population, they constitute nearly half of the new middle class. But this also means the representation of upper castes has reduced in today's middle class, for the old middle class was almost entirely constituted by them.

Further, Sheth notes a change in the situation as far as inclusion of 'lower castes' in the middle class is concerned, that is, at least in the recent past:

> About half of the middle class population came from different lower-caste social formations, i.e. the dalits (SCs), the tribals (STs), the backward communities of peasants and artisans (OBCs) and the religious minorities. Considering that members of all these social formations constituted 75 per cent of the sample population, their 50 per cent representation in the middle class is much lower than that of the upper and intermediate castes. But seen in the context of their inherited lower ritual status in the traditional hierarchy, this is a significant development. Even more significant is the fact that when members of the lower-castes, including those belonging to castes of 'ex-untouchables', acquire modern means of social mobility, such as education, wealth, political power, etc. their low ritual status does not come in the way of their entering the middle class and, more importantly, acquiring the consciousness of being members of the middle class.

Further, there is marked change in the 'new middle class' in terms of its nature. The new 'recruits' are bringing in their social group values into the middle class.

> The Indian middle class today has a significant rural component, thanks to the earlier inclusion in it of the rural based dominant castes and now of the members of the lower castes participating in modern economy and administration. In brief, the middle class in India today is not a simple demographic category comprising of certain ritual-status groups. It is a social-cultural formation in which as individuals from different castes and communities enter, they acquire new economic and political interests, and lifestyles, in common with the other members of that 'class'. Within this new middle class, caste identities of its members survive, but operating in conjunction with the new, overarching identity of middle class, they acquire a different political and cultural meaning.

THE CASE FOR AND OF DALIT MIDDLE CLASS

There are few studies dealing with Dalits who have benefited from the government policies of protective discrimination and other development programmes, leading to the emergence of a new social category among them, namely, Dalit elites (Abbasayulu, 1978; Roy and Singh, 1987; Sachidananda, 1974) or a segment of the 'middle classes' (Kulke, 1976; Ram, 1988). The earlier studies on the theme of Dalit middle class and Harijan elites looked into the incongruity between the social and economic mobility of Dalits in a context of the general process of social mobility in the Indian society. Kulke's (1976) study of 'Integration, Alienation and Rejection: The Status of Untouchables' dealt with 300 SCs and non-SCs from Dhanbad in Bihar. Ram's study (1988) on 'Rise of a New Middle Class' among the Scheduled Castes has 240 respondents from various occupational backgrounds varying between sweepers and Class I services. Roy and Singh's (1987) study, dealing with Harijan elites caught up 'between two worlds', has 55 respondents in occupations such as political leaders, caste leaders, bureaucrats, doctors, engineers, lawyers, teachers and businessmen.

Two of the studies were located in cities in Uttar Pradesh and were carried out during the mid-1980s. They deal with social and economic mobility and the identity question of the Dalits in an urban setting with intergenerational educational and occupational upward mobility, their level of assimilation into the middle class lifestyle and the problems involved therein. Such studies suggest the rise of a new section among the Dalits, namely, Dalit middle class or elites who are perceived to be in an extraordinary situation of identity crisis and increased aspirations, who are on the move but have not reached their destination as yet.[9]

Kulke (1976) studied the 'Status of Untouchables' or the beneficiaries of the reservation policies introduced by the post-independence Indian state, to look at the processes *of Integration, Alienation and Rejection* with reference to 'Accommodation, Confrontation and Rejection of Scheduled Castes vis-à-vis the Hindu society'.[10] He found that the social background of middle class 'untouchables' was predominantly from a few Scheduled Castes. Middle class Dalits' social environment was different from the community of their origin and they were not fully integrated into 'main stream' middle class culture, which is largely dominated by upper castes. Middle class Dalits generally lived in Dalit neighbourhoods. Caste continued to be an important factor in assessing their social status. However, with upward economic mobility, they could avail services from others and neither did they feel the need of *sanskritizing* their ritual life. He also observed that in contrast to most of the illiterate Dalits who identified themselves with Gandhian ideology, the middle class Dalits identified more with Ambedkar.

He predicts, 'India will have to face a social conflict of unpredictable proportions if its 75 million untouchables cannot be integrated socially, economically, and politically' (1976: 244). There have been two different approaches to solve the problem of untouchables. They are Ambedkar's concept of segregation and confrontation, and Gandhi's concept of integration. The Indian Government took the latter approach as the official policy and provided concessions and reservations in the name of 'protective discrimination' to untouchables to achieve the same.

Kulke's study shows that the state policy had a positive effect on a considerable number of individuals among the Scheduled Castes in terms of moving into higher social positions. However,

(1) most of the middle class Dalits are predominantly from a few Scheduled Castes. (2) Occupation of the father has a lot to do with the children's higher positions; it shows that there is no sudden/direct development in switching over from the caste occupation to higher social position in one's life, but father's occupation – other than caste occupation, preferably a small job – is the first step to achieve a higher social and economic position/status in one's life. (3) The social environment of 'successful untouchables' is different from that of their community of origin. As they move on to a higher social and economic status, they have become distanced from their community of origin. Yet, in spite of this process, most of these untouchables have not evolved social contacts with the upper strata. (4) They dwelt largely in the neighbourhood of untouchables, preferably with their own community, as upper castes were not prepared to mingle with them. Even so, the middle class untouchables tended to prefer their own community people on the one condition that they were also educated and belonged to their class. (5) Friendship with upper castes in offices or outside is not possible for all untouchables but only for untouchables with higher social and economic status. (6) Family friendships are higher between higher social and economic status (SES) untouchables and higher SES upper-caste people, than in the case of lower SES untouchables and upper castes. (7) Higher economic status gives more chances of getting served by barbers, washer man and so on, on par with caste-Hindus. (8) Higher social status draws middle class untouchables away from their community of origin. (9) Higher SES/middle class untouchables do not give great importance to getting 'Sanskritized'. (10) Untouchability as a concept works as a psychological barrier. It depends not only on one's own experiences in the case of middle class untouchables, but also on other's experiences of keeping them away from the Hindu society. (11) Attachment towards Gandhi or Ambedkar among untouchables shows the middle class attachment to Ambedkar: the minimum educated have an attachment to both and illiterates mostly prefer only Gandhi. Among the youngest generation (the then Graduates) attachment towards Ambedkar is diminishing. (12) Another obstacle to the integration of untouchables into the larger society is that they have

to identify themselves as untouchables in order to get jobs, promotions and other benefits. (13) Middle-class untouchables' status now lies between partial acceptance and rejection, between integration, frustration and aggression. (14) This dilemma leads middle class untouchables to 'we consciousness' and they form associations to discuss common interested matters and to celebrate occasions such as Ambedkar's birthday. (15) Caste still is a relevant social dimension of status consciousness among middle class untouchables who otherwise attempt to overcome caste barriers (i.e. due to psychological barriers or the failure of the Gandhi's approach to integration). (16) The degree of perception of untouchability increases with a rising educational standard. This does not necessarily depend on any personal experience of untouchability; it is rather a consciousness of the discrimination suffered by their group of origin. Untouchability thus remains a psychological barrier against integration, also on the part of the untouchables themselves (Kulke, 1976: 249).

The desire to rise socially and to be accepted in the new middle class milieu leads to certain limitations. In the case of the untouchables, the mobility process clearly has a secular character, that is, the possibilities for and the efforts to obtain religious and ritual recognition are minimal. In general, all untouchables demonstrate a low religious activity, which decreases even further with professional or educational status mobility. This incipient process of change in the case of untouchables thus does not fit into Srinivas's Sanskritization scheme (Kulke, 1976: 249).

The consciousness of having repeatedly to suffer discrimination and of belonging to a group that is branded untouchable manifests itself in the form of latent psychological barriers, which hinders the efforts of socially mobile Scheduled Castes members towards social integration. Frequently, this consciousness is not even based on direct personal experience, but rather on unconscious group solidarity or the conscious efforts to detach and efface oneself from the group of origin. In any case, the adoption of a detached and neutral attitude towards their caste of origin is very difficult for the socially mobile (Scheduled Castes) members (Kulke, 1976: 247–248).

The identification of mobile Scheduled Castes varies with their education level and social status. Thus, those who favour Gandhi as the leader of SCs also prefer the usage of the term 'Harijans'. While the majority of the moderately mobile untouchables preferred the neutral official characterization 'Scheduled Castes'; and the most educated and most successful social climbers chose self-characterizations such as 'Indian', 'Hindu' or simply 'human being' (Kulke, 1976: 251–252). Measurement of political radicalization tested with the given options yielded figures such as political system – democratic (46.7%), dictatorial-totalitarian (14.6%) or revolutionary (38.7%) – in terms of which option suits the best to solve the problems of untouchables. With the increase in educational level, the option for revolution increases (Kulke, 1976: 252).

Ram (1988) prefers the category 'middle class' for the beneficiaries of reservation policies and observes that there are a small number of Scheduled Castes individuals who have benefited from the policy of protective discrimination and consequently acquired a better socio-economic status. Their employment in white-collar jobs meant upward mobility in the class structure. While they were forging new patterns of social relationships with people in their workplace and elsewhere – irrespective of caste and community considerations – the degree and direction of their mobility was not clear. Quoting Saberwal (1972: 114), Ram regards mobile people as those who 'Have either been upwardly mobile earlier or are upwardly mobile now, or are getting equipped for upward mobility in the foreseeable future'. Ram argues that the middle class among the Scheduled Castes is different from the old middle class. Since the economic mobility of Scheduled Castes does not necessitate an equal social mobility, there is an incongruity between their social and economic mobility.

Further, Ram (1988) has attempted to measure upward social mobility among the Scheduled Castes. He employs measures such as Socio-economic Status (SES) Scale, Caste Status Ranking (CSR) Scale and Social Distance (SDS) Scale. In correlation of social status and economic status, Ram argues, however, that the dominant pattern of social stratification in India has been that of caste. The hierarchies of caste and class have not functioned, so far, in a parallel direction. It seems the class structure is inclusive of caste structure and vice versa. Consequently, the mobility of a person in the class structure has not always led to his mobility in the caste structure. This has happened more in the case of the lower and particularly the lowest castes because the latter had suffered immensely from numerous social and religious disabilities in the past. Complete social mobility had neither occurred in the past nor is occurring in the present – it is possible only through a rigorous political action involving, 'a civic value oriented social system instead of a family, caste, religion and language oriented one'.[11]

Compared to the early stages of its formation, the Dalit middle class today is more assertive of its identity and more firm on its ideological foundation. In spite of witnessing mobility in economic status, mobility in social status eluded the middle class Dalits. Since then, the course of social mobility has remained a contested ground between the Dalits and others. Amidst resentment and rejection on the one hand and intermittent allurements to suppress their caste identity in exchange of admission into the inner circles of the middle class on the other hand, most of the Dalit middle class individuals had clung to their Dalit identity. This was mainly due to the very initiation process that embedded Dalit consciousness and Dalit ideology in them.

However, the characteristics of the Dalit middle class are not uniform. They have different backgrounds and different locations now. Such diversity in backgrounds and locations necessitates a variation in their identity patterns. In this regard, Omvedt explains:

> Not all of the new Dalit middle class are radicals. Many are simply enjoying the benefits of the new life. They call themselves Hindus and are trying to live as others do. Some are living far from home and are unwilling to reveal their humble backgrounds. Some are living calm lives with relatives, not connected with any causes. Nor are they all second generation; some are first-generation educated while some are living and working so far away from their rural homes that they are able to hide their identity. It is only now that they are beginning to come out. (Omvedt, 2001: 27)

Further, Omvedt (2001) differentiates between 'old' and 'new' Dalit middle classes and she elaborates:

> The earlier Dalit middle class fought against casteism, but were often concerned with personal survival to do much. During the 1970s and 1980s Dalit protests were expressed by fighting riots and resisting atrocities physically. The new generation is now coming into their own and discovering a new pride in being Dalit. (Omvedt, 2001: 27)

Referring to the 'new Dalit middle class', she observes:

> This generation is, in part, a product of the policy of reservations. Even if there were no state policies to promote the education and employment of ex-untouchables, a middle class would have evolved because of the new opportunities for mobility in a more open and equalitarian society. But it is certain that it would have happened much more slowly, with deprivation and bitterness involved in the process ... This generation is, in part, a product of the policy of reservations. Even if there were no state policies to promote the education and employment of ex-untouchables, a middle class would have evolved because of the new opportunities for mobility in a more open and equalitarian society. But it is certain that it would have happened much more slowly, with deprivation and bitterness involved in the process. (Omvedt, 2001: 27)

The middle class Dalits are in the similar status of being the discriminated sections of the society in relation to caste-Hindus, as they too experience discrimination along with other Dalits. Omvedt opines:

> But these differences, apart from the apparent alienation between the middle class leaders and the Dalit proletariat, pale before the fact that all sections of Dalits, whether professors, professionals, clerks or agricultural labourers, have experienced the humiliations and exploitations of casteism at crucial points in their life. (Omvedt, 2001: 27–28)

The qualitative difference here being in terms of their endurance and the means and capacity to fight caste-based exploitation. The middle class Dalits possess the leadership qualities mainly provided by their social and economic mobility from which the Dalit masses could benefit. She further clarifies:

> Exploitation takes different forms, but people at every level, from labourer to highly educated, have experienced discrimination because they don't have the same degree of influence, money and family linkages of the upper castes. It is this unpalatable experience of Brahminism, which holds together the various Dalit middle class communities and factions. Holding them together is also a simple economic fact: the 'middle class' is not a solidary group. Instead, there is a ladder and a sliding scale of privilege and attainment. At all levels, Dalits aspire to a better life, and this may mean a higher pay or a little land for agricultural labourers, a higher position in the bureaucracy and more prestige for the educated. One does not necessarily see the other's success as cutting off his opportunities. But Dalits clearly distrust their political leadership. (Omvedt, 2001: 28)

However, the emergence of the Dalit middle class is not the panacea for all the problems the Dalits face today. Thus, she opines:

> The rise of Dalit middle class does not mean the end of casteism and oppression; a growing middle class of an oppressed group simply strengthens the overall fight against oppression. The new Dalit millennium will be an interesting one! (Omvedt, 2001: 30)

Indeed, the Dalit middle class is a product of social justice or protective discrimination policy of the Indian state, and the enabling environment coupled with their inner urge to rise above their disadvantageous situation that accelerated their recruitment into the middle class in such a large scale within a short span of time. Quoting Mendelsohn and Vicziany (2000) as Jodhka (2010: 16) observes:

> over the years the size of Dalit middle class grew, thanks largely to the policy of reservations in government jobs and educational institutions. As they grew in numbers they also felt more confident in articulating their experiences of discrimination at the workplace and the continued caste based prejudice against their communities in the society at large. They began to form separate associations of Scheduled Caste employees and mobilized themselves in events of discriminatory experience of their caste fellows.

However, the process of social change was inadequate in reaching all the Dalits and, at the same time, the opportunities provided for their social and economic mobility are meagre compared to the rising aspirations among them. The incongruity in social and economic mobility of the middle class Dalits is a hurdle that has a bearing on the very process of their social mobility.

ARE MIDDLE CLASS DALITS ELITES TOO?

The earlier studies on the theme of Dalit middle class and Harijan elites looked into the ambiguity in the social and economic mobility of Dalits in the process of their social mobility. Ram's study on 'rise of a new middle class' among the scheduled castes has 240 respondents from various occupational backgrounds varying between sweepers and class I services. Roy and Singh's (1987) study dealing with Harijan elites caught up 'between two worlds' has 55 respondents in occupations such as political leaders, caste leaders, bureaucrats, doctors, engineers, lawyers, teachers and businessmen. Both the studies were located in the cities in Uttar Pradesh and were carried out during mid-1980s. They deal with the social and economic mobility and the identity question of the Dalits in an urban setting with intergenerational educational and occupational upward mobility and the level of assimilation into a middle class lifestyle and the problems involved therein.

Such studies suggest a rise of new section among Dalits middle class or elites as it perceived to be in a strange situation of identity crisis and increased aspirations. They are on the move and not reached the destination yet.[12] At the same time, many recent studies that dealt with social change, social mobility and Dalit politics have not focused on the Dalit middle class in a full-fledged manner. They have focused on either mobility or political consciousness. So far, there have been only two empirical studies on the Dalit middle class (Kulke, 1976; Ram, 1988). Both the studies suggest the formation of a new Dalit middle class and its existence in many senses independent of the general middle class and poor Dalits. Even among these two, Nandu Ram's study was more intensive in looking at the socio-economic mobility and identity patterns among the Dalit middle class. These two studies concentrated on North India, especially few towns in Uttar Pradesh. So far, no such studies exist in South India.

The word 'Elite'[13] first used in the sixteenth century meant a 'choice'. In the seventeenth century, it was used to describe 'commodities of particular excellence'; and later on to denote 'superior social groups' such as crack military units or the higher ranks of the nobility. According to Oxford English Dictionary, the earliest use of 'elites' is in 1823, denoting social groups. Until the nineteenth century, the term did not become famous in the social and political writings of Europe or until the 1930s in Britain[14] and America (Bottomore, 1964).[15] The term came into vogue towards the close of the nineteenth century in the socio-political literature of Europe, Britain and America, and in 1930, through sociological writings, especially those of the Italian sociologist Pareto. The term was used to mean many things and to describe certain fundamental features of organized social life.

Pareto's[16] theory of the elite suggests that 'in every society there are people who possess in a marked degree the qualities of intelligence, character, skill, and capacity of whatever kind'. Mosca (1933)[17] divided elites into (1) governing elite (directly in government positions) and (2) non-governing elite (intellectuals). According to Lasswell (1952),[18] there are as many elites as there are values. According to Kerr et al. (1960),[19] there are five categories of elite in the industrialization process: (1) a dynamic elite, (2) the middle class, (3) the revolutionary, (4) the colonial administrators and (5) the nationalist leaders. Mosca delineates factors, which help a person or group to emerge as elite. He says wealth is the main factor. In some societies, the priestly class will emerge as the elite and in some other, the hereditary castes. Mosca stressed that wealth and military valour are the characteristic features of the dominant class.

Weber (1953) classified the elite into political as well as intellectual; they are feudal and charismatic in nature. Similarly, Pareto[20] describes that recruitment to elite consists in merit and reorganization. From the lower classes too, an elite could be recruited. The following are the factors in elite recruitment: (1) hereditary (birth in aristocratic families); (2) wealth (richness); (3) religious dominance; (4) education and (5) individual ability.

However, in a complex society like India, these characteristics do not help in identifying the elites as they are broad in nature. Lal (1995: 148–157) observes that the problem of identifying elites is not new to social scientists today. Studies conducted in this sphere have mostly been conducted in Western communities following three broad approaches: (a) positional, (b) reputational and (c) issue participation approaches to the identification of elites.[21] Sau (1986: 123–124) notes that there is rapid expansion of white-collar employees in India compared to the industrial workers. Moreover, Shah (1990: 161) adds that a large majority of the members of the middle class belong to the upper middle castes.

In Indian society, princes, priests, landlords and top persons in the upper castes may be regarded to form the groups of traditional elites. In the nineteenth century, education was mainly responsible for the creation of new groups: of civil servants, legal and medical practitioners, engineers, university teachers, journalists and creative writers. In the post-independence period, with the expansion of administration, education and the growth of the centres of administration, now, new groups of elites have also emerged. Actually, the area of elite recruitment has widened (Dubey, 1971: 29–30).

Analysing the term elite under all these definitions, we can arrive at the conclusion that the elements such as superiority, power and organization are important in defining the term elite. Thus, we may think of the elite as those who are regarded as superior, influential and are held in high esteem by the people; they may or may not have formal positions in politics and the government, but they are in a position to influence the decision-making process, set values and uphold them. It is here that the imminent question arises, whether all communities have a free access into the elites, more specifically, do the Dalits become elites? Heimsath (1964: 5) argues that in India, social reform did not ordinarily mean a reorganization of the structure of society at large, as it did in the West, for the benefit of the underprivileged social and economic classes. Instead, it meant the infusion into the existing social structure of new ways of life and thought, which determined that the society would be preserved, while its members would be transformed.

Navlakha (1989) argues that elite formation in India can be understood by studying industrial managers, civil servants and academicians because these are the areas the elite aspirants are generally attracted to. He mainly focused on the following:[22]

> (1) caste background, (2) urban versus rural background, (3) economic background, (4) father's income, (5) work/employment of fathers and (6) fathers' education.

His study shows that 79 per cent of the respondents are from socially and economically advantageous backgrounds, while the rest are from moderately advantageous backgrounds and none from socially and economically disadvantageous backgrounds. The other studies conducted on similar themes cited by Navlakha are background of students (Jayaram, 1977; Sharma, 1976), students' enrolment in IITs (King, 1970), Indian students abroad (Jesudason, 1977), Urban Elite of Jodhpur (Lal, 1974), Indian Managerial elite (Jain, 1971), etc. He argues that all these studies show that the aspirants as well as the settled elites hail from somewhat advantageous backgrounds only, and lower sections of society are not represented in these even if it is marginal. Another important observation made from the study is that 'as a consequence of Western education, the upper castes like Brahmins, Kayasthas, Baniyas, etc. and some Muslims have emerged as middle class and from these middle classes most of the elite, including political bureaucratic, military and business have emerged' (Navlakha, 1989: 23).

Sharma (1994: ix) observes that there are two main sources of mobility for Scheduled Castes, namely, (1) the welfare measures and (2) certain socio-cultural movements.[23] Patwardhan[24] as cited in Sharma (1994: 246–47) observes: 'The overall perspective is that there is an increasing possibility for upward mobility for all the Harijans'. She states, 'there are two processes of mobility: (1) through corporate efforts; and (2) by competing between castes and within a caste'. Patwardhan also notices that migration, education and white-collar jobs particularly outside the village have been the main sources of social mobility among the SCs. The challenge to the ideology of Varna and the construction of a counter-ideology is made possible only with the emergence of new

Dalit elite, which is separated from and no longer depended on the traditional order and its political economy. In many senses, the ideology that is fashioned is the product of these elite and has relevance largely within that social context. Yet, the legitimacy of that ideology and of those who are elite is defined in terms of its relationship to the Dalit masses. Hence, the articulation of a new Dalit consciousness rests on a fundamental paradox; it is not a mass consciousness, but depends for its validity on posited connection with the masses (Gokhale, 1990: 212–213).

The idea behind the Harijan or Scheduled Castes elites had developed from the observation of the 'widening gap' between some SCs[25] and the rest of the untouchables, for whom the policies such as positive discrimination were meant (Dushkin, 1972: 212). K.L. Sharma argues: 'the realization that unevenness exists among the Scheduled Castes has led to the exploration of what is popularly known as "Scheduled Castes Elites"' (1986: 56). The development of very few persons or families from the SCs, who having utilized all the programmes and block others who are more needy in availing of the same programmes, leads to 'gaps' within the SCs. Thus, some families form as elites or middle classes and the rest remain poor. Consequently, various constitutional measures have produced and will produce, with the existing rate of progress, only a minority of the middle classes among the Scheduled Castes, and the majority of the Dalits have remained and will remain a relatively poor working class. There are elites among SCs, but the question is who these elites are? What is their socio-economic background? How they reach elite positions? Do they take up the cause of the advancement of their fellow men? What are the differences between them and the non-Scheduled Caste elite? In a sense, it refers to those who are included/involved to a greater or smaller extent in the decision-making process, which implies the exercise of the intellect and rational judgement on their part (Abbasayulu, 1978). The economic mobility of Scheduled Castes, which had its origins in the British period itself, registered an improvement only after independence. Again, this improvement was only among those castes, individual families among them, who have acquired land, utilized various government facilities and those are concentrated mostly in urban areas (Ram, 1995: 41). There are quite a few studies on Dalit elites (Harijan or Scheduled Caste elites as they were called earlier). K.L. Sharma (1986: 56) lists the following studies:

> Herold's *India's Ex-Untouchables,* Saberwal's *Scheduled Caste Elites of Punjab,* Sachchidanand's *The Harijan Elite* and Deshpande's *Scheduled Caste Elites and Social Change* are some of the most well known titles on this theme. Issacs interviewed fifty educated persons from the Scheduled Castes; Saberwal added eight more that is, he interviewed fifty eight, Sachidananda interviewed 200. Deshpande slid down much below Issacs, and interviewed only twenty-nine Harijan elites.

He observes:

> Two points of methodological and substantive nature emerge from these studies of Scheduled Castes and their elites: (1) The reliance is on the information which the researchers could gather from their respondents (elites in this case); and (2) it is by and large realised that the 'unevenness' among the Scheduled Castes, inherently prevalent as well as created by the implementation of policies and programmes for their welfare, is mainly responsible for their backwardness. (Sharma, 1986: 56)

Abbasayulu (1978) studied the elite Dalits in Andhra Pradesh, in which he evolved a criterion to recognize elites.[26] Those who are involved to a greater or smaller extent in the decision-making process, which implies the exercise of intellect and rational judgement on their part, are elites. Thus, (1) those who are elected/nominated to both the legislative assembly and legislative council, etc. including ministers; (2) those Scheduled Caste members who have been recruited to the IAS cadre; (3) those who are employed as lawyers and judges; (4) those working as doctors and engineers and (5) those employed as teachers in the three old[27] universities. He further categorizes those from the categories (1) and (2) as political elites, (3) as administrative elites and (4) and (5) as the intellectual elite. He recognizes the role of the elites in the development of Scheduled Castes in general. He observes that the Scheduled Castes elites or elite Dalits represent the grievances of Scheduled Castes at the different fora such as the legislative assembly and the political parties.

Sachidananda (1974) carried out a study of *The Harijan Elites* in Bihar. He considered educated Harijans for this study. He also evolved a criterion to recognize elite Dalits. For him, 'any Harijan who is a matriculate and lives in a village is an elite', and a 'Harijan who is a graduate and lives in a town or a city is considered as an elite'.[28] He finds elite Dalits as 'torch bearers' of social change, for they are most active and powerful agents of social transformation. They are the catalysts of change. Similarly, Roy and Singh in their study of Harijan elites deal with, the 'dilemma that the Scheduled Castes face today', in the context of 'transformation of the social system on the slippery path of socio-economic status upgradation', they observe that the Scheduled Castes now remain suspended 'between the two poles of rebellion and silence (Roy and Singh, 1987: v–iv). The Scheduled Caste elite are concerned with community problems; the issue of reservations; community solidarity and the upliftment of the community.

Roy and Singh (1987: 12–13) observe that the impact of modernization created spaces for Scheduled Castes to become elites. The journey of Scheduled Castes 'to the promised land of economic security, equality and dignity' continues contrary to the expectation that it would end up on the availing of facilities such as reservations in education and in the services. The worldview introduced by the British Raj lit a ray of hope among 'untouchables' to overcome their 'fateful condition and their status of passive subjects to that of active citizens', and it sets up a new goal to be achieved, that is, 'equality democratically'. Roy and Singh (1987: 20) further posit a view that Harijan elites are 'caught between the two worlds of trouble; some past which they cannot completely give up and the uncertain future which they must go on trying to share'. 'The Harijan Elites', they say, 'as the most knowledgeable, articulate and advanced sector of the untouchables, are in a better position to express their community's concerns and the way to realize them'.

Modern consciousness, which contradicts the caste system and 'untouchability', is gaining importance in India. However, there are several threats posed by the upper strata whose interests lie with the perpetuation of the caste system, who want the traditional values to be continued. The Dalits, realizing that their future will be with the opposition of the caste system, will fight against it. There are two strategies, which they may employ for development. One is collective political action and other is personal or individual salvation. The Dalit elites prefer the path of individual salvation through upward social mobility, better jobs and access to power and positions through different political parties. The Dalit elites who emerged from their depressed positions to acquire elite status are caught between these two worlds. On the one hand, they aspire to be different, while on the other hand, they are blamed for maintaining a distance from their own community.

Aggarwal (1983) presented the cases of educated Scheduled Castes who did well in their respective fields; he worked with the categories of students, peons, clerks, officials, doctors, engineers and politicians in his study *Halfway to Equality* conducted in Delhi in 1983. The study deals with the successful Scheduled Castes persons from Delhi, as well as from the other states, drawing upon information pertaining to: their personal family background, their mobility 'up from the bottom', the government benefits for SC students, the hardships they faced in the process of reaching present positions, their views on untouchability, personal experiences, friendship with upper castes and its consequences, their attachment to their community, and so on; all these were recorded in their own words and narrative style. The author presents all the narratives to the reader and asks them to decide themselves whether or not these 'educated, aspired Harijans' achieved equality on par with other castes. In his opinion, these educated SCs derived some privileges, are hopeful about their future and possess greater tolerance with regard to the existing conditions than their counterparts, that is, rest of the SCs who have not benefited similarly. Aggarwal's theorization of the status of mobile Dalits, once they move up from their original socio-economic statuses, is that 'they are half way to equality'. He provides the examples: (1) individual men and women with education and good jobs are being accepted by the high castes as equals; (2) they still carry the stigma of their caste and (3) back in their villages, being untouchables, they are afraid of encountering insults due to the upper castes' jealousy of their achievements.[29] On the issue of 'identification', he observes that most of the respondents do not want to hide their identity and further reports that their experiences reveal that it is futile to hide or pass over their identity. 'Most people, however, neither announce their caste voluntarily, nor hide it when asked. Something analogous to America's "Black is beautiful" is happening'.[30]

Further, according to Aggarwal, the educated Harijan elites hailing from different regions and having settled in Delhi maintain relationships through meetings at conferences and festivals. Interest in Ambedkar and Buddha bonds them together, and they utilize this occasion for tasks such as matchmaking because there is a scarcity of educated SCs. One more observation that is interesting in this regard is that 'most educated Harijans are from the villages' and that 'rural Harijans are more upwardly mobile than their urban cousins'. He further adds that 'a large proportion of urban Harijans are sweepers whose employment opportunities as well as wages have improved over the years. Consequently, they have failed to strive for better positions in society'. Deshpande (2003), who has worked on the problem of social change and the role of elites among Scheduled Castes, observes that the position of the weaker sections is precarious in the caste hierarchy. To prove their status, they have to scale at least some heights in the caste hierarchy. The climb up would become possible only when the elites play a magnificent role for the betterment of Scheduled Castes. The main thrust of Deshpande's argument is that social change among SCs occurs through elites. Discussing the emergence of the capitalist class in modern India, Harish Damodaran (2008) observes that a capitalist class failed to emerge among the Dalits except a nascent bourgeoisie class:

> The group that has, nevertheless, been bypassed in this churning of capital and widening of its social base are the Dalits. In our study we did not come across a single Dalit industrialist even in the South. Recent reports suggest the rise of a nascent Dalit bourgeoisie, concurrent with the Bahujan Samaj Party (BSP) becoming a formidable force and occasionally ruling Uttar Pradesh via coalitions since the 1990s, and currently with a clear majority of its own. (Damodaran, 2008: 315–316)

The process of social change in India has resulted in social mobility among the 'lower castes' especially the Dalits. Such social mobility has been lacking in uniformity and has some limitations. It has not been able to effect changes in all the sectors equally, namely, social, economic, political and cultural. Similarly, it has not effected change among all the communities. However, in the case of the Dalits, it has resulted in the formation of a small section of 'Dalit elites' or Dalit middle class, mainly due to the mobility witnessed by them in education and employment. Drawing inspiration from the Ambedkar-led Dalit movement, the beneficiaries of the reservation policy after forming a new Dalit middle class engaged themselves in defining, redefining and sustaining Dalit ideology and identity. The immediate context for such articulations is the continuation of caste discrimination and perception of relative deprivation. In the absence of assimilation, these mobile individual Dalits keep to other Dalits with similar economic background.

NOTES

1. See Singh (1985: 2).
2. As quoted in Singh (1985: 27).
3. Dahrendorf (1959: 53).
4. See Singh (1985: 26).
5. See Prasad (1968). The study was carried out during 1958–1960 covering 500 middle-class families of five big towns of Uttar Pradesh (namely, Kanpur, Agra, Varanasi, Allahabad and Lucknow with 100 families from each town).
6. See Chibbar (1968).
7. See Singh (1985).
8. He studied Civil and Railway Officials, College teachers, Doctors, Engineers, Lawyers and University teachers in the city of Gorakhpur.
9. See Kulke (1976), Ram (1988), Roy and Singh (1987) and Aggarwal (1983) for this line of argument.
10. A similar study was carried out by Khan (1994) in Karnataka to inquire into identity formation and self-identity.
11. For further details, see Ahmed and Ahmed (1964: 244).
12. See Kulke (1976), Ram (1988), Roy and Singh (1987) and Aggarwal (1983).

13. Chandra (1987) traces the history of the concept of elite, 'During the 16th century, the term "elite" was used simply to mean a choice. In the 17th century, it signified commodities of a particular excellence. Later it was used to describe the superior social groups' (Bottomore, 1964: 25). According to Manheim (1940), 'elites' are those minorities, which are set apart from the rest of the society by their pre-eminence in one or more of these various distributions.
14. In Great Britain, it was used to denote non-political group, that is, those with assured entry into 'high society' were designated as elites. The term was used to indicate the superiority and exclusiveness pertaining to personal relationships (Cole, 1955: 102–103).
15. Bottomore (1964).
16. Pareto employed this term to designate a class, which held a high status and commanded influence in the community. He suggests: 'Let us assume that in every branch of human activity each individual is given an index which stands as a sign of his capacity, in very much the same way as grades are given in the various subjects in examination in schools ...'. So let us make a class of the people who have the highest indices in their branch of activity and to that class give the name of the elite (as quoted by Bottomore, 1964).
17. Mosca (1933: 53) defines the elite as an organized minority, obeying a single impulse, which holds domination over the unorganized majority.
18. For Lasswell (1952: 6), the members of the elite are 'the holders of high positions in a given society'. Cole (1955) refers to the elites as 'groups, which emerge to positions of leadership and influence at every social level'. Nadel (1956: 415) has defined the elite as a 'Whatever else we may mean by elite, we obviously mean a body of persons enjoying a position of pre-eminence over all others. "High status" or "superiority" seem to be only other words for the same thing'. Aron (1950) believes that 'the minority which in each of the enumerated professions, has succeeded best and occupied high positions'.
19. Kerr (1960: 50).
20. As quoted by Bottomore (1964).
21. (a) The *Positional Approach* (which was popular prior to 1953) is one in which 'those holding position of authority actually make key decisions while those who do not occupy such positions, do not make key decisions' (Those who are occupying objectively defined top positional positions), (b) in the *Reputational Approach* the influ-

ential persons in the community play a significant role and can get things done for the community and (c) the *Issue Participation Approach* (i.e. 'event analysis' or decision-making approach) is based on the assumption that those who actually participate in the decision-making process are the elites because they have shown the influence in real-life situations.

22. The study revealed the following:

(1) Caste background

Caste Background (% of Respondents from)	*Population Percentage*	*Elites (in %)*
Upper Castes	9.9	81.3
Middle Castes (cultivating)	24.1	6.8
Lower Castes	45.1	3.5
Scheduled Castes	20.9	1.1
Others	—	0.2
Not stated	—	7.1

(2) Urban versus rural background: 86.5 per cent of the respondents were of urban origin, whereas the total urban population percentage is 18 per cent. (3) Economic background: 84.3 per cent respondents come from high, well-to-do families, whereas the population percentage of this category is around 5 per cent. (4) Father's income: 61.6 per cent of respondents' fathers' income was more than ` 250. About 31.6 per cent of respondents' fathers' income was less than that. (5) Work/employment of father: 87.5 per cent hailed from non-manually engaged families. About 54.3 per cent came from high occupational stratum and 9.9 per cent came from manual strata. (6) Father's education: 89.3 per cent have modern education.

23. Based on the innumerable caste studies, the main features of the caste system include a common name, common descent, hereditary calling and homogeneity of caste members (Sharma, 1995: 42). While criticizing the class studies in the Indian society he opines that 'Class has existed along with caste and as an inseparable phenomenon forming the overall system of social stratification' (Sharma, 1995: 45).
24. Patwardhan (1973: 186).
25. Ram (1988) refers to them as 'fortunate'.
26. Abbasayulu (1978: 47) evolves a new criterion for defining elites. According to him, 'elites are those who have intellect and rational

judgment while participating in decision-making process and occupy some position of trust and responsibility'.

27. They are Osmania University, Andhra University and Kakatiya University.
28. Mendelsohn (1986: 508) comments on this classification and observes that contrary to this articulation the Harijan elite '... are only an elite relative to the mass of their caste fellows ...'
29. Aggarwal (1983: 6–8).
30. Ibid.

CHAPTER 3

Dalit Middle Class

An Empirical Analysis

The socially and economically upwardly mobile section among the Dalits, the Dalit middle class, as has been discussed in depth in the earlier chapters, is unique in terms of its class composition, disposition, lifestyle and political opinions. Dalit middle class, as is considered by various scholars, is distinct from the global as well as the Indian middle class. The Dalit middle class is identified and defined in terms of its marked differences with the 'general' Indian middle class.[1]

The life circumstances of this class are manifestly different from others, especially the general Indian middle class. Considering the abundant accounts that profiled middle class in India,[2] the Dalit middle class satisfies all the important features, while other specific features are unique to this class alone. This uniqueness is generally attributed to its atypical location, which necessitates it to deal with varied forms of caste-based discrimination as well as achieving economic mobility. In order to reach the middle class positions, the Dalits need to attempt social as well as economic mobility simultaneously. While the 'caste-Hindu middle class' enjoys a privileged social status independent of its economic attributes, middle classes in other societies as well are not subjected to this kind of socially hierarchical and unequal circumstances.

The studies on general middle class in India, again enumerated at length earlier, largely dealt with the profiling of the members of the middle class by way of providing socio-economic profiles of individuals (and in some cases families), their perceptions on various issues concerning their own lives and also the society, their interests and identification with various socio-political issues.[3] Similarly, the studies on Dalit middle class also engaged with such issues in addition to laying emphasis on caste and identity.[4]

Given the foregoing framework, this chapter outlines and collates various characteristics and the specificities/particulars of the Dalit middle class by juxtaposing it against the general features of the middle class. The objective here is to focus broadly on socio-economic profiles (occupation, age, gender, sub-caste, marital status, educational qualifications, religion and work career) of the middle class Dalits. The same attributes are also compared with the education, occupation, employment and income of their families (spouse and children) and their paternal families (parents, grand-parents and siblings). In addition, other determinant factors of their socio-economic status such as number of dependents and the nature of their dependence, education patterns in the paternal family, residential locality, status of residential accommodation, consumption patterns, economic status in terms of income, savings and debts, landholding patterns, changes in lifestyle and other criteria are analysed as part of the social background of middle class Dalits.

SOCIAL AND ECONOMIC LOCATION OF MIDDLE CLASS DALITS

The foremost determinant of Dalit middle class is the occupation of its members. Dalits – especially those who got access to modern education, which provided avenues for employment in modern occupations and professions and had consequences for their social and economic upward mobility – became part of the emerging middle class within their community. They are largely concentrated in government service, autonomous institutions, government and private-teaching and research institutions, public sector units such as banks, railways, electricity department and APSRTC (Andhra Pradesh State Road Transport Corporation). They are also engaged in independent professions such as law and medicine as well as employed in the private sector mainly non-governmental organizations (NGOs) and the print media.[5] Few of them are also in business and entrepreneurship. The demarcation between occupation and profession blur often, in the case of the middle class Dalits of the present study, the same is more evident in the case of many technically qualified professionals often taking up jobs. In such instances, the clear indicator was about the sectors – government, autonomous, private and other sectors – in which they have been and are employed. Professionals from law and medicine fields find themselves subject to this phenomenon and the switching between being an employee and an independent professional is evident. In the case of doctors, they start their career as an independent professional and later to switch over to becoming independent professionals. In other cases, it is vice versa.

Occupation

The middle class Dalits in the present study have been drawn from eight occupational categories, namely (1) officer cadre, (2) clerical cadre, (3) advocates, (4) doctors, (5) university faculty, (6) NGO professionals, (7) bank employees and (8) journalists. While all the categories had 15 middle class Dalits each, the number of doctors and journalists totalled 10 and 5, respectively, for reasons mentioned earlier in Chapter 1. While the first two categories were from the government sector, categories 5 and 7 represented autonomous and the public sector, respectively. Among the categories 3 and 4, which primarily represented independent professionals, there were fewer employees in both the government sector and the judiciary. Categories 6 and 7 completely fell under the private sector and few among them were independent professionals too.

Throughout the present study, middle class Dalits from these various sectors, comprising both – occupations and professions – were treated as merely representative of either occupational or professional categories, irrespective of whether or not they were employed or pursuing their profession/enterprise independently. The middle class Dalits included in the study were found to have a monthly income ranging from ₹ 8,000 to ₹ 23,000. Among them, the independent professionals had less income than the employees. In Table 3.1, a comparison of the middle class Dalits' occupation and gender distribution has been provided.

Table 3.1 *Occupation-Professional Distribution of Middle Class Dalits*

Occupation of Respondents	*Gender*		*Total*
	Male	*Female*	
Officer Cadre	11 (10.5)*	4 (3.8)	15 (14.3)
Clerical Cadre	10 (9.5)	5 (4.8)	15 (14.3)
University Faculty	11 (10.5)	4 (3.8)	15 (14.3)
Bank Employee	11 (10.5)	4 (3.8)	15 (14.3)
NGO	8 (7.6)	7 (6.7)	15 (14.3)
Advocate	15 (14.3)	—	15 (14.3)
Doctor	9 (8.6)	1 (1)	10 (9.5)
Journalist	5 (4.8)	—	5 (4.8)
Total	80 (76.2	25 (23.8)	105 (100)

* In all tables in this chapter, figures in parenthesis indicate rounded off percentages.

Very few Dalit women have entered into modern professions and occupations and the same is reflected in the sample. The figures indicating the general gender profile in employment among the Dalits reveal that[6] the gender profile of the middle class Dalits in the sample is 80 males and 25 females. Women's representation in the present sample is nearly half in officer cadre, clerical cadre, university faculty and banks and in the case of NGOs, almost equal to that of men. Reflecting the general absence or negligible presence of Dalit women in professions such as law, medicine and journalism, their representation in the present study is also either absent or marginal.

Among those employed in these occupations and professions, very few women were forthcoming in identifying themselves as Dalits and many displayed a reluctance to be interviewed unless strongly recommended to do so by their male colleagues or relatives. It could be partly because of the gender setting, added to the general unwillingness to reveal their caste identity to strangers, especially for research purposes. However, women who agreed to be interviewed were as articulate as the male middle class Dalits were.

Education

Education is the means for achieving social and economic mobility and middle-class status in general. It is the same for the Dalits as well.[7] It is evident from the sample that in certain occupations, technical educational credentials are a prerequisite to obtain/achieve it. In the case of the current constitution of Dalit middle class, education is a deciding factor for membership. The educational profile of the middle class Dalits of the present study also reflects these claims.

Since the middle class Dalits belonged to diverse occupational categories ranging from clerks to university faculty, accordingly, their education profile too reflects these variations. It ranges from matriculation to Ph.D. As part of reservations in employment in the government sector, the Dalits are provided with concessions pertaining to minimum qualification for eligibility to these posts. However, the middle class Dalits of the present study possessed minimum and in some cases additional educational qualifications. None of the middle class Dalits seem to have utilized such concessions.

The educational profile of respondents is presented in Table 3.2.

Table 3.2 *Education*

Respondents' Occupation	*Education*					*Total*
	Below Graduation	*Graduation*	*Post Graduation*	*Technical Degree*	*PhD*	
Officer Cadre	—	2 (1.9)	10 (9.5)	1 (1)	2 (1.9)	15 (14.3)
Clerical Cadre	1 (1)	6 (5.7)	7 (6.7)	1 (1)	—	15 (14.3)
University Faculty	—	—	3 (2.9)	—	12 (11.4)	15 (14.3)
Bank Employee	—	3 (2.9)	12 (11.4)	—	—	15 (14.3)
NGO	—	3 (2.9)	8 (7.6)	4 (3.8)	—	15 (14.3)

Cont'd...

...*Cont'd*

Advocate	—	—	—	15 (14.3)	—	15 (14.3)
Doctor	—	—	—	8 (7.6)	2 (1.9)	10 (9.5)
Journalist	—	1 (1)	3 (2.9)	1 (1)	—	5 (4.8)
Total	1 (1)	15 (14.3)	43 (41)	30 (28.6)	16 (15.2)	105 (100)

As seen in Table 3.2, more than half of the respondents have higher levels of educational qualifications, that is, post graduation or more. While 30 have a technical qualification, one is an undergraduate and 15 are graduates. Interestingly, there are 16 PhDs spread across university faculty in the sample, officer cadre and doctors. Ideally, PhD is a desirable qualification for university faculty alone. However, the fact that there are two officer cadre employees and two doctors with a doctorate degree indicates their individual interest and motivation in pursuing higher studies and their learning aptitude, which high-profile professions demand.

Higher the educational qualification of an individual, the higher is his/her social status among the Dalits. Highly educated Dalits are greatly admired within the community. Even among the respondents, the display of admiration for highly educated Dalits was evident in their constant reiteration that education had been the sole factor contributing to their social and economic mobility. Until very recently, in spite of having the facility of reservations in education and employment, very few Dalits could make an entry into the modern occupations and professions. Owing to which, the average age of middle class Dalits in these occupations and professions is less compared to other communities among these categories in the middle class.

Age and Gender

The majority of middle class Dalits in the sample has an average 6–10 years of service in their occupation or profession, with nearly half of them falling under the age group of 36–45 years. Signifying the first *en masse* entry of Dalits into these occupations and professions during 1980s, there are 21 who are between 46 and 55 years and there is only one respondent above 56 years. There are 11 in the age group of 25–30 years and 26 in 31–35 years age group. This trend is common to both genders according to their representation in the sample, as can be seen in Table 3.3.

Table 3.3 *Age and Gender*

Age Group	*Gender*		*Total*
	Male	*Female*	
25–30 years	6 (5.7)	5 (4.8)	11 (10.5)
31–35 years	17 (16.2)	9 (8.6)	26 (24.8)
36–45 years	36 (34.3)	10 (9.5)	46 (43.8)
46–55 years	20 (19)	1 (1)	21 (20)
56+ years	1 (1)	—	1 (1)
Total	80 (76.2)	25 (23.8)	105 (100)

Comparatively, Dalit men have forged ahead in the realms of education and employment in comparison to Dalit women. In the higher echelons of education and employment, Dalit women are thus inadequately represented compared to Dalit men. The sample is representative of such a trend.

Sub-Caste and Religious Profile

To start with, a general overview of the Dalit communities and their religious profile has been provided, which has been further employed to locate them in a regional context. There are 59 communities (sub-castes) among the Scheduled Castes (Dalits) in Andhra Pradesh. Four of them, namely, Chamar, Chalavadi, Madiga and Mala are spread throughout the state, while the rest of them are concentrated in specific regions or districts of the state. Most of them are small in number and are confined to a few districts. Among the Scheduled Castes, Madiga and Mala are numerically large and dominant. Both Madiga and Mala together constitute nearly 80 per cent of the total Dalit population in the state (50 and 30% respectively). With these two communities in the lead, the rest of the 57 communities are broadly divided into *the right hand* and *left hand castes*. Among them, some numerically small communities are traditionally *satellite castes* (related in a patron-client relationship) to Malas or Madigas.

Hyderabad city alone has 50 sub-castes from among the Dalits, with a total population of 307,248 Scheduled caste persons. Among these, 90 per cent hail from Madiga and Mala castes – with 50 per cent of Madigas and 40 per cent of Malas. According to the 2001 census, the urban population of Andhra Pradesh state is 20,808,940 (27.3%) and urban population of Hyderabad is 3,829,753 persons. The Dalit population in the state is 12,339,496 (16.2%) persons. The urban Dalit population consists of 2,120,087 (10.2%) persons. The Dalit population in Hyderabad city totals 307,248 people (8%).[8]

Middle class Dalits predominantly originate from a few Scheduled Castes.[9] In correspondence with the general pattern of Dalit population in Andhra Pradesh, the Dalit middle class in the state, especially in Hyderabad, is largely constituted in terms of the two numerically dominant castes, namely, Mala and Madiga. As they are numerically dominant, these two major communities access all the available mobility options and form 85 per cent of the Dalit middle class. It is widely recognized that the Malas, who are slightly few in terms of population compared to Madigas, have overtaken them not only in terms of constitution of the middle class but also in general social and economic mobility.[10] Among the numerically smaller sub-castes, Adi-Andhras are in a better position, similar to the Malas. The sub-caste-wise distribution in the sample is: Mala 46, Madiga 44, Adi-Andhra 7 and other sub-castes 8 (they include Manyam, Pambala and Relli).

Table 3.4 *Sub-Caste and Religion*

Sub-Caste	*Religion*				*Total*
	Hindu	*Christian*	*Buddhist*	*Atheist*	
Mala	31 (29.5)	9 (8.6)	2 (1.9)	4 (3.8)	46 (43.8)
Madiga	37 (35.2)	5 (4.8)	1 (1)	1 (1)	44 (41.9)
Adi-Andhra	6 (5.7)	—	1 (1)	—	7 (6.7)
Other*	5 (4.8)	—	2 (1.9)	1 (1)	8 (7.6)
Total	79 (75.2)	14 (13.3)	6 (5.7)	6 (5.7)	105 (100)

* Other sub-castes include Manyam, Pambala and Relli.

The presence of religious groups, other than Hindu, is prevalent among the Dalits, as many of them have chosen to convert to other religions during various periods in history for a variety of reasons (Table 3.4). Since the nineteenth century, social consciousness and political awareness has been increasing among the Dalits, especially among Dalit Christians, Dalit Muslims and Neo-Buddhist Dalits,[11] compared to Dalits who follow the Hindu religion. In fact, conversions to other religions in recent times have largely to do with such consciousness and awareness rather than any other reason.

Now, the Dalits constitute a considerable number among the Christians as well as the Buddhists. Since these Dalits would lose the benefits of reservations and other facilities, if their conversion to either Christianity or Islam was officially admitted, the number of Christians reported in many official surveys is likely to be less than the actual numbers. However, a considerable number of Christians and Buddhists were present in the present study. Their religious affiliations demonstrate that a majority – 79 – followed or claimed affiliation to Hindu religion, while 14 were Christians, 6 were Buddhists and another 6 claimed to be atheists.

However, comparatively speaking, there is not much variation in terms of distribution of communities (sub-castes) or belonging to different religious groups. They are distributed more or less proportionately in terms of different communities within various religious groups. The same was found among those who claimed to be atheists.

Marital Status

All the middle class Dalits in the present study are well above the legal age of marriage. Their marital status shows that 96 (75 males and 21 females) were married, 6 (4 males and 2 females) were unmarried, while 2 were divorcees (1 male and 1 female) and 1 was widowed (female). All the unmarried were in the age groups of 25–30 years and 31–35 years (three in each category), of which, four were males and two were females. Of the 99 (94.3%) who were married, 58 (55.2%) have been married to persons selected by their families or relatives, whereas the remaining reportedly exercised their choice in selecting their spouse. This trend was more or less common to all occupations and age groups. There was no differentiation in terms of occupation as far as type of marriage (arranged or self-chosen/love marriages) was concerned. The number of love marriages/self-choice of spouse was around half the number of arranged marriages. This trend was observed between both male and female across all occupations and age groups. In all the cases where the partner hailed from a different community, without exception it was a love marriage. This trend of love marriage with other caste persons was confined to only a few Dalits who were employed in prestigious jobs.

The correlation between age and type of marriage shows that in the 25–30 years age group (from a total of 11) 6 had arranged marriages, while 2 had love marriages and 2 others did not specify their marriage type. In the 31–35 years age group, 14 had arranged marriages and 8 had love marriages. Among the 36–45 years age group, 26 had arranged marriages and 15 had love marriages. Among the 46–55 years age group, 11 had arranged marriages and 10 had love/self-chosen marriages. The lone respondent in 56+ year age group had an arranged marriage. The variation in terms of age and arranged or love/self-chosen marriages suggests that around the period between 1970s and 1980s, the economically mobile Dalits, especially the males, exercised their 'freedom' in selecting or choosing their spouse independent of and sometimes contrary to the wishes of their family.

A comparison between gender and type of marriage shows that of the 76 married males, 44 had arranged marriages and 27 had love marriages and another 4 did not specify the type of marriage. Among the 24 married females, 14 had arranged marriages, 6 had love marriage and another 3 did not specify their marriage type. In comparison to Dalit men, the phenomenon of exercising their will in choosing their spouse is a recent one among the Dalit women. In spite of a relative freedom they possess due to educational and economic mobility, the Dalit women are controlled by the patriarchal values regarding choice of spouse.

Table 3.5 *Respondents' Spouse Community*

Gender	*Respondents' Spouse Community*					*NA (Un-married)*	*Total*
	Within SC		*Other than SC*				
	Same Sub-Caste	*Different Sub-Caste*	*Scheduled Tribe*	*Other Backward Classes*	*Other Community*		
Male	61 (58.1)	10 (9.5)	1 (1)	—	4 (3.8)	4 (3.8)	80 (76.2)
Female	21 (20)	1 (1)	—	1 (1)	—	2 (1.9)	25 (23.8)
Total	82 (78.1)	11 (10.5)	1 (1)	1 (1)	4 (3.8)	6 (5.7)	105 (100)

The pattern of marriage among them illustrates that while arranged marriages were the norm (55.2%), love marriages too (31.4%) were prevalent among the upwardly mobile Dalits. Among these upwardly mobile Dalits, marriages were arranged with partners, not only within but also outside their community, with friends and acquaintances acting as mediators. In the case of love marriages, marriage with a partner from outside the community was the norm, despite a considerable number of love marriages occurring with partners from within the community. The reasons for having an arranged or love/self-chosen marriage range from: in the case of 58, it was the wish of family members and for 30 it was a personal choice. Of the 11 who did not specify reasons for the type of marriage they had, three of them had love marriages (Table 3.5).

SOCIAL BACKGROUND OF MIDDLE CLASS DALITS

In this section, the social background of middle class Dalits and the patterns of dependence of their ancestral family and others are outlined. This dependency factor largely characterizes the economic 'difference' between the middle class Dalits and their paternal families. The capability of middle class Dalits to fulfil the economic needs of their extended families, their willingness to do the same, and instances and the extent to which such a practice exists among them constitutes the foregoing analysis in this section.

Paternal Family and the Dependents

Paternal family plays a pivotal role in the middle class Dalits' education and employment, thereby being responsible for their entry into the middle class. At the same time, it also has a bearing on their present economic status. In this regard, education, occupation, employment, monthly income and dependence patterns of middle class Dalits' parents, grandparents and siblings were analysed.

Parents and Grandparents

The socio-economic background of the parents has a direct bearing on their children. It manifests itself in terms of their children's level of social and economic mobility. In the case of Dalits, such a desire on the part of their parents motivates them to achieve a higher level of social and economic status compared to that of their parents. Given the levels of their economic affordability, the parents' contribution towards their children's mobility might sometimes be in terms of encouragement alone. It is widely acknowledged that many Dalits who entered into modern occupations and thereby into the middle class have had modest origins. In many instances, they are the sole educated and employed persons in the entire family. However, the socio-economic background of the parents does play a major role in the children's socio-economic status.[12]

The educational profile of the middle class Dalits' parents and grandparents suggests that the majority of the middle class Dalits were first-generation educated. In a few instances, wherein either the parents or the grandparents were educated, they are benefited in terms of resources and guidance with respect to their education and career. Second- or third-generation educated middle class Dalits were highly educated in comparison to the first-generation educated among them.

While the education levels among the middle class Dalits range from under graduation to Ph.D., among parents and grandparents, education levels ranged mostly from graduation to school level, respectively. Among them, fathers were comparatively highly educated. This indicated that Dalits had access to education only in recent times. Apart from that Dalit men had the privilege of being highly educated in comparison to Dalit women. The educational profile of the fathers, mothers and grandparents shows that the majority among all the three categories are predominantly illiterate. In a few cases the fathers, mothers and grandparents had been educated up to the school level, which were 26.7 per cent, 25.7 per cent and 1 per cent, respectively. There were 6.7 per cent graduates among fathers and mothers. One per cent of the mothers had completed graduation and 4.8 per cent of the fathers had technical education as well (Table 3.6).

Table 3.6 *Education Profiles of Respondents, Their Parents and Grandparents*

Education Levels	*Respondent*	*Father*	*Mother*	*Grandparents**
Illiterate	—	55 (52.4)	73 (69.5)	98 (93.3)
Literate	—	10 (9.5)	4 (3.8)	2 (1.9)
School Level	—	28 (26.7)	27 (25.7)	1 (1)
Below Graduation	1 (1)	—	—	—
Graduation	15 (14.3)	7 (6.7)	1 (1)	—
Post Graduation	43 (41)	—	—	—
Technical Education	30 (28.6)	5 (4.8)	—	—
PhD	16 (15.2)	—	—	—
No Response	—	—	—	4 (3.8)
Total	105 (100)	105 (100)	105 (100)	105 (100)

* In cases of variation in educational qualification among grandparents, only the highest education of one or more grandparents has been counted.

The pattern of occupation too corresponds with that of education, placing fathers over mothers and grandparents. Similarly, Dalit men were better placed in modern occupations compared to Dalit women.

Table 3.7 shows that at least one-third of the middle class Dalits were second-generation employed, nearly half of them hailed from families with a predominantly agricultural background, while very few had fathers who had pursued modern occupations.

Fifty-one reported that their fathers had been agriculturists, while 70 reported that their grandfathers had been agriculturists. This perhaps could be an indicator of an occupational shift away from agriculture in the last two generations. In the case of 13 middle class Dalits, their fathers were currently employed and earning a monthly income, while only in 5 cases the mothers are currently employed. Of them, in 10 instances the fathers were earning a monthly income of ₹ 5,000 and in 3 instances the fathers were earning between ₹ 8,001 to ₹ 15,000. In the case of mothers, all five who were employed were earning an income of ₹ 5,000 per month. In the case of grandparents, both maternal and paternal grandparents have been categorized together. There was very little difference between the education and economic status of the grandparents of both male and female middle class Dalits.

Table 3.7 *Occupations of Respondents and Their Parents*

Occupation	*Father*	*Mother*	*Grandparents**
Agricultural Labour	28 (26.7)	18 (17.1)	68 (64.8)
Agriculture	23 (21.9)	14 (13.3)	2 (1.9)
Caste Occupation	2 (1.9)	1 (1)	1 (1)
Government Service	38 (36.2)	9 (8.6)	7 (6.7)
Independent Profession	3 (2.9)	—	5 (4.8)
Business	1 (1)	—	1 (1)
Other	4 (3.8)	—	—
Homemaker	—	59 (56.2)	—
NR/NA	6 (5.7)	4 (3.8)	21 (20)
Total	105 (100)	105 (100)	105 (100)

* Only the highest occupation of one or more grandparents is counted.

Comparison of Own Economic Status with Paternal and Maternal Families

The economic status of a family plays a major role in shaping the future of its members. The role of the middle class Dalits' familial economic status in their lives (those who underwent social and economic upward mobility due to their families' capacity to afford their education) needs to be examined. With a view to compare their economic mobility with that of their families, they were asked to identify the economic status of their own family, paternal family and maternal family (Table 3.8).

Table 3.8 *Economic Status of Own Family in Comparison with Paternal Family, Maternal Family and Sub-Caste*

Family	*Perceived Economic Status*					*Total*
	Upper Middle Class	*Middle-Middle Class*	*Lower Middle Class*	*Poor*	*No Response*	
Own Family	22 (21)	59 (56.2)	12 (11.4)	—	12 (11.4)	105 (100)
Paternal Family	—	20 (19)	42 (40)	29 (27.6)	14 (13.3)	105 (100)
Maternal Family	—	16 (15.2)	40 (38.1)	35 (33.3)	14 (13.3)	105 (100)

The majority of the respondents identified themselves as 'the middle class proper' (i.e. middle-middle class), their paternal and maternal families as lower middle class and sub-caste as a whole in the category of 'poor'. An intergenerational comparison of economic status shows that 29 of them and 34 others with poor paternal and maternal family backgrounds had respectively moved into the middle class. From among the 29 who identified with an economically poor paternal family background, 15 of them had moved into the upper middle class, 8 respondents into middle-middle class category and 6 respondents had moved into lower-middle class category.

Similarly, of the 35 with an economically poor maternal family background, 15 of them had moved into the upper middle class, 13 others in the middle-middle class and another 7 into the lower middle class. Of the total 42 who had a lower-middle class paternal family background, 3 had moved into the upper-middle class category and 33 into middle-middle class category. Of the 20 respondents with a middle-middle class paternal family background, 4 had moved into the upper middle class. Similarly, of the 40 belonging to a lower-middle class maternal family background, 7 had moved into the upper middle class and another 28 into the middle-middle class category. In all such instances, there is an upward mobility among the respondents compared to their paternal and maternal families. The same is articulated by them as an improvement in the economic status of their own family compared to their paternal and maternal families.

Education in Paternal Family

Education is a very important indicator of social and economic mobility, particularly in the case of Dalits who had been kept away from access to education earlier for centuries together. It had been strongly advocated during the Nationalist Movements and the socio-religious reform movements that education among the Dalits would empower them to overcome their social, economical and political disadvantages. Similarly, post-independence Indian state too laid emphasis on the development of Dalits through education. Hence, the reservations in employment and political representation were considered more important rather than economic development.

It is evident from such efforts by the government that there is a steady progress in literacy among Dalits, though such progress is sluggish and slight compared to other communities. Independent of this effort, education among the Dalits began one or two generations earlier due to other factors. It was random in nature and confined to very few regions, communities and often to individual families. At a general level, efforts towards education began only recently and it is still a comparatively recent phenomenon. Consequently, the educated among the Dalits in general are predominantly first-generation educated.

In the case of the respondents of the present study, more than half were second-generation educated. However, the previous generation's level of education was very less. In a few instances, such a background helped them to set high goals for themselves with regard to education. In a few other instances, their siblings, especially elder brothers, had been educated, thereby motivating and encouraging them to set higher goals educationally for themselves (Table 3.9).

In two-thirds of cases, the education in their families had begun with other family members. While in 34 instances, they were the first to be educated, in cases where the other members of the family were the first to be educated, the figures were father, 41 instances; brother, 15 instances; sister, 1 instance and paternal grandfather, 14 instances. A comparison between males and females shows that the female were mostly second-generation educated, the proportion of educated women in their families had risen by almost three times the original figure and in the case of males, the proportion of educated men had doubled. Thus, significant changes seem to have occurred for women in comparison to men, in terms of access to education, motivation and encouragement from family members, which was absent earlier. Another important factor is that access to education becomes possible for Dalit women only when a relative in the previous generation had availed education. This becomes significant when we find that 28 males and 5 females were first-generation educated.

Table 3.9 *Education in Respondents' Paternal Family Started With*

Respondents' Occupation	*Who Received Education First?*					*Total*
	Respondent	*Father*	*Brother*	*Sister*	*Paternal Grandfather*	
Officer Cadre	6 (5.7)	6 (5.7)	—	—	3 (2.9)	15 (14.3)
Clerical Cadre	5 (4.8)	5 (4.8)	3 (2.9)	1 (1)	1 (1)	15 (14.3)
University Faculty	4 (3.8)	7 (6.7)	2 (1.9)	—	2 (1.9)	15 (14.3)
Bank Employee	3 (2.9)	5 (4.8)	3 (2.9)	—	4 (3.8)	15 (14.3)
NGO	4 (3.8)	6 (5.7)	2 (1.9)	—	3 (2.9)	15 (14.3)
Advocate	7 (6.7)	5 (4.8)	3 (2.9)	—	—	15 (14.3)
Doctor	3 (2.9)	5 (4.8)	2 (1.9)	—	—	10 (9.5)
Journalist	2 (1.9)	2 (1.9)	—	—	1 (1)	5 (4.8)
Total	34 (32.4)	41 (39)	15 (14.3)	1 (1)	14 (13.3)	105 (100)

An occupation-wise comparison shows that those who are employed as officer cadre, university faculty, bank employees, NGO professionals and journalists were second-generation educated, while in the case of clerical cadre and advocates, the majority were first-generation educated. Only in the case of doctors, equal numbers of first- and second-generation educated were found. The present generation had entered into a diverse range of occupations, partly facilitated by the attempts made by the earlier generation to acquire some level of education.

Dependents from Paternal Family: Their Shelter and Economic Needs

Being the most economically successful compared to their ancestral family, other relatives, friends and acquaintances, middle class Dalits were dependent on them for various needs such as shelter, economic support, career advice and recommendation. An overwhelming majority of respondents from the present study reported that among other forms of help, they had given shelter to paternal family members as well as other relatives under their roof at some point of time or the other.

The dependency patterns of the paternal family showed that while in some instances they had lived with the respondents and had been economically dependent on them as well, in other instances, they lived separately, but were nonetheless dependent upon the respondents for the fulfilment of their economic needs. In many instances, it was the paternal family members, that is, parents as well as siblings, who were dependent.

Siblings and Their Dependence Patterns

Siblings played a crucial role in terms of either contributing to the upward mobility of the respondents or becoming dependent on them for their economic needs. Sibling dependency for education and employment needs examination to establish their economic bearing on the respondents. Table 3.10 illustrates the number of siblings (brothers and sisters) the respondents had.

A total of 11 (10 males and 1 female) respondents did not have siblings. Of those who had siblings, 22 of them (17 males and 5 females) had only brothers, 7 (6 males and 1 female) had only sisters and the remaining 65 (47 males and 18 females) had both brothers and sisters (Table 3.11).

Table 3.10 *Number of Siblings (Brothers and Sisters)*

Respondents' Gender	*Number*				*Total*
	No Siblings	*Have Only Brothers*	*Have Only Sisters*	*Have both Brothers and Sisters*	
Male	10 (9.5)	17 (16.2)	6 (5.7)	47 (44.8)	80 (76.2)
Female	1 (1)	5 (4.8)	1 (1)	18 (17.1)	25 (23.8)
Total	11 (10.5)	22 (21)	7 (6.7)	65 (61.9)	105 (100)

Table 3.11 *Respondents' Education, Occupation and Monthly Income in Comparison with Their Siblings*

Gradation	*Comparison with Brothers and Sisters*		
	Education	*Occupation*	*Monthly Income*
Similar	3 (2.9)	6 (5.7)	9 (8.6)
Lower	60 (57.1)	54 (51.4)	64 (61)
Higher	2 (1.9)	—	—
Some Higher and Some Lower	29 (27.6)	34 (32.4)	21 (20)
Not Applicable*	11 (10.5)	11 (10.5)	11 (10.5)
Total	105 (100)	105 (100)	105 (100)

* No Siblings.

A comparison of the respondents' and their siblings' education, occupation and monthly income showed that in the majority of the cases, the siblings had lower levels of education (57.1%), occupation (51.4%) and monthly income (61%) compared to the respondents. In the case of other respondents, where some siblings had higher and lower levels of education (27.6%), occupation (32.4%) and monthly income (20%), the figures shown were significant due to their implications for the social and economic mobility of the respondents. In two cases, the respondents' siblings had higher levels of education than the respondents did; however, this difference is absent in the occupation and monthly income categories.

There are no instances of both parents and siblings being dependent on respondents. In the 37 (35.2%) cases, only parents were dependent on respondents. Among these, in four cases, parents were dependent on the respondents, but they (the respondents) had no siblings, in another four of these cases, parents were not dependent and in one case parents were no longer alive. Similarly, in five cases, only the siblings were dependent on the respondents. There were only 13 cases, where both parents and siblings were not dependent upon the respondents. Significantly, among the cases where the respondents did not have siblings, in four cases, the parents were dependent on respondents, in one case the parents were not dependent and in six cases, the parents were no longer alive. Similarly, in one case, parents were no longer alive, but the siblings were dependent; in 43 cases, siblings were not dependent and the parents were no longer alive; and in six cases respondents had no siblings and parents were also no longer alive.

Table 3.12 *Nature of Dependence of Respondents' Paternal Family*

Dependents from Paternal Family	*Nature of Dependence*				*Total*
	Living with Respondents' Family	*Economic Dependence*	*No Dependence*	*Not Applicable**	
Parents	7 (6.7)	30 (28.6)	18 (17.1)	50 (47.6)	105 (100)
Siblings	5 (4.8)	—	89 (84.8)	11 (10.5)	105 (100)
Total#	12 (11.4)	30 (28.6)	107 (101.9)	61 (58.1)	105 (100)

* Not Applicable denotes parents not alive and no siblings.
# Totals do not tally to 100 per cent.

In no instance, were siblings dependent on respondents for economic needs alone. Their dependence was in terms of shelter, all unmarried, and were either pursuing their studies or seeking employment. The instances of siblings being dependent on respondents were only in five cases, they are staying with the respondents but not dependent economically. In another seven instances, the parents are staying with the respondents. In yet another 30 instances, the parents were dependent for economic needs. In total, there were dependents in 42 cases. It is important to note that out of 44 instances in which the parents (both or one) are alive, but only in 7 cases, they were staying with the respondents' family and only in 30 instances they were dependent for economic needs. Of them, 10 out of 13 single parents alive were economically dependent on respondents. In total, 37 parents were dependent on respondents in terms of economic needs as well as living with the respondents' family (Table 3.12).

A comparison in terms of respondents' gender and dependence by their siblings shows that both male and female respondents have siblings as dependents on them, irrespective of their own marital status and having their own family. In the case of parents, 24 male respondents and 6 female respondents had their parents dependent on them. Another six male respondents and one female respondent had their parents living with them. Similarly, four male respondents and one female respondent had their siblings staying with them. In most cases, the dependency was not only due to the 'need factor' but also due to the relatively better economic status of the respondents compared to their parents or siblings. There were instances where respondents, who were relatively well off financially, had more than one sibling who were solely dependent on them.

A comparison with respondents' occupation and paternal family dependency shows that respondents from all occupations and professions had dependents. Higher the occupational status of respondents (read income), higher the dependency of paternal family members on them. In the case of less represented professions, such as doctors and journalists, the number of dependents was also less. On an average, five to seven respondents from each occupation or profession reported such dependency.

All the above figures assume significance since the dependency of parents and siblings impacts the middle class Dalits from enjoying the full benefits of their occupational status and upward mobility in terms of improved standard of living compared to the general middle class. Moreover, it also reveals the close emotional ties with and commitment to parents and siblings, in addition to their own families.

Other Dependents

There were few other dependents from among close relatives, distant relatives, acquaintances and friends from the respondents' native place for both economic needs and shelter. Most of the dependents from others category were students pursuing studies, appearing for government exams, searching for employment and so on. Many respondents informed that they provided economic assistance to relatives and friends on need basis and had sheltered some relatives in the past. However, currently there are not many relatives and friends staying with them. It would be useful to understand the kind of social relations the respondents were maintaining with their relatives and their friends since childhood (Table 3.13).

Table 3.13 *Dependents Other than Family Members and Nature of Dependence*

Other Dependents	*Nature of Dependence*			*Total*
	Staying with Respondent	*Economic Needs*	*No Dependence*	
Close Relatives	6 (5.7)	12 (11.4)	—	18 (17.1)
Distant Relatives	—	1 (1)	—	1 (1)
Acquaintances and Friends	—	3 (2.9)	—	3 (2.9)
No Dependents	—	—	83 (79)	83 (79)
Total	6 (5.7)	16 (15.2)	83 (79)	105 (100)

A total of 22 respondents had shouldered responsibility for their relatives and friends by assisting them for their various needs. Of them, six had close relatives (other than paternal family members) staying with them and 16 had distant relatives, acquaintances and friends depending on them for economic needs. All these figures are a significant indicator of the respondents' degree of attachment to their extended family, friends and other acquaintances in their community. It reflects a concern for the well-being, not only of their immediate family members, but also the other members of their community. This strong 'community orientation' also perhaps singles out the Dalit middle class from the general middle class.

The social background of middle class Dalits, particularly the respondents, suggest that, in general, compared to their present socio-economic status, their paternal family's socio-economic background is low. The education, occupation and income levels of the respondents are higher than their paternal families. There is a visible upward mobility in the case of respondents. At the same time, their paternal family's low socio-economic status has a bearing on their upward mobility.

Middle Class Dalits and Their Families

A family's social and economic status is determined based on its members' education, employment and income patterns. Accordingly, respondents' spouse and children's education, employment and income patterns were analysed to understand the likely implications for family's economic and social status.

Spouse

While 75 males and 21 females have a spouse, 9 did not have a spouse, of which 2 were divorcees, 1 was a widow and 6 were unmarried, of these, 5 are males and 4 are females. In Table 3.14, education, occupation and monthly income of the respondents' spouse are analysed. In the case of occupation and monthly income, spouses of respondents who were employed in lower occupational categories and those who are not employed were classified under lower occupation and monthly income category.

Table 3.14 *Respondents' Education, Occupation and Monthly Income with That of Their Spouses*

Spouse's	*Grading*								*Total*
	Lower		*Equal*		*Higher*		*NA*		
	*SMR**	*SFR***	*SMR*	*SFR*	*SMR*	*SFR*	*SMR*	*SFR*	
Education	64 (61)	—	11 (10.5)	17 (16.2)	—	4 (3.8)	5 (4.8)	4 (3.8)	105 (100)
Occupation	65 (61.9)	17 (16.2)	6 (5.7)	1 (1)	4 (3.8)	3 (2.9)	5 (4.8)	4 (3.8)	105 (100)
Monthly Income	64 (61)	18 (17.1)	7 (6.7)	—	4 (3.8)	3 (2.9)	5 (4.8)	4 (3.8)	105 (100)

* SMR = Spouse of Male Respondent.
** SFR = Spouse of Female Respondent.

The education levels among the males were either equal to or higher than their spouse, while in the case of females, not only their spouse's education, but also occupation and monthly income were equal or higher compared to their own. In the case of males, education of their spouse was less than theirs (68.6%), while in the case of females, it was equal (14.3%) or more (8.6%) compared to their spouse. Similarly, occupation and monthly income of male were more than their spouse in comparison to female was. The figures reveal that in the case of occupation and monthly income of a spouse, female were better off compared to male since it had implications for social and economic status in terms of a higher standard of living.

Children

The children were grouped into broad categories – number of children, age group, education level, marital status, employment and monthly income – mainly to ascertain their dependence patterns and contribution to social and economic status of the family. Among the total 99 married middle class Dalits (including divorcees and widowed), 90 had children. The respondents without children were distributed across various age groups, one person in the 25–30 years age group, six persons in the 31–35 years age group and two persons in the 36–45 years age group. The majority of the respondents without children were in the age group of 31–35 years. This may be an indication of their late settlement in jobs or late marriages. In the case of number of children: with one child were distributed in all age groups, namely, in 25–30 years age group one; in 31–35 years age group six and in 36–45 years age group 11. Overall, having more than one child was the norm and the same was evident among the majority of the middle class Dalits across all age groups (Table 3.15).

Of the total 11 in the age group of 25–30 years, eight are married, of which only one respondent was childless while one had one child and another six had more than one child. In the age group of 31–35 years, among 26 excluding the 3 unmarried, 6 did not have children, another 6 had one child and 11 had more than one child. In the age group of 36–45 years, only 2 did not have children out of another 46. The remaining 44 were distributed among the categories of 6 with one child and 15 who had more than one child.

There was only one respondent in the age group of 56 years and above with more than one child.

Table 3.15 *Respondents' Age and Number of Children*

Respondents' Age Group	*Number of Children*				*Total*
	No Children	*One Child*	*More than One Child*	*Not Applicable*	
25–30 years	1 (1)	1 (1)	6 (5.7)	3 (2.9)	11 (10.5)
31–35 years	6 (5.7)	6 (5.7)	11 (10.5)	3 (2.9)	26 (24.8)
36–45 years	2 (1.9)	11 (10.5)	33 (31.4)	—	46 (43.8)
46–55 years	—	6 (5.7)	15 (14.3)	—	21 (20)
56+ years	—	—	1 (1)	—	1 (1)
Total	9 (8.6)	24 (22.9)	66 (62.9)	6 (5.7)	105 (100)

Respondents' children when broadly categorized into two age groups, namely, below 25 years and 26 years and above, only two had children above 25 years of age while another 88 have children under 25 years of age. A comparison between age and education of respondents' children showed that of the 90 who had children, there was similarity in terms of age group distribution and education among respondents' children. While 77 of them were under 25 years of age and pursuing their studies, children of one respondent in 26 and above age groups had completed their studies, and one respondent had children in both age groups, with some pursuing their studies and some who had completed their studies. Marriage patterns among respondents' children show that in many cases, respondents' children were below the marriageable age. Only one respondent's child was above 26 years age group and had gotten married. With respect to the remaining 89 respondents (of which in one case, the children come under both age groups), marriages of the children had not taken place yet. These figures are again significant because they show that in the majority of the cases, the income of the respondents are spent not only towards educating their children, but also towards providing economic and social support for their parents and siblings, and in some cases friends and acquaintances as well (as discussed in detail earlier). This perhaps may have consequences for the kind of education they are able to provide their children due to these multiple demands made on their income, though this could not be brought out clearly from the available data.

In this regard, the problems faced in terms of children's education at school, college and university levels were analysed in order to understand the nature of such problems and the coping mechanisms adopted. Respondents' children who were pursuing school-level education had problems. The majority of these problems were related to learning and a few were related to fees and the standard of the school. These implied their economic inability to afford fees and thereby access to good schools, though it could not be ascertained whether this was due to multiple demands on their limited income. However, in some cases, respondents' children were pursuing studies at college and university levels, but problems were not reported in these cases, indicating general affordability among these respondents to provide their children with a good education.

The comparison between occupation and monthly income of respondents and their children showed that though 90 respondents had children, only two respondents' children were employed. While one respondent's children earned a monthly income, which was lower than his income, the other respondent had children with a higher income level.

Aspirations Regarding Children's Future

Aspirations regarding children's future are reflective of the Dalits' own achievements and their aspirations for future generations. The higher the occupational status and income, higher are the aspirations for their children. Along with stability, high income and social prestige, there are other expectations of the children's career. In the case of those social groups among the Dalits, which have achieved a certain level of social and economic mobility, their children are expected to either achieve more or keep up with their own level. Thus, employment in a similar or a higher occupational category is a normal expectation of the children's future (Table 3.16).

Significantly, the respondents who wanted their children to take up occupations similar to theirs were in government or public

Table 3.16 *Aspirations for Children's Future*

Respondents' Occupation	*Aspirations for Children's Future*						*Total*
	Government Job	*Settling Abroad*	*Independent Professional*	*Entrepreneurship*	*Children's Own Choice*	*No Response*	
Officer Cadre	9 (8.6)	—	1 (1)	—	—	5 (4.8)	15 (14.3)
Clerical Cadre	4 (3.8)	—	2 (1.9)	—	6 (5.7)	3 (2.9)	15 (14.3)
University Faculty	4 (3.8)	—	3 (2.9)	1 (1)	4 (3.8)	3 (2.9)	15 (14.3)
Bank Employee	4 (3.8)	1 (1)	3 (2.9)	—	1 (1)	6 (5.7)	15 (14.3)
NGO	4 (3.8)	—	1 (1)	—	4 (2.9)	6 (5.7)	15 (14.3)
Advocate	5 (4.8)	—	4 (3.8)	—	2 (1.9)	4 (3.8)	15 (14.3)
Doctor	2 (1.9)	—	3 (2.9)	—	3 (2.9)	2 (1.9)	10 (9.5)
Journalist	2 (1.9)	—	—	—	2 (1.9)	1 (1)	5 (4.8)
Total	34 (32.4)	1 (1)	17 (16.2)	1 (1)	22 (21)	30 (28.6)	105 (100)

sector jobs. Irrespective of occupation and profession, the majority wanted their children to be settled in secure occupations such as government service. Among all occupational categories, the major tilt was towards a government job or an independent profession that was secure and remunerative. Other options such as business or settling abroad are still a distant dream for the Dalit middle class given their relatively lower level of achievement with respect to economic and social mobility. However, 22 respondents wanted their children to exercise their own choice with regard to career options. Among the 30 respondents who did not respond in this regard, half of them were unmarried and the remaining did not have any children.

Utilization of Reservations in Education and Employment

The very emergence of Dalit middle class has its roots in the reservation system. Without reservations in education and employment, almost none of the present members of the Dalit middle class would have made it into the middle class at all. Even in the case of those respondents who had not availed of reservations, their earlier generations might have utilized reservations.

Utilization of reservations comes about only after the individuals from the eligible communities are able to complete their matriculation. Prior to that, admissions into educational institutions are largely open to all since there is sufficient infrastructure to meet the requirements of all the students. Reservations in education are meant to safeguard the interests of students from weaker sections. It enables them to further their interests pertaining to higher education in various disciplines or courses that are normally not within their reach, given the limited number of seats and high fees for these courses. Reservations for students from weaker sections, including the Dalits, are in the form of seats in proportion to their population and fee waivers, free books and scholarships and other benefits. Irrespective of the nature of the course, many poor and lower-middle class Dalit students avail reservations in education after matriculation, beginning with securing a seat to availing a stipend (popularly known as scholarship). In the field of technical education, children of economically well-off Dalits also avail reservations in order to secure admissions, which is otherwise not possible for them.

In this context, it becomes important to look into the reservations availing pattern among the Dalits that essentially has a bearing on their employment pattern. Table 3.17 indicates a reservations utilization pattern among the respondents in comparison to their occupations.

Table 3.17 *Stages at Which Reservations Were Availed*

Respondents' Occupation	*Stages at Which Reservations Were Availed*				*Total*
	Education	*Employment*	*Education and Employment*	*Not Availed*	
Officer Cadre	1 (1)	1 (1)	13 (12.4)	—	15 (14.3)
Clerical Cadre	1 (1)	5 (4.8)	8 (7.6)	1 (1)	15 (14.3)
University Faculty	2 (1.9)	5 (4.8)	8 (7.6)	—	15 (14.3)
Bank Employee	3 (2.9)	4 (3.8)	8 (7.6)	—	15 (14.3)
NGO Professional	13 (12.4)	—	—	2 (1.9)	15 (14.3)
Advocate	10 (9.5)	—	5 (4.8)	—	15 (14.3)
Doctor	6 (5.7)	1 (1)	3 (2.9)	—	10 (9.5)
Journalist	5 (4.8)	—	—	—	5 (4.8)
Total	41 (39)	16 (15.2)	45 (42.9)	3 (2.9)	105 (100)

In the present study, 102 had availed reservations in education, employment or both. Of which 41 availed only education, 16 only employment and 45 both education and employment. Three respondents had not availed reservations in either education or employment. A comparison of paternal family economic background and reservations utilization pattern among the respondents is analysed in Table 3.18.

A comparison between the pattern of utilization of reservations and paternal family economic background showed that the respondents hailing from poor economic background needed reservations for both education and employment. Among these, 20 had availed of reservations as against 15 respondents from lower-middle class families and 8 from middle-middle class families. Eight professionals in law and medicine had availed reservations in employment too, as they were in government service.

Table 3.18 *Paternal Family's Economic Status and Utilization of Reservations*

Economic Status of Paternal Family	*Stages at Which Reservations Were Availed*				*Total*
	Education	*Employment*	*Education and Employment*	*Not Availed*	
Middle-Middle Class	7 (6.7)	5 (4.8)	8 (7.6)	—	20 (19)
Lower Middle Class	17 (16.2)	10 (9.5)	15 (14.3)	—	42 (40)
Poor	9 (8.6)	—	20 (19)	—	29 (27.6)
No Response	8 (7.6)	1 (1)	2 (1.9)	3 (2.9)	14 (13.3)
Total	41 (39)	16 (15.2)	45 (42.9)	3 (2.9)	105 (100)

MIDDLE CLASS BY PROFESSION: CAREER TRAJECTORY AND PROBLEMS

As the average age of the respondents of the present study suggests, many of them had 6–10 years of work experience. The number of respondents with less than 2 years experience in the present job or profession was 12, 21 had 2–5 years of experience, 32 had 6–10 years of experience, 17 had 11–15 years of experience and 23 had around 16 years work experience (Table 3.19).

Table 3.19 *Years of Service in Present Job/Profession and Number of Years Remained Unemployed/Without Work*

Years of Service in Present Job/Profession	*Number of Years Remained Unemployed/ Without Work*				*Total*
	Less than 2 years	*2–5 years*	*6–10 years*	*Never*	
Less than 2 years	2 (1.9)	3 (2.9)	—	7 (6.7)	12 (11.4)
2–5 years	3 (2.9)	4 (3.8)	3 (2.9)	11 (10.5)	21 (20)
6–10 years	6 (5.7)	2 (1.9)	1 (1)	23 (21.9)	32 (30.5)
11–15 years	3 (2.9)	4 (3.8)	1 (1)	9 (8.6)	17 (16.2)
Above 16 years	7 (6.7)	1 (1)	2 (1.9)	13 (12.4)	23 (21.9)
Total	21 (20)	14 (13.3)	7 (6.7)	63 (60)	105 (100)

Intriguingly, the comparison between years of service and years of unemployment among the respondents shows that the majority of the respondents in all occupational categories, that is, 63 had been unemployed at some point in time after completion of studies. The majority of the respondents had directly entered into the present job or profession after completing their studies. Forty-two respondents had remained unemployed for varying periods. Of them, 21 had been unemployed for less than 2 years, 14 for nearly 5 years and 7 for 10 years. Overall, 60 have had changes in the job or profession. Among these, while 28 had had one change of job, another 31 had changed two jobs and 1 person had changed jobs more than three times (Table 3.20).

Table 3.20 *Previous Jobs or Professions*

Number of Previous Jobs/Professions if Any	*Type of Jobs/Professions Held Previously*					*Total*
	Similar	*Lower than Present*	*Higher than Present*	*Higher and Lower*	*NA*	
Nil	—	—	—	—	45 (42.9)	45 (42.9)
One Job	15 (14.3)	12 (11.4)	1 (1)	—	—	28 (26.7)
2–3 Jobs	10 (9.5)	16 (15.2)	—	5 (4.8)	—	31 (29.5)
More than 3 Jobs	—	—	—	1 (1)	—	1 (1)
Total	25 (23.8)	28 (26.7)	1 (1)	6 (5.7)	45 (42.9)	105 (100)

A comparison between present job or profession and the earlier ones in terms of high-low category showed that 25 had held a similar job earlier, while 28 held jobs lower than the present one, only 1 had a job higher than the present and another 6 held a mixture of higher and lower jobs in the past. The number of respondents who had directly entered into the present job or profession was 45. These figures related to the respondents' career trajectory and prospects assume significance in the context of caste discrimination against Dalits, sometimes overt, sometimes subtle, which varies in its form and intensity.

Experiences of Caste Discrimination

Untouchability, a distinct demarcation between Dalits and caste-Hindus is still a problem for rural or urban, illiterate or educated Dalits. Like other Dalits, the middle class Dalits too face or perceive untouchability and other forms of caste discrimination in their everyday life and in their occupational realms as well. Caste discrimination is pervasive in all spheres of life. In rural areas, it is more visible and often turns into a confrontation, but in cities, such instances are underplayed by both perpetrator and the recipient. In this regard, the respondents were asked to narrate incidences of caste discrimination in various facets of life, namely, workplace, career growth, neighbourhood and public places.

Middle class Dalits, who hail predominantly from a rural background, have experience of varied forms and intensity of caste discrimination. Memories of such experiences are fundamental in shaping their collective consciousness as a community. Having been removed from such a social and economic setting, the middle class Dalits may or may not perceive caste discrimination in their present setting. Those who perceive caste discrimination might be having a sufficient basis for the same or it could be because of their experience that they perceive it larger than its original proportion. Thus, their present social setting prompts them to act against it or tolerate it.

Table 3.21 *Caste Discrimination at Workplace and in Career Growth*

Caste Discrimination at Workplace by	*Form of Discrimination Experienced in Career Growth*					*Total*
	Casteism	*Personal Rivalry/ Jealousy*	*Non-Caste Groupism*	*All of Them*	*No Discrimination*	
Superiors	15 (14.3)	1 (1)	—	—	1 (1)	17 (16.2)
Colleagues	2 (1.9)	—	1 (1)	—	—	3 (2.9)
Both	4 (3.8)	—	—	—	2 (1.9)	6 (5.7)
No Discrimination	11 (10.5)	1 (1)	1 (1)	2 (1.9)	64 (61)	79 (75.2)
Total	32 (30.5)	2 (1.9)	2 (1.9)	2 (1.9)	67 (63.8)	105 (100)

One observes from Table 3.21 that less than half of the respondents felt discriminated based on caste. Among those who had experienced such discrimination, the discrimination based on casteism was in the majority, when compared to other forms of discrimination they had encountered in their workplace. A comparison between caste discrimination experienced by the respondents at the workplace and discrimination experienced in career growth (in terms of denial of promotion, career advancement, etc.) shows that 26 felt that they were facing caste discrimination: 15 from their superiors, 3 from their colleagues and another 6 from both superiors and colleagues. On the other hand, 38 had experienced discrimination related to their career growth in various forms such as *casteism* (30.5%), personal rivalry/jealousy (1.9%), non-caste reason such as *groupism* (1.9%) or all of them (1.9%). However, though in both these instances, the majority of the respondents did not perceive caste-related discrimination, it is important to take into account the perceptions of those who felt discriminated based on caste, as this had a bearing on their work and personal life, thus limiting their mobility. It was observed in the case of a majority of the respondents that such experiences had led them towards collective action (through the formation of SC/ST Welfare Associations to fight such problems).

The middle class Dalits are empowered economically, socially and politically in comparison to the Dalit masses. However, the Dalit middle class too faces caste prejudices and biases despite its economic mobility, in fact, more often because of such mobility. The significant aspect here is that their experiences of caste discrimination are in various new forms. As middle class Dalits, they are mainly subjected to *casteism* that affects their career growth. When faced with caste discrimination, in some cases (wherein which they were assertive about their community identity) they had challenged it, and in other cases (where they were not assertive and were concealing their identity in order to pass off as non-Dalits), they became more vulnerable to such discrimination. The degree of reluctance to reveal/assert one's identity is perhaps related to the degree of such discrimination.

The following instance is an example. An engineer at a university, who was a third-generation educated and hailed from an upper-middle class background, was concealing his community identity, due to which, he felt, he had been saved from the trouble of being subjected to caste-based discrimination. His perception was that due to his upper-middle class family background and because of not having utilized reservations in education and employment, there was no likelihood of him being subjected to caste discrimination, which he feared was otherwise imminent for a Dalit. Since he had not utilized reservations and as there was no mobilization of Dalits during the initial stages of his career at the university, he had not identified himself with the Dalits. Concealing caste identity, he claimed, had not been intentional on his part; however, people had mistaken him for an 'upper caste', mainly due to his physical features and lifestyle. By the time a strong mobilization of SC/STs had emerged in the university, he had been established as a non-Dalit beyond suspicion. Throughout, a few other Dalit employees had known about his 'true identity' but had never made it an issue with him or the others. On his part, though, he did not directly involve himself in the activities of the SC/ST Employees Association in the university, he had supported its causes without being subjected to suspicion about his caste identity by the employees from the other castes. He also intended to retain the non-Dalit image that had been mainly conferred on him by the '*casteist* non-Dalits', as long as possible (Table 3.22).

In another instance, an employee in a government office revealed that he had initially concealed his caste identity, similarly fearing caste discrimination, only to realize later that with a strong Dalit mobilization in the office, there was no need for him to do so. However, having embarked on the stance of concealment, there was no way he could retract from his earlier position due to the repercussions involved. This had led him to persist with his adopted non-Dalit image. Thus far, he had never faced any situation involving the revelation of his Dalit identity. However, he had also realized the delicacy of the situation and the futility of revealing his caste identity under the circumstances, as it would lead to repercussions from the non-Dalits once his claims about his identity were proved wrong. If such a situation arose, he admitted, he would not be able to fall back on his community's support since they would be equally embarrassed by it.

Table 3.22 *Caste Discrimination Experienced by Respondents in Neighbourhood and Public Places*

Form of Caste Discrimination in Neighbourhood	*Form of Caste Discrimination in Public Places*					*Total*
	Refusal of Entry	*No Interaction*	*Insult/Derogatory Comments*	*All of Them*	*No Discrimination*	
Casteism	5 (4.8)	2 (1.9)	—	—	12 (11.4)	19 (18.1)
Non-friendship	—	3 (2.9)	1 (1)	—	12 (11.4)	16 (15.2)
Refusal of House for Rent	—	—	—	2 (1.9)	9 (8.6)	11 (10.5)
Untouchability	—	—	—	—	1 (1.9)	1 (1)
All of Them	1 (1)	4 (3.8)	—	—	—	5 (4.8)
No Discrimination	—	—	—	—	53 (50.5)	53 (50.5)
Total	6 (5.7)	9 (8.6)	1 (1)	2 (1.9)	87 (82.9)	105 (100)

In addition to discrimination related to their professional locations, some respondents perceived that, as individuals and members of the Dalit community, they were at a disadvantage in their neighbourhood and public places as well. Nearly half of the respondents had experienced caste-based discrimination in their neighbourhoods, varying from casteism (18.1%), non-friendship (15.2%), refusal of houses for rent (10.5%), untouchability (1%) or all of the above-mentioned forms of caste discrimination (4.8%). In contrast, with regard to discrimination in public places, they perceived that though the extent of caste discrimination here was relatively less, they had experienced it in various forms such as the refusal of entry (5.7%), no interaction (8.6%), insults/derogatory comments (1%) or all of them (1.9%). All these instances testify that in spite of their progress in the fields of education and employment, Dalits still experience caste discrimination in conventional and sometimes newer forms. The locations of such discrimination have expanded even as Dalits have forged an entry into diversified and newer locations.

Help Received from Others in Education and Career Planning

In understanding the Dalit middle class, it also becomes important to analyse the influence of others (members of their own and other communities) on their lives. Friends and other well wishers play a significant role in the lives of upwardly mobile Dalits, along with their paternal family. In the present study, the contribution of these individuals towards the upward mobility of the respondents in their student days and formative stages of their careers was perceived as being very significant in more ways than one. The influence of the persons who assisted them had not only influenced their careers or aided their upward mobility, but also had a bearing on their social relations in their new location.

In order to understand the nature of assistance extended to them during their student days, as well as in their careers, the caste and occupational profiles of the individuals who helped them were analysed. These individuals, who extended assistance to the respondents in the above-mentioned ways, mostly belonged to a higher economic and social position in comparison to the respondents and their paternal families. In the course of receiving help from these individuals, some respondents were also motivated to forge an entry into their benefactors' occupations. Nearly half of the respondents had received help from individuals (other than family members) during the pursuit of their studies and before embarking on their careers. In all such instances, more than one person had extended help to the respondents. No respondent reported benefiting only from a single individual.

The help received varied from psychological (by way of emotional support or encouragement to pursue education and/or career guidance), economic and motivation/inspiration to reach present occupations. An analysis of caste profiles shows that 7 had received help from persons belonging to the same sub-caste, 17 respondents from persons from other sub-castes and another 15 from other caste persons (non-Dalits). On the other hand, 58 respondents had not received any such help. The figures once again illustrate a significant 'community orientation' among the Dalit middle class (Table 3.23).

Table 3.23 *Caste and Occupation of Persons Who Helped the Respondents*

Caste Background of Persons Who Helped	*Occupational Status of the Persons Who Helped*				*Total*
	Similar	*Higher*	*Mixed**	*No Response*	
Same Sub-Caste	4 (3.8)	3 (2.9)	—	—	7 (6.7)
Different Sub-Caste	5 (4.8)	10 (9.5)	2 (1.9)	—	17 (16.2)
Other Castes	6 (5.7)	5 (4.8)	4 (3.8)	—	15 (14.3)
Mixed	—	—	8 (7.6)	—	8 (7.6)
No Response	—	—	—	58 (55.2)	58 (55.2)
Total	15 (14.3)	18 (17.1)	14 (13.3)	58 (55.2)	105 (100)

* Similar, higher and lower.

The occupational profiles of individuals who extended such help to the respondents show that in the case of 15, the benefactors belonged to the same occupational category; in the case of 18, they are from an occupation higher in economic and social status compared to their occupation and in the case of another 14, they are from various other occupations (Table 3.24).

Table 3.24 *Caste Background of Persons Who Helped and Nature of Help*

Caste Background of Persons Who Helped	*Nature of Help*					*Total*
	Financial Help	*Career Guidance*	*Recomm-endation*	*Introduction for Job*	*No Response*	
Same Sub-Caste	3 (2.9)	2 (1.9)	1 (1)	1 (1)	—	7 (6.7)
Different Sub-Caste	—	4 (3.8)	8 (7.6)	5 (4.8)	—	17 (16.2)
Other Castes	—	6 (5.7)	3 (2.9)	6 (5.7)	—	15 (14.3)
Mixed	—	4 (3.8)	—	4 (3.8)	—	8 (7.6)
No Response	—	—	—	—	58 (55.2)	58 (55.2)
Total	3 (2.9)	16 (15.2)	12 (11.4)	16 (15.2)	58 (55.2)	105 (100)

Help had been extended in various forms such as in the case of 3, it was financial support during the period of studies, for 16 it was career guidance, in the case of 12 it was formal/informal recommendation for jobs and introducing the respondents informally/through letters to their employers in the case of another 16. While tangible assistance to these middle class Dalits had been provided by the members of their sub-caste, mainly in the form of financial assistance, nontangible assistance in the form of career guidance, introduction to employers and recommendations had been provided by members belonging to other sub-castes in their community and other castes (Table 3.25).

Individuals from occupational backgrounds similar to the respondents had provided them with financial help and recommendations for jobs, individuals with higher occupational status had largely provided career guidance and mentoring, and persons belonging to diverse occupations had provided assistance by way of introducing them to different career prospects.

Table 3.25 *Occupation of Persons Who Helped and Nature of Help Extended*

Occupation of Persons Who Helped	*Nature of Help*					*Total*
	Financial Help	*Career Guidance*	*Recomme-ndation*	*Introduction*	*No Response*	
Similar	3	2	9	1	—	15
Higher	—	10	3	5	—	18
Mixed	—	4	—	10	—	14
NR/NA	—	—	—	—	58	58
Total	3	16	12	16	58	105

MIDDLE CLASS DALITS AND THEIR ECONOMIC STATUS

This section features the middle class characteristics of the respondents and their households with particular reference to the background of reservations that had facilitated their socio-economic mobility, the economic constraints they had experienced and their lifestyles, in general, their conditions of existence.

ECONOMIC STATUS

The economic status of the middle class Dalits is not in congruence with their income. Some of the reasons for this have been outlined in the earlier sections. Unlike, most members of the general middle class, most members of the Dalit middle class would not benefit merely from a limited economic mobility, entry into a modern profession/occupation. Due to the demands made on them, financially and otherwise, from their relatives, friends and acquaintances and because they solely depend on the income, they earn from their present occupation or profession to support themselves and these other individuals. The income and expenditure patterns among the respondents suggested that they were largely distributed in income groups ranging below ₹ 1 lakh to ₹ 2–3 lakh per annum. Most of them were located in the ₹ 1–2 lakh per annum group. In most cases, the respondents were the sole earning members of their family, the main source of income being their occupation or profession. Their lives were organized around the incomes earned from their occupations. Comparatively, government and public sector employees had larger incomes, and the majority of them were distributed in ₹ 1–2 lakh and ₹ 2–3 lakh income groups. On the other hand, the majority of the professionals, especially, those in the NGO sector, legal and journalism fields were concentrated in below ₹ 1 lakh income category. Among the professionals, doctors were relatively well placed economically, owing to the greater prestige of the profession and due to the nature of their employment (Table 3.26).

Table 3.26 *Details of Family Income (per annum from all sources)*

Respondents' Occupation	*Family Income*					*Total*
	Below ₹ 1 lakh	*₹ 1 to 2 lakh*	*₹ 2 to 3 lakh*	*₹ 3 to 4 lakh*	*₹ 4 to 5 lakh*	
Officer Cadre	—	11 (10.5)	3 (2.9)	1 (1)	—	15 (14.3)
Clerical Cadre	5 (4.8)	6 (5.7)	4 (3.8)	—	—	15 (14.3)
University Faculty	—	11 (10.5)	2 (1.9)	2 (1.9)	—	15 (14.3)
Bank Employee	6 (5.7)	8 (7.6)	—	—	1 (1)	15 (14.3)
NGO	9 (8.6)	3 (2.9)	3 (2.9)	—	—	15 (14.3)
Advocate	7 (6.7)	3 (2.9)	5 (4.8)	—	—	15 (14.3)
Doctor	1 (1)	5 (4.8)	4 (3.8)	—	—	10 (9.5)
Journalist	4 (3.8)	—	—	1 (1)	—	5 (4.8)
Total	32 (30.5)	47 (44.8)	21 (20)	4 (3.8)	1 (1)	105 (100)

Considering the fact that many of the respondents belonged to the first generation of the economically upward mobile in their families, they had financial and other responsibilities towards their paternal family, and their expenses generally exceeded their income. Except a few, almost all respondents fell in the range of an annual income of ₹ 1–2 lakh. Among them, a considerable number had an income below ₹ 1 lakh per annum (Table 3.27).

With regard to expenditure, a major chunk went towards household expenses, expenditure directed towards creation of assets, on children (especially for education) and other needs formed a negligible percentage (Table 3.28).

Table 3.27 *Family Income and Consumption Pattern*

Family Income per Annum from All Sources (in ₹)	*Respondents' Family Consumption Pattern*			*Total*
	High	*Moderate*	*Low*	
Below ₹ 1 lakh	2 (1.9)	13 (12.4)	17 (16.2)	32 (30.5)
₹ 1 to 2 lakh	1 (1)	42 (40)	4 (3.8)	47 (44.8)
₹ 2 to 3 lakh	5 (4.8)	15 (14.3)	1 (1)	21 (20)
₹ 3 to 4 lakh	2 (1.9)	2 (1.9)	—	4 (3.8)
₹ 4 to 5 lakh	—	1 (1)	—	1 (1)
Total	10 (9.5)	73 (69.5)	22 (21)	105 (100)

Table 3.28 *Details of Income per Annum from All Sources and Average Monthly Expenditure of Respondents' Families*

Income per Annum (in ₹)	*Monthly Expenditure*				*Total*
	Expenses	*Assets*	*On Children*	*Other*	
Below ₹ 1 lakh	30 (28.6)	1 (1)	1 (1)	5 (4.8)	37 (35.2)
₹ 1 to 2 lakh	36 (34.3)	1 (1)	3 (2.9)	3 (2.9)	43 (41)
₹ 2 to 3 lakh	17 (16.2)	2 (1.9)	—	—	19 (18.1)
₹ 3 to 4 lakh	3 (2.9)	—	—	—	3 (2.9)
₹ 4 to 5 lakh	1 (1)	—	—	—	1 (1)
No Response	2 (1.9)	—	—	—	2 (1.9)
Total	89 (84.8)	4 (3.8)	4 (3.8)	8 (7.6)	105 (100)

Savings and Indebtedness

Savings and insurance for emergencies were a common phenomenon among the regular income groups (salaried employees). Almost all these respondents had some savings and/or subscribed to various insurance schemes. Overall, not much variation was found in this practice among different occupational groups, except that the number of subscriptions to insurance schemes and savings were relatively greater among the salaried employees in comparison to professionals due to their irregular income (Table 3.29).

Table 3.29 *Investments and Savings for Emergencies*

Savings/Investments	*Insurance Schemes*					*Total*
	LIC	*Health Schemes*	*Chit Funds*	*All*	*No Response*	
Investment in Agriculture/House Assets	7 (6.7)	4 (3.8)	—	2 (1.9)	—	13 (12.4)
Savings in Shares/Chit Funds	29 (27.6)	5 (4.8)	2 (1.9)	—	—	36 (34.3)
Mandatory Government Saving Schemes	4 (3.8)	1 (1)	2 (1.9)	5 (4.8)	—	12 (11.4)
Investment and Savings in Agriculture/House Assets and Government Saving Schemes	2 (1.9)	1 (1)	—	11 (10.5)	—	14 (13.3)
Shares/Chit Funds and Government Saving Schemes	—	—	—	1 (1)	—	1 (1)
Savings in Banks	1 (1)	—	—	1 (1)	—	2 (1.9)
No Savings	1 (1)	—	—	3 (2.9)	—	4 (3.8)
No Response	5 (4.8)	4 (3.8)	—	—	14 (13.3)	23 (21.9)
Total	47 (44.8)	17 (16.2)	4 (3.8)	23 (21.9)	14 (13.3)	105 (100)

Respondents had generally invested a portion of their earnings in various savings-related schemes, shares and chit funds. The majority had opted for private savings schemes such as chit funds and investments in shares, which were perceived as flexible and more attractive compared to other institutionalized savings sources such as government savings schemes and schemes offered by the banks. However, four respondents have reported that they are not having any savings/investments, mainly due to economic constraints. The insurance schemes that the respondents preferred to subscribe were those of the public sector, with a large number of them subscribing LIC, in addition to other health-related schemes. These figures indicate that their priorities and outlook with regard to savings/subscriptions scheme largely mirror those of the general middle class.

Except in the case of 28 respondents, others had incurred debts ranging from below ₹ 1 lakh to ₹ 10 lakh and above. Among these, 21 had incurred debts below ₹ 1 lakh; six of them ₹ 1 to 2 lakh; 12 ₹ 2 to 5 lakh; five 5 to 10 lakh and another three had incurred debts above ₹ 10 lakh. The sources of credit for these debts were formal, informal and both: 46 had borrowed money from formal sources (banks, place of employment, other institutions), 11 had borrowed the money from informal sources (family, relatives, friends and acquaintances) and 10 had obtained the money from both these sources (Table 3.30).

Table 3.30 *Details of Standing Debts*

Amount	*Debts and Their Source*					*Total*
	Formal Sources	*Informal Sources*	*Both*	*No Debts*	*No Response*	
Below ₹ 1 lakh	15 (14.3)	3 (2.9)	3 (2.9)	—	—	21 (20)
₹ 1 to 2 lakh	5 (4.8)	1 (1)	—	—	—	6 (5.7)
₹ 2 to 5 lakh	8 (7.6)	2 (1.9)	2 (1.9)	—	—	12 (11.4)
₹ 5 to 10 lakh	1 (1)	2 (1.9)	2 (1.9)	—	—	5 (4.8)
₹ 10 lakh and Above	2 (1.9)	1 (1)		—	—	3 (2.9)
No Response	15 (14.3)	2 (1.9)	3 (2.9)	—	—	20 (19)
Not Applicable	—	—	—	28 (26.7)	10 (9.5)	38 (36.2)
Total	46 (43.8)	11 (10.5)	10 (9.5)	28 (26.7)	10 (9.5)	105 (100)

The debts are incurred for various needs and reasons, mostly personal in nature. However, not much information could be obtained from the respondents in this regard.

Residential Locality/Neighbourhood

One of the basic features of the middle class is that of residing in a locality, which can also be termed as a predominantly 'middle class', with all the attendant amenities and facilities a middle class income group requires and desires. There are distinctly middle class, posh and poor localities in Hyderabad city, which are defined in terms of their residents' economic class. However, such localities are not separated geographically based on these classifications. They may be at times located next to each other, sometimes as islands. A poor neighbourhood is not uncommon in the midst of a posh locality and the reverse is true.

The respondents of the present study, having a predominantly middle class income and lifestyle, though sharing a common social background with the people living in poor localities, had chosen middle class localities for residential purposes. With respect to the poor localities, it is generally perceived that the majority dwelling there hail from socially disadvantaged sections, largely the Dalits. The members of the Dalit middle class, at least those who are locals, might be having relatives living in these poor localities. Thus far, it has been the other communities, who have had possession of the middle class and posh localities and Dalits are the new entrants into such localities, predominantly composed of other communities. In this context, it becomes important to understand their arrival into such a locality and most importantly their experiences in their neighbourhood (Table 3.31).

Table 3.31 *Residential Locality*

Current Residential Locality	*Number of Years Living in the Present Place of Residence*			*Total*
	0–5 years	*5–10 years*	*10+ years*	
Middle Class Locality	36 (34.3)	32 (30.5)	35 (33.3)	103 (98.1)
Poor Locality	2 (1.9)	—	—	2 (1.9)
Total	38 (36.2)	32 (30.5)	35 (33.3)	105 (100)

When asked to classify their present and past residential localities as posh, middle class and poor localities, the respondents chose to classify them as markedly middle class locality. All, except two respondents, lived in middle class localities. Even these two respondents had shifted from a poor to a middle class locality in the last 5 years. This could be partly because the majority of these individuals had migrated to the city, for purposes of either education or employment, that had necessitated them to take up residence in a middle class locality. Unlike in the past where the majority of Dalits who migrated to the city were illiterate and sought employment in unskilled sectors, the new migrants were educated and employable in modern occupations. Even in the case of 12 local (predominantly second- or third-generation migrants) respondents, their families had migrated long back and undergone some upward economic mobility; therefore, they were now placed in a middle class locality.

An examination of the respondents' house ownership status in relation to their neighbourhood showed that both in cases where respondents possessed own house or were living in rented houses; they were mostly concentrated in either non-Dalit localities or localities with Dalit and other communities, in comparison to exclusively Dalit localities (Table 3.32).

Table 3.32 *House Ownership Status and Neighbourhood*

Ownership of House	*Neighbourhood*				*Total*
	Dalit	*Non-Dalit*	*Both*	*No Response*	
Own House	6 (5.7)	12 (11.4)	21 (20)	—	39 (37.1)
Rented House	7 (6.7)	19 (18.1)	38 (36.3)	2 (1.9)	66 (62.9)
Total	13 (12.4)	31 (29.5)	59 (56.2)	2 (1.9)	105 (100)

The reasons proffered for choosing their present locality/neighbourhood in the case of respondents to own house ranged from easy availability for 17 respondents, economic affordability for 14, allotments by the office/employer in the case of 4 and other reasons for 4 respondents (Table 3.33).

Table 3.33 *Reasons for Choosing the Neighbourhood in the Case of Own House*

Respondents' Neighbourhood is Predominantly	*Reasons*					*Total*
	Easy Availability	*Economic Affordability*	*Allotted by the Office/ Employer*	*Other*	*Not Applicable*	
Dalit	1 (1)	1 (1)	—	—	11 (10.5)	13 (12.4)
Non-Dalit	6 (5.7)	5 (4.8)		2 (1.9)	18 (17.1)	31 (29.5)

Cont'd...

...Cont'd

Both	10 (9.5)	8 (7.6)	4 (3.8)	2 (1.9)	35 (33.3)	59 (56.2)
NR	—	—	—	—	2 (1.9)	2 (1.9)
Total	17 (16.2)	14 (13.3)	4 (3.8)	4 (3.8)	66 (62.9)	105 (100)

Type of House

In comparison to their paternal families, the majority of the respondents were first-generation migrants to Hyderabad city, who had arrived largely for purposes of education and/or employment (Table 3.34).

Table 3.34 *Type of House and Status of Residential Accommodation*

Type of House	*Status of Residential Accommodation*		*Total*
	Own	*Rental*	
Independent House	28 (26.7)	48 (45.7)	76 (72.4)
Flat in an Apartment	11 (10.5)	18 (17.1)	29 (27.6)
Total	39 (37.1)	66 (62.9)	105 (100)

Initially, some of them had resided in rented houses and later had purchased a place of their own. Presently, 39 respondents owned a house in the city, while 66 are residing in rented houses (Table 3.35).

Table 3.35 *Type of House and Number of Rooms*

Number of Rooms	*Type of House*		*Total*
	Independent House	*Flat in an Apartment*	
Single Room	2 (1.9)	—	2 (1.9)
Single Bedroom	14 (13.3)	4 (3.8)	18 (17.1)
Double Bedroom	21 (20)	13 (11.4)	34 (32.4)
More than 3 Rooms	31 (29.5)	5 (4.8)	36 (34.3)
No Response	8 (7.6)	7 (6.7)	15 (14.3)
Total	76 (72.4)	29 (27.6)	105 (100)

The type of residential accommodation that the respondents had largely indicated that the majority, that is, 76 preferred residing in an independent house compared to an apartment only by 29 of them (Table 3.36).

Table 3.36 *Status of Residential Accommodation*

Present Market Value in Case of Own House (₹ in Lakh)	*Status of Residential Accommodation*		*Total*
	Own	*Rental*	
Below 1	8 (7.6)		8 (7.6)
Below 2	7 (6.7)	—	7 (6.7)
2 to 5 lakh	6 (5.7)	—	6 (5.7)
5 to 10 lakh	13 (12.4)	—	13 (12.4)
More than 10 lakh	5 (4.8)	—	5 (4.8)
NA/Not Own House	—	66 (62.9)	66 (62.9)
Total	39 (37.1)	66 (62.9)	105 (100)

An examination of the present market value of the houses owned by respondents showed that: of 39 who owned a house, the majority of them, that is, 26 owned houses worth below ₹ 5 lakh, while another 13 owned houses worth between ₹ 5 and 10 lakh, and only 5 of them owned houses worth more than ₹ 10 lakh.

Consumption Pattern

Owning assets is an important cultural marker for the middle class. It also reflects their consumption patterns and lifestyle. The consumption pattern among the respondents showed that the majority of the respondents, that is, 73 (69.5%) had a moderate tendency towards consumerism. Consumption patterns of the respondents were measured in relation to the number of consumer durables used and their prices. Luxurious items such as a car, refrigerator, washing machine, VCR/VCP and computer were accorded high rank, while motor bike/moped, dining table, cell phone and credit card were given a moderate rank and TV (Colour TV/Black &White TV), telephone and bicycle were given a low rank.

While there were 9 respondents with a high propensity for consumption of these durables, a considerable number, that is, 23 of them were at a low level of the overall consumption index. This trend has a bearing largely on their income and their responsibilities towards their paternal families. Those respondents who did not have to shoulder the economic responsibilities of their paternal families lived comfortably with a moderate consumption pattern, which also corresponded with their income level (Table 3.37).

Table 3.37 *Consumption Patterns based on Rank Given to Consumer Goods*

Respondents' Consumption Pattern	*Frequency and Percentage*
High	9 (8.6)
Moderate	73 (69.5)
Low	23 (21.9)
Total	105 (100)

Almost all respondents possessed at least one each of the consumer durables mentioned and cases of ownership of more than one of these durables were rare and occurred mostly in the form of low ranked consumer durables.

Landholding Pattern

Ownership of land is an important indicator of economic status in rural areas. Dalits' major source of livelihood in rural areas is agriculture labour. Traditionally, they do not belong to the land-owning population. Except for the traditional *Inam* lands (community land gifted to Dalits in recognition of their services to village community), many Dalits did not possess agricultural land. Only in the post-independence period, after other traditional land-owning communities moved away from agriculture, some Dalits gained ownership of agricultural land in rural areas. However, such landholdings of Dalits' are largely composed of lands distributed by the government as part of land reforms.

In cities, it is a remote possibility of Dalits owning lands, except those who migrated one or two generations earlier. In a few cases, they had such ownership of land; however, it had reduced significantly, owing to various reasons (urban land ceiling, growth in family size, slow-paced economic mobility among those families, etc.). Non-locals or the first-generation migrants to the city do not have landholdings in the city, except land acquired by some of them for housing purpose. The landholding pattern among respondents shows that 45 have landholdings of varying kinds. Of which five of them have land in the city and 40 at their native place. Among those 42 who do not own any land, 6 are locals and 36 come from different parts of the state. However, a considerable number of them, that is, 18 did not respond to the question. Among the respondents, almost equal numbers of respondents have or do not have landholdings.

Table 3.38 *Landholding Pattern*

Respondents' Occupation	*Landholding Pattern*			*Total*
	Yes	*No*	*No Response*	
Officer Cadre	6 (5.7)	6 (5.7)	3 (2.9)	15 (14.3)
Clerical Cadre	6 (5.7)	8 (7.6)	1 (1)	15 (14.3)
University Faculty	10 (9.5)	3 (2.9)	2 (1.9)	15 (14.3)
Bank Employee	4 (3.8)	6 (5.7)	5 (4.8)	15 (14.3)
NGO	6 (5.7)	7 (6.7)	2 (1.9)	15 (14.3)
Advocate	6 (5.7)	5 (4.8)	4 (3.8)	15 (14.3)
Doctor	6 (5.7)	3 (2.9)	1 (1)	10 (9.5)
Journalist	1 (1)	4 (3.8)	—	5 (4.8)
Total	45 (42.9)	42 (40)	18 (17.1)	105 (100)

Analysis of land ownership in their native place has some significance, that is, to ascertain respondents' tendency towards investments in agriculture and shouldering agriculture-related responsibilities. Land ownership, as indicated in Table 3.38, takes the form of mostly agricultural land of their native places. The practice (out of interest and/or as responsibility towards the ancestral family) of sending part of their income to native place was found among a few respondents. However, such a practice is in decline now. Except few, the majority of the respondents do not have stakes in these lands as they are the most economically well off in their families and have given up their share for their siblings' or parents' subsistence needs. In the absence of lands in their native place, many respondents have had to shoulder the economic dependence of their paternal family. A few others showed interest in family-related agricultural activities by providing not only financial inputs sporadically, but also expected returns from such investments.

EXPERIENCING THE LIFESTYLE CHANGES

Each social and economic class has a distinctive lifestyle. Members of a class follow the normative-material[13] practices of that class and generally adhere to the class character. The educated Dalits, after entering into an occupation/profession that provides them with a middle class income, naturally takes to a middle class lifestyle, until other circumstances force them towards their own community circles. Depending on the result of their initial attempts to interact with others, they either get assimilated in the general middle class or get alienated and move towards forming their own Dalit middle class.[14]

A few lifestyle aspects such as food habits and dressing, usage of a particular accent, tone in the language or usage of English; religious practices, making or leaving out friends and acquaintances and family outing for cinema, eating out have been analysed with an assumption that there would be a change in their lifestyle with their entry into the middle class, especially in the case of those who come from a poor economic background. Though most of the respondents were not alien to these lifestyle practices of the middle class, those who had come from rural and poor backgrounds had also experienced or witnessed them during their pursuit of education, well in advance, to acquaint themselves with the middle class lifestyle. For the majority of the respondents, changes in these lifestyle aspects were not sudden occurrences, but had taken place over a period of time.

In Table 3.39, the lifestyle changes in terms of increase or decrease in lifestyle, as perceived by the respondents, are presented.

There was a noticeable surge in terms of qualitative changes in the respondents' lifestyle after entering into their present occupation/profession; these were largely related to food habits and dressing among 65 and language among another 66 of them.

Interestingly, these two aspects either witnessed an increase in terms of quantity and quality or remained same. However, 40 respondents found no change in their consumption pattern and 39 had found no change with respect to language, since these individuals had been acquainted with these lifestyle patterns from their student days, in either their hostels or the hotels they frequented. In contrast, in the case of religion and family outings, 2 respondents perceived a decline in their frequency of visits to temples and 10 found a decline in the frequency of their family outings. The circle of friends and acquaintances had widened for 80 of them, remained the same for 20 and decreased for another 2 of them. These new friends were generally from other communities. There is thus a marked increase in the interaction of middle class Dalits with members of other communities (Table 3.40).

Table 3.39 *Aspects of Lifestyle that have Undergone Changes*

Aspects of Lifestyle that Have Undergone Changes Over the Years	*Increased*	*Remained Same*	*Decreased*	*Total*
Consumption Pattern: Food Habits, Dressing, etc.	65 (61.9)	40 (38.1)	—	105 (100)
Language: Adoption of Accent, English, etc.	66 (62.9)	39 (37.1)	—	105 (100)
Religion: Visiting Temples, Worshipping New Deities, etc.	26 (24.8)	77 (73.3)	2 (1.9)	105 (100)
New Friends and Acquaintances	83 (79)	20 (19)	2 (1.9)	105 (100)
Family Outing: Cinema, Hotel, etc.	40 (38.1)	55 (52.4)	10 (9.5)	105 (100)

Table 3.40 *Reasons Proffered for Lifestyle Changes*

Respondents' Occupation	*Changes in Lifestyle Can Be Attributed to Factors Like*					*Total*
	Economic Status	*Social Status*	*Occupation/ Profession*	*All of These*	*No Response*	
Officer Cadre	5 (4.8)	—	4 (3.8)	6 (5.7)	—	15 (14.3)
Clerical Cadre	5 (4.8)	—	—	9 (8.6)	1 (1)	15 (14.3)
University Faculty	9 (8.6)	—	2 (1.9)	3 (2.9)	1 (1)	15 (14.3)

Cont'd...

...Cont'd

Bank Employee	9 (8.6)	—	1 (1)	4 (3.8)	1 (1)	15 (14.3)
NGO	6 (5.7)	1 (1)	2 (1.9)	6 (5.7)	—	15 (14.3)
Advocate	7 (6.7)	—	2 (1.9)	6 (5.7)	—	15 (14.3)
Doctor	4 (3.8)	—	—	5 (4.8)	1 (1)	10 (9.5)
Journalist	2 (1.9)	—	—	3 (2.9)	—	5 (4.8)
Total	47 (44.8)	1 (1)	11 (10.5)	42 (40)	4 (3.8)	105 (100)

The paternal family economic status of the respondent's paternal family had a bearing on their perceptions regarding changes in their lifestyle. Most of the respondents, whose origins were either modest or poor, had been motivated by their life experiences in their paternal family to bring about improvements in their lifestyle. Generally, economic status was perceived by 47 respondents to be the main factor that had motivated them to bring about changes in their lifestyle compared to social status or occupation/profession. The acquisition of economic status combined with other factors seemed to have led to significant changes in the lifestyle of another 42 of them.

In this chapter, the socio-economic status of the middle class Dalits was analysed in relation to various factors such as number of dependents and their nature of dependence, education pattern in the paternal family, residential locality, status of residential accommodation, consumption pattern, economic status in terms of income, savings and debts, landholding pattern and changes in lifestyle. The next chapter deals with the respondents' perceptions on various social, economic and political issues with an intention to ascertain their patterns of ideology and identity.

NOTES

1. Kulke (1976), Ram (1988) and Omvedt (2002).
2. Misra (1961), Prasad (1968) and Singh (1985).
3. Prasad (1968) and Singh (1985).
4. Kulke (1976), Ram (1988), Srinivas (1996) and Saavala (2001).

5. Jeffrey (2001) argues that Dalits so far are limited only to regional languages newspapers, mainly as stringers and not many have made it into the English print media and higher levels.
6. See Jain et al. (1997: 154) for employment pattern among Dalit women.
7. Ram (1988: 18) observes that education plays a pivotal role in social mobility of Dalits.
8. Census of India (2001).
9. Kulke (1976: 245) observes it as a major characteristic of Dalit middle class.
10. Ramaswamy (1974: 1158) suggests several factors contributed to the unequal development of Malas and Madigas in Andhra Pradesh.
11. Webster (1992: 32) traces the history of Dalits' conversion to other religions, especially to Christianity during the nineteenth century.
12. Malik (1979: 29) also finds similar correlation between fathers' and sons' occupational statuses.
13. See van Dijk (1998: 152).
14. Kulke (1976: 252) explains how the attempts of Dalit middle class to integrate in the general middle class do not materialize and consequently lead to 'rejection' and 'alienation'.

CHAPTER 4

Middle Class Dalits and Their Ideology and Identity

Caste as a system and as an ideology, and practice was or is a priori condition of structural discrimination, which is omnipotent and omnipresent in the Indian society. The structural discrimination continues to affect everyday lives of the Dalit community strongly across all the sections and classes. Middle class Dalits face many kinds of discriminations and disadvantages in their social relations and career. To understand the nature of Dalit middle class within the given context, its ideology and identity, lifestyle, life circumstances and priorities, and politics of the members are important. In this chapter, an attempt is made to comprehend the life circumstances that lead members of the Dalit middle class to gravitate towards Dalit identity and ideology. The analysis outlines the life experiences and life circumstances of middle class Dalits across modern occupations and various facets of their social life – in the 'secular-modern' context – to understand various situations that create a *Dalit collective conscience* to organize and identify themselves as Dalits. van Dijk (1998: 120) explains,

> Ideologies are essentially shared and hence need to be defined at group level. The same is true for the social or collective 'identity' of the group as a group. Usually, identity is taken in an individualistic fashion in terms of representations and identification processes of group members. However, in the same way as groups may be said to share knowledge, attitudes

and an ideology, we may assume that they share a social representation that defines their identity or 'social self' as a group.

The Dalit middle class in its pursuit of an identity formulates its own ideology in order to justify its location, beliefs, values and politics. Jonathan Friedman (1992: 837) asserted self-definition of identity 'is decisively a question of empowerment'. It is true in the case of Dalits and especially the middle class Dalits, whose location of origin and present locations equally shape their life situation, identity, ideology and politics. Here, an attempt is made to understand the ideology and identity formation among the Dalit middle class at four levels, which are: (1) life situation (circumstances, experiences and expectations), (2) identity pattern (personal and social), (3) ideology formation (social, economic and political) and (4) politics (pragmatic and ideological). In the first level, an attempt to understand life situation (circumstances, experiences and expectations) was carried out through analysis of their interpersonal relationships, social relations, community connections, their interaction with other 'successful' Dalits and own collective/individual efforts towards development of Dalits.

At the second level, their identity patterns (personal and social) were taken up, in which, their self-description, identity patterns and status differentiation with others and criteria for identifying Dalits were analysed. At the third level, their ideology (social, economic and political) formations of the middle class Dalits were constructed through enquiring into their views and perceptions on the progress made by Dalits since independence, status of Dalit women, Dalit movement, Dalit leaders and greatest personalities of the twentieth century.

And finally, their politics (pragmatic and ideological) were analysed with the help of their membership in organizations/political parties, their preference to effective models/strategy for overall development of Dalits, views on reservations, views related to political options before the Dalits for achieving equality, knowledge about issues/measure related to Dalits, prioritization of socio-economic and political issues and their views on some important socio-economic and political issues in understanding their identity and ideology.

MIDDLE CLASS DALITS AND THEIR LIFE SITUATION (SOCIAL MILIEU)

As part of understanding the life situation (circumstances, experiences and expectations) of the Dalit middle class, their interpersonal relationships, social relations, community connections, their interaction with other 'successful' Dalits and own collective/individual efforts towards development of Dalits are analysed.

Middle Class Dalits and Their Interpersonal Relations

Interpersonal relations (mostly a collaboration at work, forging of alliances other than friendship, camaraderie or acquaintance) in various occupations and professions were generally formed on caste lines. In some instances, they were direct and openly visible, and in others, they were discreet and hard to prove. On the lines of caste-based mobilizations for political and social occasions, at the workplace too, individuals belonging to the same community come together and have more trust in each other compared to individuals from other communities. At times, if there is competition and clash of interests among these individuals, then they fall back on individuals from other communities who share their temperament, views and political understanding. In all these instances, same caste or same *varna*[1] and similar interests form basis for interpersonal relations at workplace in that order (Table 4.1).

Among the respondents, only 36 felt interpersonal relations at their workplace were formed on caste lines, while the majority 52 did not find caste influencing interpersonal relations at the workplace. On the other hand, the number of respondents who were not sure about such a tendency was seven. Another 10 respondents did not respond to the query. Compared to the findings from earlier studies, where the Dalit employees were subjected to alienation at the work place, the situation is slowly improving in this regard. Many of the Dalit employees are now part of SC/ST Employees Welfare Associations that are well organized to fight caste discrimination, and offer comradeship at the same time. With such support structures to deal with alienation and discrimination based on caste, the middle class Dalits are trying to arrest the spread of 'older' problems into newer locations.

Table 4.1 *Caste and Interpersonal Relations in the Office/Workplace*

Respondents' Occupation	*Interpersonal Relations in the Office/Workplace Are Formed on Caste Lines?*				*Total*
	Yes	*No*	*Cannot Say*	*No Response*	
Officer Cadre	5 (4.8)*	7 (6.7)	2 (1.9)	1 (1)	15 (14.3)
Clerical Cadre	4 (3.8)	11 (10.5)	—	—	15 (14.3)
University Faculty	7 (6.7)	8 (7.6)	—	—	15 (14.3)
Bank Employee	5 (4.8)	2 (1.9)	3 (2.9)	5 (4.8)	15 (14.3)
NGO	5 (4.8)	7 (6.7)	1 (1)	2 (1.9)	15 (14.3)
Advocate	6 (5.7)	6 (5.7)	1 (1)	2 (1.9)	15 (14.3)
Doctor	3 (2.9)	7 (6.7)	—	—	10 (9.5)
Journalist	1 (1)	4 (3.8)	—	—	5 (4.8)
Total	36 (34.3)	52 (49.5)	7 (6.7)	10 (9.5)	105 (100)

* In all tables in this chapter, figures in parenthesis indicate percentages.

Social Relations in Workplace and Neighbourhood

Social relations at the workplace are indicative of their attempts to rise above caste barriers. Social relations in terms of friendship with colleagues from different socio-economic backgrounds in everyday interactions are an indication in this direction. Regarding personal friendships, the Dalits exhibit no particular preference for their own community; they have friends from all castes. In the process of naming five close friends at the work place, the respondents informed that they had friends from all communities; nevertheless, their closest friends were Dalits. On an everyday basis, in their work as well as personal needs, they interacted with a few colleagues whose interests were similar to their own. As part of their professional vocation, they interacted with people from all communities and thus had friends across all communities. However, the proximity of such friendship varied between friends from own and other communities. In some cases in which the respondents had to work in a group or had a collective work responsibility, they seem to enjoy the partnership of persons from other communities. Having friends from other communities was not a problem for the majority of the respondents, in a few instances; however, they did have difficulty in seeking out friends from other communities (Table 4.2).

Table 4.2 *Particulars of Respondents' Friends in Office/Workplace*

Respondents' Friends in Office/Workplace	*Particulars of Respondents' Friends in Office/Workplace*				*Total*
	Similar	*Different*	*Mixed*	*No Response*	
Occupation	—	—	75 (71.4)	30 (28.6)	105 (100)
Age	—	—	75 (71.4)	30 (28.6)	105 (100)
Gender	47 (44.8)	—	28 (26.7)	30 (28.6)	105 (100)
Caste	12 (11.4)	6 (5.7)	54 (51.4)	33 (31.4)	105 (100)
Religion	52 (49.5)	—	23 (21.9)	30 (28.6)	105 (100)

Occupational position and age seemed to pose no barriers in forming friendships across various gender, class, caste and age groups for the respondents compared to gender, caste and religion. Respondents' friends in the office/workplace belonged to various occupational categories and age groups, while 47 of them had same gender friends and 52 of them had friends from the same religion. In the case of caste, 12 respondents had persons from their own caste as friends and 6 had only other caste persons as close friends. Others considered none of these aspects while choosing friends, they had friends across occupation, age group, gender, caste and religions. This indicated the kind of commonality they had with middle class members from other communities. Social integration had taken place as far as friendship was concerned. However, these social interactions were individual in nature, did not involve their families and were not an indication of the assimilation of different communities. These relationships were secondary in nature.

On the other hand, the choice of friends in the neighbourhood was marked by certain limitations, compared to the office or workplace. Forming friendships on mutually agreeable terms in the neighbourhood, suiting all their interests was difficult compared to an office or the workplace. As can be seen in Table 4.2, the friendship patterns in their place of residence, neighbourhood or the city in general showed that the respondents engaged more with their persons from their own community for family-level interactions and community-level interactions. As family-level interactions involved social and religious occasions, their preferences lay towards their own community rather than other communities (Table 4.3).[2]

Table 4.3 *Particulars of Respondents' Friends in the City with Whom Respondents Interact at Personal and Family Levels*

Particulars of Respondents' Friends in the City	*In Comparison with the Respondents*				*Total*
	Similar	*Different*	*Mixed*	*No Response*	
Occupation	5 (4.8)	5 (4.8)	57 (54.3)	38 (36.2)	105 (100)
Age	—	17 (16.2)	50 (47.6)	38 (36.2)	105 (100)
Gender	59 (56.2)	3 (2.9)	5 (4.8)	38 (36.2)	105 (100)
Caste	10 (9.5)	13 (12.4)	44 (41.9)	38 (36.2)	105 (100)
Religion	48 (45.7)	—	19 (18.1)	38 (36.2)	105 (100)

In contrast to the nature of friendships in the office or workplace that were largely secondary in nature, friendships in the neighbourhood required a broad-based social acceptance of not only individuals but also their families. Social interactions at family level between Dalits and non-Dalits were still bound by many caste-based prejudices, notions of hierarchy and purity and pollution. Except in a few cases, where the Dalits were employed in high government positions or the non-Dalits had disbanded such purity-pollution, hierarchical notions, and interaction at family levels were taking place. On their part, many Dalits did not feel disconcerted over the denial of such occasions for interactions with the non-Dalits. The very fact that many of them had non-Dalit friends at the office and the workplace and not as many at the family level suggests that the middle class Dalits do not intend to pursue it in haste. Social relations are mutual, largely sustained by reciprocity from both the sides. In the case of social relations between Dalits and non-Dalits, there is a gradual progress in terms of the numbers of Dalits and non-Dalits seeking friendship and trust from each other.

Middle Class Dalits' Interaction with Own Community

The most important criticism on the middle class Dalits has been about 'forgetting roots' and not caring for their own community after moving up on the economic ladder. It is generally felt by almost all the middle class Dalits that they were not making their best efforts to empower the Dalit masses. Dalits' position becomes delicate when they get embedded into the middle class. They try to retain close community-based connections with their Dalit colleagues on the one hand and the other acquaintances living in the city on the other hand. Those who have strong familial bonding in the rural areas try to retain them as well. Since their assimilation into the general middle class is uncertain, many middle class Dalits seem to be giving priority to their social relations within their own community.

Table 4.4 *Respondents Visiting Their Native Place and People from Native Place Visiting Them*

Respondents Visiting Their Native Place	*People from Native Place Visiting Respondents*				*Total*
	Visiting Frequently	*Visiting Rarely*	*Not Applicable*	*No Response*	
Visiting Frequently	49 (46.7)	12 (11.4)	—	—	61 (58.1)
Visiting Rarely	22 (21)	15 (14.3)	—	—	37 (35.2)
Not Applicable	—	—	2 (1.9)	—	2 (1.9)
No Response	—	—	—	5 (4.8)	5 (4.8)
Total	71 (67.6)	27 (25.7)	2 (1.9)	5 (4.8)	105 (100)

Among the majority of respondents of the present study, visiting community members either in native place or in the city was a regular practice. The reverse trend was also prevalent (Table 4.4). As the majority of the respondents were migrants to the city, whose kith and kin were not present in the city, maintaining connections with them became important for them. The frequency of visits on both sides was used as an indicator to measure connections with individuals from their community (Table 4.5).

There were 61 respondents who made visits to their native place frequently, whereas 71 of them were visited frequently by the people from their native place. Similarly, 70 respondents made visits to people from their community in the city and 84 were visited by their community people in the city. In some instances, the respondents' visits to the people belonging to their community were rare; in other instances, the level of reciprocity from the other side was lower compared to the respondents who frequented their homes on a regular basis. In the case of three respondents, where there were no visits on both sides, the respondents were maintaining connections with the members of their community within the city itself (Table 4.6).

Table 4.5 *Respondents Visiting Community People in the City and Community People (from the City) Visiting Them*

Visiting Community People in the City	*Being Visited by Community People (from the City)*				*Total*
	Visiting Frequently	*Visiting Rarely*	*Not Applicable*	*No Response*	
Visiting Frequently	70 (66.7)	2 (1.9)	—	—	72 (68.6)
Visiting Rarely	16 (15.2)	14 (13.3)	—	—	30 (28.6)
Not Applicable	—	—	2 (1.9)	—	2 (1.9)
No Response	—	—	—	1 (1)	1 (1)
Total	84 (80)	16 (15.2)	2 (1.9)	1 (1)	105 (100)

Table 4.6 *Respondents' Visits to Their Native Place and Community People in the City*

Respondents Visiting Their Native Place	*Respondents Visiting Community People in the City*				*Total*
	Visiting Frequently	*Visiting Rarely*	*Not Applicable*	*No Response*	
Visiting Frequently	54 (51.4)	7 (6.7)	—	—	61 (58.1)
Visiting Rarely	14 (13.3)	23 (21.9)	—	—	37 (35.2)
Not Applicable	—	—	2 (1.9)	—	2 (1.9)
No Response	4 (3.8)	—	—	1 (1)	5 (4.8)
Total	72 (68.6)	30 (28.6)	2 (1.9)	1 (1)	105 (100)

As seen in Table 4.5, the majority of the people visiting their native place also visited the homes of persons belonging to their community in the city, who were not related to them. Similarly, the majority of the respondents whose visits to their native place were rare also made very few visits to the homes of people belonging to their community in the city. Thus, keeping connections with members of their community was important for the majority of the respondents who had made their homes in the city. The majority of their social relations at the family level were confined to their own community people and this aspect assumes importance. Their close interaction with community people constituted an important part of their social relations. However, it need not be seen as purely ethnocentric behaviour, due to the fact that many of these individuals were residing away from their native place, where social relations are more or less formed on caste lines.

Middle Class Dalits' Interaction with 'Successful' Dalits

Middle class Dalits, especially the respondents, were successful Dalits themselves in a sense. Compared to their parents and grandparents' generation, the respondents had achieved significant social and economic mobility. They are considered successful by the poor Dalits. It is interesting to note that the standards set for success by the middle class Dalits included achievement in terms of political leadership, high rank bureaucratic positions and economically successful business/enterprise ventures. Respondents named persons who had achieved such success in various fields, who were known to them personally. The majority of the respondents named a few individuals, who were known to them personally and/or with whom they interacted on a regular basis in this regard. The persons thus named were commonly those who had made it big in the fields of government service and/or as political leaders.

The successful Dalits, named by the respondents, who had achieved success in social, economic and political fields, were not their own relatives, in the majority of the cases, they were not known to them since childhood. Similarly, they did not belong to their native place and/or to their present occupation. The majority of the respondents considered these individuals as having achieved a higher degree of social and economic mobility compared to their own. Most of the respondents interacted with them regularly. It indicates that such 'successful' Dalits have a strong psychological influence on the respondents for emulation as role models. In case the respondents cannot aspire to achieve such 'success' themselves, in all probability, their children would be encouraged to do so (Table 4.7).

Table 4.7 *Field of Excellence of Ten Successful Dalits Whom the Respondents Know Personally*

Respondents' Occupation	*Field of Excellence of Successful Dalits*				*Total*
	Government Service	*Professionals*	*Various Fields*	*No Response*	
Officer Cadre	—	2 (1.9)	7 (6.7)	6 (5.7)	15 (14.3)
Clerical Cadre	—	—	9 (8.6)	6 (5.7)	15 (14.3)
University Faculty	—	—	6 (5.7)	9 (8.6)	15 (14.3)
Bank Employee	1 (1)	—	9 (8.6)	5 (4.8)	15 (14.3)
NGO	—	—	8 (7.6)	7 (6.7)	15 (14.3)
Advocate	—	1 (1)	6 (5.7)	8 (7.6)	15 (14.3)
Doctor	—	—	5 (4.8)	5 (4.8)	10 (9.5)
Journalist	—	—	2 (1.9)	3 (2.9)	5 (4.8)
Total	1 (1)	3 (2.9)	52 (49.5)	49 (46.7)	105 (100)

Respondents from all occupational groups personally knew the successful Dalits from various social, economic and political fields. In the case of 15 respondents, the successful Dalits named by the respondents belonged to their own community and in the case of 41 respondents to other sub-castes. Significantly, 49 of them had not interacted with the successful Dalits whom they regarded as role models on a personal level. Among the 56 respondents, who named successful Dalits known to them personally, 19 of them mentioned the names of 10 successful Dalits, while 18 named between 5 and 9 persons, 17 named 2 and 4 persons and 2 of them mentioned just 1 successful Dalit.

Middle Class Dalits' Initiatives for Development of Dalits

Individual and collective activities for development of Dalits, in which respondents had participated, show that the respondents were involved in many initiatives for the economic and educational benefit and moral encouragement of the Dalits, which had as their objectives, the development of the community. An examination of the number and types of collective/individual activities the respondents were involved in reveals that 17 respondents were involved in at least one such activity and 54 of them were involved in more than one activity. Another 32 were not involved in any such activities and 2 persons did not respond.

These activities range from financial help in their individual capacity, showing solidarity and playing an active role as part of an existing collective body. However, not all preferred being part of already established organizations and few of them launched a new individual or small collective efforts. This is in consonance with the views expressed by some of them that in a collective form, the Dalit middle class has not been able to accomplish much. Hence, their individual efforts were most important for the development of Dalits (Table 4.8).

The individual/collective efforts aimed at the development of Dalits that had been initiated by the respondents involved their contribution, which varied from participation in meetings to organizing them, from personally extending monetary support to mobilizing financial resources, from membership in an association to launching such organizations and heading them. It is quite interesting to note that many respondents believe that the smallest of gestures on their part in terms of responding to local issues would also contribute to the development of Dalits.

The individual/collective activities (for development of Dalits) in which the respondents had participated included participation in various socio-political mobilizations to organizing the same; membership in various organizations to launching or heading such organizations and individual financial contributions to participation in campaigns for greater economic benefits from the government. The individual/collective activities the respondents had taken part in included the following:

1. *Writings*: Writings on Dalits (books, newspaper articles, etc.), the publishing of books written by Dalit writers and literature on Ambedkar.

Table 4.8 *Collective/Individual Activities for Development of Dalits*

Number of Activities	*Nature of Activities*						*Total*
	Financial Help and Economic Development Oriented	*Activities Related to Education and Skill Development*	*Solidarity and Motivation Oriented*	*Political Mobilization*	*Mixed*	*Not Applicable*	
Only One	12 (11.4)	—	—	1 (1)	4 (3.8)	—	17 (16.2)
More than One	1 (1)	1 (1)	3 (2.9)	41 (39)	8 (7.6)	—	54 (51.4)
Nil	—	—	—	—	—	32 (30.5)	32 (30.5)
No Response	—	—	—	—	—	2 (1.9)	2 (1.9)
Total	13 (12.4)	1 (1)	3 (2.9)	42 (40)	12 (11.4)	34 (32.4)	105 (100)

2. *Legal aid to Dalits*: Fact finding in cases of atrocities upon Dalits, reporting on atrocities on SCs/STs, extending support to the victims of atrocities, etc.
3. *Meetings*: Attending national and international conferences related to Dalits to represent Dalit cause, namely, Durban Conference and Bhopal Conference, initiating and participating in seminars on reservations, organizing national/state-level workshops on Dalit concerns, participation in workshops-related SC/ST Atrocities Act, etc.
4. *Trainings*: Training for Dalits and Dalit political representatives, organizing awareness programmes for leather workers, etc.
5. *Help to Dalit students*: Providing financial help to poor students, providing free education, admitting Dalit boys and girls to social welfare hostels, initiating self-employment projects for the youths, promotion of Dalits' admissions in university, encouragement to SCs in hostels, career counselling for Dalit students, organizing night schools, coaching provided to unemployed youths for appearing in competitive exams, conducting sports/games and quiz competitions for village children, etc.
6. *Associations/organizations*: Dalit NGOs and volunteers networks, the APSC Welfare Association, SC/ST Welfare Trusts, SC/ST Employees' Welfare Association, SC/ST Cell in-charge in a university, Member of B.R. Ambedkar Open University Center for Dalit studies, Solving employees' problem, National Campaign on Dalit Human Rights, coordinator of DVAF, member of Sakshi (Dalit Human Rights Network, AP), etc.
7. *Campaigns/mobilizations for a cause*: Uniting Dalits, campaigning for Bahujan Samaj Party, human rights campaigns, campaigns against communal riots, campaigns/dharnas for reservations as part of SC/ST protection forum, campaigns for abolition of Jogini and bonded labour, etc.
8. *Economic development oriented:* Encouraged an NGO to work for Dalits, land allotments to SCs, community hall for SCs in native village, financial contribution to poor Dalits, distribution of clothes to the poor, flood relief programmes, counselling and free medical treatment to poor Dalits, etc.

9. *Political mobilizations*: Participation in Dalit movement, supporting Dalit candidates in elections, dissemination of Ambedkar's ideology, etc.
10. *Participation in various social mobilizations*: Anti-arrack movement, participation in Dandora (Madiga Reservation Porata Samithi's struggle for SC reservations categorization in Andhra Pradesh) movement, participation in political movements, meetings, functions of Ambedkar birth anniversary, awareness camps, capitation movement, participation in Asian Social Forum in January 2003, Jashuva birthday celebrations, participation in anti-caste movements, fighting for employees' rights, participation in movement against rustication of Dalit students in a Central University, etc.
11. *Reservations:* Filed a case in court on behalf of Dalit employees seeking reservation in promotions, pro-reservation movement, etc.
12. *Land struggles:* Struggle for land distribution.
13. *Miscellaneous:* Participation in Budget Analysis in 2002 with regard to Special Component Plan for SCs, literacy development, etc.

The *life situation* of middle class Dalits is influenced and shaped by various circumstances, experiences and expectations. The extent and nature of influence of caste on their *interpersonal relations;* changes in the nature of their *social relations;* their *community connections;* their personal *interaction with other 'successful' Dalits* and, finally, *their own collective/individual efforts towards development of Dalits* are analysed to understand how all these have an impact in shaping of their identity.

IDENTITY PATTERNS AMONG THE MIDDLE CLASS DALITS

In order to understand personal and social identity patterns among the respondents, their self-description, identity patterns and status differentiation with others and criteria for identifying Dalits were analysed.

Self-Description of Personality Type and Expectations from Others

Self-description of respondents in socio-psychological terms brought out their personality in individual terms as opposed to the community or group identity. In this regard, their own personal traits and the personality traits they liked in others were analysed. The respondents, in more or less similar numbers, described themselves as composed, serious or jovial personality types. Similarly, the personality traits they liked in others were related to behaviour/attitude, morals and discipline/nature. When the respondents' self-description of their personality type were contrasted with the personal qualities they appreciated in other persons, respondents who described themselves as composed and jovial types of persons accorded more importance to morals and the respondents who described their personality type as serious rated good behaviour as being the most important quality that was appreciated by them (Table 4.9).

Table 4.9 *Self-Description of Type of Personality and Most Appreciated Qualities in Others*

Self-Description of Type of Personality	*Most Appreciated Qualities in Others*				*Total*
	Attitude	*Behaviour/ Morals*	*Discipline/ Nature*	*No Response*	
Composed	14 (13.3)	18 (17.1)	2 (1.9)	—	34 (32.4)
Serious	15 (14.3)	6 (5.7)	2 (1.9)	—	23 (21.9)
Jovial	10 (9.5)	15 (14.3)	3 (2.9)	3 (2.9)	31 (29.5)
Other*	3 (2.9)	—	—	2 (1.9)	5 (4.8)
No Response	—	1 (1)	—	11 (10.5)	12 (11.4)
Total	42 (40)	40 (38.1)	7 (6.7)	16 (15.2)	105 (100)

* Combination of two personality types mentioned above.

Middle Class Dalits and Their Identity Patterns

Identification is a social act. Every individual has multiple identities to choose from. However, it is not merely dependent upon the individual's choice since sometimes others too influence and impose identities on an individual.[3] Nevertheless, how an individual prefers to identify himself/herself in a social setting is more important than the ascribed identities. Personal identity has two forms – (a) a mental representation (personal) of the 'self' as a unique human being with its own personal experiences as represented in accumulated mental models and (b) a mental representation of the social self as (being part of) a collection of group membership, and the identification processes that are related to such membership representations (van Dijk, 1998: 119).

Gyanendra Pandey poses this question at a different level, he observes,

> It is the issue of double consciousness and the blurred lines between public and private, overt and covert, violence that I attend to in the remainder of this essay. I do so through a brief consideration of aspects of the *dalit* middle class's struggle in contemporary India, a struggle that returns to the question, am I *dalit*, or am I middle class? Are ex-slaves/ex-untouchables allowed to be middle class? Can they allow themselves to be middle class? The violence and the double consciousness lodged in these questions may be demonstrated in a wide range of arenas. I take up two for analysis here: the question of political constituency (whom the subaltern middle classes might speak for) and the matter of 'passing,' which in the case of the *dalits* in India often takes the form of a struggle over naming oneself and one's family. (Pandey, 2009: 330)

It is in this context that exploring the identity choices of middle class Dalits becomes important. The middle class Dalits belonged to multiple social groups and perform various social roles, hence it becomes important to examine their preferred identify in the context of their social and economic mobility and their life circumstances. Few broad identity categories were provided to the respondents to rank those according to their preference (see Table 4.10) with an assumption that given their social and economic background the respondents primarily belonged to the middle class.

As seen in Table 4.10, a comparison of identity preferences reveals that the highest number of them had an urge to be recognized as an individual with no specific group identity, this category included 36 respondents who identified themselves in terms of a non-caste identity. While 35 others preferred to identify themselves as Dalit, 16 chose to identify themselves in terms of their sub-caste identity; those who identified themselves in terms of their occupation were 13. Interestingly, no one preferred to be identified as an individual purely belonging to middle class.[4] For them middle class was a given identity that led them nowhere since such a clear identification with only the 'middle class' would lead to their alienation from other communities and rejection by the Dalits. In the present context, taking up of a middle class identity as an alternative to their community identity was not helpful to the respondents in any way. The reasons provided for ranking a particular identity over others were more in terms of reiteration of their identity preferences rather than those of an explanatory nature.

Table 4.10 *Identification Patterns*

Social Categories	*Identification Patterns*						*Total*
	Rank 1	*Rank 2*	*Rank 3*	*Rank 4*	*Rank 5*	*No Rank*	
With Sub-Caste	16 (15.2)	5 (4.8)	10 (9.5)	12 (11.4)	31 (29.5)	31 (29.5)	105 (100)
As a Dalit	35 (33.3)	9 (8.6)	12 (11.4)	38 (36.2)	—	11 (10.5)	105 (100)
As a Person Belonging to Middle Class	—	8 (7.6)	52 (49.5)	13 (12.4)	15 (14.3)	17 (16.2)	105 (100)
With Occupation	13 (12.4)	63 (60)	10 (9.5)	6 (5.7)	4 (3.8)	9 (8.6)	105 (100)
As an Individual With No Specific Group Identity	36 (34.3)	11 (10.5)	4 (3.8)	17 (16.2)	24 (22.9)	13 (12.4)	105 (100)
Total	100 (95.2)	96 (91.4)	88 (83.9)	86 (81.9)	72 (68.5)	81 (77.1)	

Ascribed Identity: The respondents perceived that the identity ascribed to them by their Dalit and non-Dalit friends and acquaintances was largely dependent on the identity of the 'ascriber' (identity provider) himself/herself. While their Dalit friends and acquaintances identified the respondents in terms of being essentially Dalits, others saw them as persons belonging to the middle class. However, in both the cases, this did not imply the negation of their Dalit identity.

Such ascription of identity could be understood in two ways. First, the members of the Dalit middle class were being accepted in the society by non-Dalits on an equal footing primarily due to their middle-class status, and second, the Dalit identity itself was being accepted in the society, thereby middle class Dalits were primarily identified as Dalits. However, a congruence of both the identities was also possible.

Table 4.11 *Identity Ascribed by Dalit and Non-Dalit Friends and Acquaintances*

By Dalit Friends and Acquaintances	*By Non-Dalit Friends and Acquaintances*				*Total*
	Dalit	*Middle Class*	*Middle Class Dalits*	*No Response*	
Dalit	23 (21.9)	18 (17.1)	12 (11.4)	—	53 (50.5)
Middle Class	4 (3.8)	15 (14.3)	—	—	19 (18.1)
Middle Class Dalits	—	2 (1.9)	27 (25.7)	2 (1.9)	31 (29.5)
No Response	—	—	—	2 (1.9)	2 (1.9)
Total	27 (25.7)	35 (33.3)	39 (37.1)	4 (3.8)	105 (100)

Table 4.11 indicates that other Dalits, which included 53 respondents, identified them largely as Dalits, compared to 27 who were non-Dalit, who gave equal importance to their dual identities of being a Dalit and a middle class individual. In both the cases, it was largely other Dalits (both middle class and non-middle class Dalits), who continued to ascribe the Dalit identity to them.

Status Differentiation with Others

Society is divided into various social groups with varied statuses. Each social group perceives its position according to its material wealth and political authority in relation to other groups. In the Indian society, in addition to those two status ranks, ritual purity-based social ranking is also in practice among the Hindus. Dalits being at the bottom in social, economic, political and ritual hierarchy were looked down upon in many ways. Only recently have the Dalits begun contesting such discriminatory ranking through assertion of identity and various forms of socio-political mobilizations. However, caste-based ranking is still in practice, and Dalits are aware of it. Now, with a comprehensible socio-economic mobility, that is taking place among the Dalits, it is important to understand this status differentiation, especially as perceived by the upwardly mobile Dalits. Perceptions of a particular group about its own status vis-à-vis others is either contested or accepted by others. Today, Dalits are contesting the definitions of their status by others. Similarly, others also contest the claims of the Dalits when the latter try to redefine them according to their own ideology, which destabilizes the former claims.

With reference to the status, the differences respondents perceived between themselves and the poor Dalits, the other middle class Dalits and the non Dalit middle class were largely related to education, economic status and social status. In relation to poor Dalits, they perceived education and economic status as major status differentiators and in comparison to other non-Dalit middle class; they perceived social status as the sole differentiator. In the case of other middle class Dalits, there were no differences except minor variations in education levels and lifestyles, as they shared the same socio-economic location. However, their articulation of status differentiation with reference to the general middle class was in terms of the latter's cultural and social capital. As articulated by many respondents, their income and education levels and lifestyles were similar to those of the general middle class. However, in terms of commanding social respectability and acceptability, they perceived themselves to be lagging behind compared to the general middle class, which was largely composed of caste-Hindus (Table 4.12).

Status differences perceived by the respondents vis-à-vis the poor Dalits and non-Dalits showed that very few respondents, that is, 19 in all, perceived status differences in status compared to other middle class Dalits. Status differentiation was perceived by 72 vis-à-vis Dalits; and 80 vis-à-vis non-Dalits, specifically in economic terms.

Table 4.12 *Status Differences between Self and Others*

Status Difference Variables	*Poor Dalits*	*Other Middle Class Dalits*	*Non-Dalits*
Education	11 (10.5)	4 (3.8)	1 (1)
Economic Status	61 (58.1)	12 (11.4)	26 (24.8)
Social Status	—	3 (2.9)	53 (50.5)
No Differences	26 (24.8)	69 (65.7)	7 (6.7)
No Response	17 (16.2)	17 (16.2)	18 (17.1)
Total	105 (100)	105 (100)	105 (100)

Criteria for Identifying Dalits by Middle Class Dalits

The term 'Dalit', which was in usage locally in Maharashtra and the Hindi spoken states in central India, has now become popular in almost all parts of the country. Its modern usage began with the neo-Buddhist Mahar writers who adopted the name 'Dalit Panthers' to propagate Ambedkar's ideology of liberation. The Dalit Panthers included all the oppressed sections of the society, including the Other Backward Classes, the poor and women from all communities, due to their social and economic subordination in order to mobilize all these sections to fight against caste hierarchy and its value system. Thus, it was developed into an ideology of liberation and was adopted by Dalit movements in various states as well as political parties. However, over a period of time, owing to the identity assertion by various oppressed groups in terms of more relativistic and specific identities that are traditionally associated with them, and also due to its specific reference to the Scheduled Castes, the term was largely being used by the original referents, the Scheduled Castes alone.

The questions 'who are Dalits' and 'what are the criteria for identifying them' assume importance for three reasons. First, the term has its origins in traditional usage, with more secular connotations[5] unlike the other terms, both traditional and invented, to denote the marginalized sections.[6] Second, in its new political usage, it is articulated to include only the politically conscious Scheduled Castes and not all of them, in other words, Dalit by consciousness and not by birth. Finally, as opposed to the second view, when articulated in official contexts, it is expected to confine only to denote marginality, exclusion and oppressed status as equivalent to the term Scheduled Castes. These three aspects can be taken as equivalent to social, political and economic identities in that order. The real problem lies in the attribution of all these meanings to the term, which is warranted by the fragile location of the Scheduled Castes today. They are still subjected to the caste discrimination, trying to fight it with the limited resources they acquired in the recent past and at the same time not yet ready to shake off the image of the marginalized. Any move to underplay one aspect and overplay the other is in all probability antithetical to their objective of achieving social, economic and political equality on par with others in the society.

The criteria to identify Dalits are a combination of social, economic, political and cultural disadvantages than any one of them in particular. Dalits consider that the criteria should be a composition, which takes into consideration all such disadvantages since they have been facing problems on all these fronts, with the continued persecution of and biases against the upwardly mobile among them.

Table 4.13 *Criteria for Identifying Dalits According to the Respondents*

Criteria for Identifying Dalits	*Frequency and Percentage*
Economic Backwardness	2 (1.9)
Social Discrimination	41 (39)
Economic and Social Disadvantages	3 (2.9)
Economic and Political Disadvantages	18 (17.1)
All	26 (24.8)
No Response	15 (14.3)
Total	105 (100)

The respondents felt that social *castification* had made the Dalits vulnerable on all fronts. Table 4.13 amply indicates the views of respondents on this score. The respondents (39%) felt that social discrimination ought to be regarded as a major criterion for identifying any of them as Dalits. However, the number of those who considered economic and political disadvantages as the main criterion was significant (17.1%), whereas some of them proposed that a combination of all these factors ought to be taken into consideration (24.8%). The number of no responses is 15 (14.3%).

At the second level in order to identify the *identity patterns* (personal and social) of the middle class Dalits, *self-description* of their personality type and the personality traits they most appreciate among others; their own *identity patterns*, in which the preference they give to various identities and the identity ascribed to them by their Dalit and non-Dalit friends; the *status differentiation* they perceive vis-à-vis poor Dalits, other middle class Dalits and the members of general middle class and, finally, their preferred *criteria for identifying Dalits* – and the reasons for the same – are analysed to understand their correlation with their ideological leanings.

DALIT MIDDLE CLASS AND THEIR IDEOLOGY

In understanding the social, economic and political components of their ideology, formations of their views and perceptions on progress made by Dalits since independence, status of Dalit women, Dalit movement, Dalit leaders and greatest personalities of the twentieth century were analysed.

Progress Made by the Dalits since India's Independence

There are divergent positions on the issue of progress made by Dalits since independence with reference to development in social, economic and political spheres. Perceivably, there is very little progress on all these spheres in terms of uniformity, quality of progress, its effectiveness and the expectations attributed to it. They felt very strongly about the mode, process and pace of progress made by the Dalits since independence. Their views were reflective of the collective notions of the community concerning the progress or quite contrarily the lack of it. Their views also represented the aspirations for progress in a much more systematic manner than it was being pursued currently. While some merely listed the kinds of changes that had affected Dalits in a positive or negative manner, others embarked on the task of precisely pinpointing the lacunas (Table 4.14).

Table 4.14 *Progress Made by Dalits since Independence*

Sector	*Progress Made by Dalits*				*Total*
	Significant	*Insignificant*	*No Progress*	*No Response*	
In Social Status	19 (18.1)	37 (35.2)	7 (6.7)	42 (40)	105 (100)
In Economic Status	1 (1)	60 (57.1)	3 (2.9)	41 (39)	105 (100)
In Political Status	2 (1.9)	59 (56.2)	2 (1.9)	42 (40)	105 (100)

The progress made by the Dalits since independence in various spheres of life, as perceived by them, is broadly in terms of social, economic and educational realms. These positive developments range from the upward mobility of a small section of the middle class among the Dalits to improvements in the level of acceptance and respectability achieved by them. The views as expressed by them in this regard have been summarized as follows.

They have perceived that though there was some progress, it was not uniform in all these above-mentioned aspects and that these differences could be identified as affecting very specific aspects of the Dalits' lives. To begin with, Dalits had 'achieved social status on par with others at least legally', which facilitated 'opportunities to earn equality in the society' with a 'new status'. With 'implementation of reservations, the education level of Dalits had witnessed a surge' and thereby 'a semi-layer was increasing among them' that could be regarded as composed of 'a section of the urban Dalit middle class' mainly comprising 'employees and businessmen', with its 'presence (in a small percentage) in the organized sector'. In a general level, 'compared to the past' there was 'improvement in respectability and acceptance' that facilitated 'both economic and social improvement', thereby resulting in the 'emergence of a class of Dalit politicians', who were acting as a 'politically strong pressure group', 'demanding equality in all walks of life'.

On the other hand, the absence of expected progress was dwelt upon with greater intensity. The same was articulated in terms of the implications that such an absence had resulted in the present status of despair among Dalits. Some of the statements made by them have been presented in a summated form in this regard. There were 'no considerable changes' 'despite governmental interventions, the progress (was) only 20 per cent attitudinal change towards Dalits'. The absence of development among the Dalits was perceived to be mainly 'due to lack of commitment by the government'. In addition, they have emphasized that 'though some progress has occurred' 'the presence of casteism (did not) allow for adequate economic progress of Dalits'. Dalits were still lagging behind when it came to social status. There was no proportionate acquisition of power vis-à-vis development in consciousness. Dalits had not received any support to reach positions of power. Progress in political status was also not as expected, and Dalits have had to fight for their rights. Progress had not been up to the expectations of Dr B.R. Ambedkar. There was still religious and cultural distance between Hindus and Dalits. Dalits were still the vote banks for political parties, and their economic status had deteriorated from occupational security to no work. These broad perceptions revealed the dissatisfaction among them with regard to the lack of sufficient progress achieved by the members of their community in social, economic and political realms.

Perceptions on the Status of Dalit Women

Dalit women constitute an important constituency within the Dalit middle class. As a community that is voicing issues related to equal rights and seeking opportunities on par with other social groups, the Dalit middle class is sensitive to the question of Dalit women. Considering the social, economic and political statuses of Dalit women in society as well as in the Dalit community, the middle class Dalits accord equal or more importance to Dalit women and the problems faced by them. There is a glaring difference between Dalit men and women in terms of levels of education, employment and participation in decision-making processes. This fact is unequivocally recognized by the members of the Dalit middle class, and they advocate giving more importance to the education of Dalit women compared to Dalit men. The status of Dalit women in the society and within the family is subservient. Therefore, they are doubly disadvantaged. Dalit women, despite their personal achievements, continue to face subservience and exploitation.

Being doubly disadvantaged on the grounds of caste and gender, the Dalit women find it difficult to fight the caste system as well as patriarchy. In spite of reservations in education and employment, many Dalit women are unable to come out of the exploitative clutches of casteism and gender discrimination that is widespread in the society, which creates numerous hurdles for them. All the measures provided by the Constitution and the government policies to mitigate gender discrimination are yet to reach the Dalit women. Though there were only 25 (23.8%) women respondents in the sample, both male and female unequivocally felt that when compared to Dalit men, Dalit women were in a disadvantageous position. Except one respondent, who felt that Dalit women were in an equal position compared to Dalit men and in a disadvantageous position in comparison to other women, all others felt that Dalit women were undoubtedly in a disadvantageous position. Such disadvantages were expressed in terms of the additional problems they faced within the family and in the society.

Additional Problems Dalit Women Face within Family and in Society

Additional problems Dalit women face within their families are largely related to patriarchy, burden of household responsibility, lack of opportunities for growth, and exploitation and violence. In the society, they face disadvantages such as caste discrimination, economic dependency, lack of opportunities and exploitation and violence. Within the family, they confront patriarchy, household responsibility and lack of opportunities for growth. In the family, Dalit women encounter a variety of problems that are largely related to their gender setting. They range from gender discrimination to lack of opportunities for development. The problems related to gender discrimination within family are male dominance, patriarchy, household responsibilities, which are solely entrusted to women, family restrictions, very less space for personal, intellectual and professional growth due to family burdens, no role in decision-making and lack of freedom. The problems directly affecting their development are inequality in education, lack of economic independence, lack of facilities, lack of opportunities to participate in social activities, political disadvantages and middle class *sanskritic* ethos. In the case of working women, they have to work outside equally with men, thus women work more than men do.

In society, the Dalit women are doubly disadvantaged with economic, social and political disadvantages (gender, caste and class discriminations). Society treats Dalit women differently, inferior to all other women and subjects them to caste cruelty. Dalit women are most prone to caste atrocities, caste discrimination, class discrimination, untouchability, harassment, sexual exploitation, insecurity and inequality. They are more prone to exploitation compared to others. Dalit women face severe social discrimination, external representation (often represented by Dalit men with regard to their caste identity and other women in terms of gender identity), financial problems, social discrimination clubbed with insecurity and all kinds of disadvantages. They also suffer due to low level of education, less access to resources, less participation in social activities, inferiority, hesitation and no respect. Despite not having the proper space in society, the work burden and socio-economic responsibilities are more for Dalit women. They are not cared for at all and are ill equipped to compete with other women. They are made followers of other women (Table 4.15).

Table 4.15 *Additional Problems Dalit Women Face Within Family and in Society*

Additional Problems Dalit Women Face Within Family	*Respondents' Gender*			*Additional Problems Dalit Women Face in Society*	*Respondents' Gender*		
	Male	*Female*	*Total*		*Male*	*Female*	*Total*
Patriarchy	24 (22.9)	8 (7.6)	32 (30.5)	Caste Discrimination	58 (55.2)	17 (16.2)	75 (71.4)
Household Responsibility	20 (19)	6 (5.7)	26 (24.8)	Economic Dependencey	7 (6.7)	2 (1.9)	9 (8.6)
Lack of Opportunities for Growth	18 (17.1)	8 (7.6)	26 (24.8)	Lack of Opportunities	6 (5.7)	1 (1.0)	7 (6.7)
Exploitation and Violence	2 (1.9)	—	2 (1.9)	Exploitation and Violence	—	2 (1.9)	2 (1.9)
No Response	16 (15.2)	3 (2.9)	19 (18.1)	No Response	9 (8.6)	3 (2.9)	12 (11.4)
Total	80 (76.2)	25 (23.8)	105 (100)	Total	80 (76.2)	25 (23.8)	105 (100)

Both males and females felt that Dalit women should not be categorized simplistically into either of those two identities. The problem of doubly disadvantaged question, they felt, ought to be dealt with as one question than two because caste and gender were interrelated questions. The important identity for Dalit women was an exclusive neither 'Dalit' nor 'woman' identity but a composite identity of Dalit women (Table 4.16).

Table 4.16 *Most Important Identity for Dalit Women*

Most Important Identity for Dalit Women	*Respondents' Gender*		*Total*
	Male	*Female*	
Dalit	4 (3.8)	1 (1)	5 (4.8)
Woman	28 (26.7)	9 (8.6)	37 (35.2)
Dalit Woman	36 (34.3)	11 (10.5)	47 (44.8)
No Response	12 (11.4)	4 (3.8)	16 (15.2)
Total	80 (76.2)	25 (23.8)	105 (100)

Despite the existing disadvantaged position of Dalit women at various levels, there was a growing awareness about the importance of Dalit women's education, employment and role in decision-making among the middle class. The same was reflected in the views expressed by the males as well as females (Table 4.17).

Table 4.17 *Importance of Dalit Women's Education, Employment and Role in Decision-Making in Comparison to Dalit Men*

Dalit Women's	*In Comparison to Dalit Men*				*Total*
	Equally Important	*More Important*	*Less Important*	*No Response*	
Education	62 (59)	42 (40)	—	1 (1)	105 (100)
Employment	66 (62.9)	38 (36.2)	—	1 (1)	105 (100)
Role in Decision-Making	78 (74.3)	22 (21)	3 (2.9)	2 (1.9)	105 (100)

Except few, the majority of them were in favour of equal or more importance for women in education, employment and role in decision-making. They have stressed on the rectification of all existing inequalities, with emphasis on equal importance to Dalit women. Among the three issues, education, employment and role in decision-making were ranked in that order. There were only three men who felt that women should play a less important role in decision-making within the household.

Middle Class Dalits and Dalit Movement

Andhra Pradesh has a long history of Dalit movement. It is one of the important states in south India, in which a vibrant Dalit movement emerged, parallel to the Dalit movement led by Dr B.R. Ambedkar in 1930s. During that time, there was a strong Dalit movement in Hyderabad state – erstwhile Nizam state – spear-headed by many local leaders, who fought against caste discrimination and sought state favours for educational development of the Dalits. Some of these movements had merged with the Ambedkar led movement later on. During the late 1930s, Ambedkar largely concentrated on Andhra Pradesh to spread his movement apart from Maharashtra. However, in the post-independence period, these movements were largely appropriated by the political parties and, hence, lost their 'movement-specific' nature. Again, during the 1980s, Dalit movement was revived in response to the major atrocities committed upon the Dalits, and in early 1990s, it was further consolidated during the Mandal agitation. Thus, Andhra Pradesh is one of the few states in India to have witnessed a strong Dalit movement. However, each time, after a glorious existence for a brief spell, these movements fell into a deep slumber.

Inspired by these movements, many associations and organizations have emerged. Some of those with a strong membership base and long-term objectives are active even today. Of late, these associations and organizations alone have assumed the capacity to launch the Dalit movements. Now, the Dalit movement is largely dependent on these associations and organizations for mass base, leadership and sometimes even the agenda. Thus, these associations and organizations have largely replaced the need for a continuous Dalit movement. Instead, they are continuing to function as an active Dalit movement. In a sense, the Dalit movement is institutionalized in the form of these associations and organizations (Table 4.18).

Table 4.18 *Most Interesting Aspects of the Dalit Movement Today*

Most Interesting Aspects of the Dalit Movement Today	*Number of Responses*
Facilitation of Unity	8 (7.6)
Fighting for Rights	23 (21.9)
Disunity	8 (7.6)
Inactivity	31 (29.5)
No Response	35 (33.3)
Total	105 (100)

Some of them were also part of the Dalit movement, either directly or through Dalit associations and organizations. In this context, their views on the Dalit movement vis-à-vis its significance and effectiveness were analysed. The most interesting aspects of the Dalit movement today were broadly categorized by them into four aspects: two positive and two negative aspects. Among the positive and interesting aspects, 8 of them dwelt upon the Dalit movements' facilitation of unity among the community members and 23 have highlighted the movement's contribution in terms of fighting for the rights of the Dalits. Similarly, the negative, but interesting, aspects as perceived by them included disunity among the practitioners of the movement in the case of 8 of them and its inactivity for 31 of them. From another 31, responses could not be obtained.

The positive aspects mentioned by them about the Dalit movement have been classified as follows:

1. Achieving rights framed in the Constitution, struggle for self-respect, ability to fight casteism, organizing resistance against atrocities, fighting for reservations (including the private sector), social justice movements, protection of Dalit rights, social justice and identity of caste with self-dignity, fighting together for a common cause,
2. Political empowerment, consolidation of Dalits as a group, political unity and integrity, educational development,
3. Respect for other suppressed castes in the process of upliftment and development (of Dalits), SC reservations categorization/MRPS, sub-caste identity assertion, taking the

shape of a movement which had asserted *jati* identity and culture,

4. Reading, writing and interpreting society from a Dalit perspective and
5. Stress on economic development.

On the other hand, the negative aspects hindering the Dalit movement today were perceived in terms of:

1. Its emptiness (lack of a political programme and *NGOization* of Dalit movement),
2. Dalit movement being sustained for individual fame,
3. Caste divisions hindering Dalit unity and
4. No real Dalit movement happening today.

Dalit Leaders' Contributions towards Development of Dalits

Leaders from the community heading the Dalit movement and the political sphere were identified by them. A total of 31 contemporary Dalit leaders were identified by them. They are spread across various fields from top-level bureaucrats in government service to leaders of mass Dalit movements to political leaders. Their contribution was assessed mainly in terms of spearheading the Dalit movement and winning various socio-economic and political rights for the Dalit community. In an attempt to understand the reasons for their admiration of the identified Dalit leaders, they were asked to list the contributions of these leaders (Table 4.19).

Of the 57 who have identified various Dalit leaders: 22 of them felt that the leaders named had contributed to the strengthening of the Dalit movement; 10 felt they were playing an integral role in the economic development of the Dalits; 2 believed that these leaders are working towards the fulfilment of political rights and another 23 emphasized that they had positively contributed towards Dalit development. However, 23 respondents believed that there was not a single person at present that they could identify as the leader of the Dalits. Significantly, the number of those who did not respond was 25. This is perhaps a reflection of the

Table 4.19 *Community of the Dalit Leaders Contributing Towards Dalit Development*

Community of Dalit Leaders Contributing Towards Dalit Development	*Contribution*					*Total*
	Strengthened Dalit Movement	*Economic Development*	*Fulfilment of Political Rights*	*Variety of Contribution*	*No Response*	
Same Community	2 (1.9)	10 (9.5)	—	1 (1)	—	13 (12.4)
Different	20 (19)	—	1 (1)	2 (1.9)	—	23 (21.9)
Mixed	—	—	1 (1)	20 (19)	—	21 (20)
No One	—	—	—	—	23 (21.9)	23 (21.9)
No Response	—	—	—	—	25 (23.8)	25 (23.8)
Total	22 (21)	10 (9.5)	2 (1.9)	23 (21.9)	48 (45.7)	105 (100)

dissatisfaction felt by the middle class Dalits with regard to the present state of the Dalit movement.

Greatest Personalities of India

The greatest Indian personalities according to the middle class Dalits belonged to the fields of politics and social service in terms of their commitment and achievements towards the Dalit cause and in general. The greatest personalities according to them were Dr B.R. Ambedkar, Mahatma Gandhi, Jawaharlal Nehru, Indira Gandhi, Kanshiram and Mayavati. The most important issues in the twentieth century were socio-political movements in relation to Dalit rights, compared to the realm of politics and development. It is evident from their naming/identification of the greatest personalities of India that the persons who had strived to social change and Dalit rights were their favourites rather than individuals who had contributed to the area of politics and development. However, the majority of them believed that the greatest personalities identified by them had contributed to both these fields (Table 4.20).

Table 4.20 *Field of Contribution of the Greatest Personalities of India*

Field of Contribution	
Movements and Dalit Rights	46 (43.8)
Politics and Development Sector	4 (3.8)
All Fields	53 (50.5)
No Response	2 (1.9)
Total	105 (100)

The importance and prominence of Dalit leaders among the greatest personalities of India is reflected in the fact that 85 of them have accorded the highest rankings to one or more Dalit leaders, 13 of them ranked them towards the middle and one respondent accorded the lowest ranking to them. Another four did not respond in this regard (Table 4.21).

An attempt was made towards measuring the popularity of Ambedkar and Gandhi[7] among the middle class Dalits, in acknowledging either of them as a greatest personality of the twentieth century, it showed that 77 of them have accorded importance solely to Ambedkar, as opposed to one respondent who accorded importance solely to Gandhi, while both of them were mentioned as the greatest personalities by 21 of them. Neither of them got a mention by four of them and two did not respond to the query. Ambedkar was perceived as a cause for the accomplishments of the Dalit middle class as well as the predominant source for the 'pricking' of its conscience. Many of them have quoted various strategies for the development of the Dalits and had inculcated their vision for the Dalit movement from Ambedkar's writings. They also drew comparisons between Ambedkar and other contemporary Dalit leaders to describe the depleted status of Dalit movement at present. They dwelt at length on the shortfalls of contemporary Dalit leaders and held them responsible for the diminishing status of the Dalit movement. A few of them who remembered other Dalit leaders (in addition to Ambedkar) had had experiences of participating in the Dalit movement in various capacities in the past and some were still actively involved in it.

Table 4.21 *Ranking of Dalit Leaders*

Number of Dalit Leaders Mentioned	*Related to Dalit Leaders*					*Total*
	Dalit Leaders Ranked among First Few	*Dalit Leaders Ranked in the Middle*	*Dalit Leaders Ranked towards the End*	*No Dalit Leaders*	*No Response*	
Only One Dalit Leader	58 (55.2)	11 (10.5)	1 (1)	—	—	70 (66.7)
More than One Dalit Leader	27 (25.7)	2 (1.9)	—	—	—	29 (27.6)
No Dalit Leaders	—	—	—	4 (3.8)	—	4 (3.8)
No Response	—	—	—	—	2 (1.9)	2 (1.9)
Total	85 (81)	13 (12.4)	1 (1)	4 (3.8)	2 (1.9)	105 (100)

The idea behind eliciting their views on the greatest personalities of the twentieth century was also to understand the levels of their awareness about and acceptance of recent developments in the Dalit movement and leadership. They were not prompted with any names. This also helped to measure their political interests as well as ideological leanings. It became evident from the responses received that the majority of them evinced interest in knowing about the developments related to political mobilizations but participation in such a mobilization was not a priority among the middle class Dalits. Leaders other than Ambedkar were referred to by many of them, indicating their interest in contemporary Dalit movements. Apart from Ambedkar, a great Dalit leader and among the most popular greatest personalities of India, 43 have mentioned other Dalit leaders as well, compared to 60 others who did not mention any other Dalit leader, while two of them did not respond.

At this level, the social, economic and political *ideology* formations of the middle class Dalits are constructed by enquiring into their views and perceptions on *the progress made by Dalits since independence*, the *status of Dalit women*, the *Dalit movement*, the *Dalit leaders* and the *greatest personalities of India*. In the next section, their involvement in the Dalit politics has been covered.

POLITICS OF THE DALIT MIDDLE CLASS

The pragmatic and ideological politics of the middle class Dalits are analysed with the help of their membership in organizations/political parties, their preference to effective models/strategy for overall development of Dalits, views on reservations, views related to political options before the Dalits for achieving equality, knowledge about issues/measure related to Dalits, prioritization of socio-economic and political issues and their views on some important socio-economic and political issues in understanding their identity and ideology.

Membership in Social/Political Organizations

Caste associations have expanded their areas of concern beyond traditional elite emulation and local politics into the wider political arenas of state and national politics. Finding power in numbers within the India's democratic system, caste groups are pulling together closely allied sub-castes in their quest for political influence. In efforts to solidify caste bonds, some caste associations have organized marriage fairs where families can make matches for their children. Traditional hierarchical concerns are being minimized in favour of strengthening horizontal unity. Thus, while pollution observances are declining, caste consciousness is not. Existence of SC/ST Employees Welfare Associations along with other employees' welfare organizations is a common phenomenon in all government offices and institutions. When there are no separate organizations for Dalits, general employees' welfare associations represent Dalits' issues. The middle class Dalits in the present study were members of Dalit organizations and political parties working with Dalit ideology. All employees (61.9%) were members of SC/ST employees' associations in their concerned organizations. Most of them among the independent professionals (28.6%) were members of more than one Dalit organization/association. The majority of them from the officer cadre – who were 12 (11.5%) in number – were members of Dalit organizations/political parties.

Table 4.22 *Organizations/Political Parties (Including Dalit Oriented) in Which the Respondents Are Members*

Respondents' Occupation	*Nature of the Organizations*					*Total*
	Work-Related Associations	*Dalit Organi-zations*	*General Political Parties*	*Dalit Political Parties*	*None/Not Applicable*	
Officer Cadre	6 (5.7)	2 (1.9)	4 (3.8)	—	3 (2.9)	15 (14.3)
Clerical Cadre	2 (1.9)	1 (1)	5 (4.8)	—	7 (6.7)	15 (14.3)
University Faculty	3 (2.9)	2 (1.9)	2 (1.9)	—	8 (7.6)	15 (14.3)
Bank Employees	2 (1.9)	—	5 (4.8)	1 (1)	7 (6.7)	15 (14.3)
NGO	3 (2.9)	1 (1)	4 (3.8)	—	7 (6.7)	15 (14.3)
Advocates	—	2 (1.9)	3 (2.9)	—	10 (9.5)	15 (14.3)
Doctors	1 (1)	2 (1.9)	2 (1.9)	—	5 (4.8)	10 (9.5)
Journalists	2 (1.9)	—	1 (1)	—	2 (1.9)	5 (4.8)
Total	19 (18.1)	10 (9.5)	26 (24.8)	1 (1)	49 (46.7)	105 (100)

While 22 of them were members of one organization; 34 of them were members of more than one organization; 18 others were not members of any organization and in 31 instances, no responses could be obtained. A comparison across occupations shows that while in the officer cadre 12 (out of 15) were members of one or more organizations; in the clerical cadre, bank employees and university faculty – all belonging to government/public sector institutions – more than half are members of some or the other organization or a political party. Among the professionals, those who are working in NGOs also have membership in organizations and political parties in similar numbers, whereas very few doctors, advocates and journalists had memberships in Dalit/political organizations (Table 4.22).

Effective Models/Strategies for the Overall Development of Dalits

Six pre-identified models/strategies that would assist the Dalits in their overall development were provided to them for ranking in an order of their preference. They were: (1) reservations, (2) socialist revolution, (3) cultural change, (4) economic development, (5) urbanization and (6) political power. Their responses are presented in Table 4.23.

The explanation offered by them for according rank 1 to a particular model or strategy was analysed. In their opinion, the most suitable model/strategy for the overall development of the Dalits should be an immediate measure for 14 others. While 18 felt it should be a permanent solution and another 12 preferred it to be a gradual progress. Others did not explain their ranking preferences. In ranking the various strategies/models in order of their preference, some of them also attempted to construct their own models for the overall development of Dalits. Broad summations of these have been presented in the form of statements, which are as follows:

1. Economic development assures development in other fields, it provides space for other kinds of development in the present situation, economic status guarantees self-respect and hence progress, economic development and education through reservations have to precede other models of development.

Table 4.23 *Effective Model(s)/Strategies for the Overall Development of Dalits*

Model	*Rank 1*	*Rank 2*	*Rank 3*	*Rank 4*	*Rank 5*	*Rank 6*	*Rank 7*	*No Rank*	*Total*
Reservations	50 (47.6)	10 (9.5)	9(8.6)	15 (14.3)	17 (16.2)	—	—	4(3.8)	105 (100)
Socialist Revolution	4(3.8)	12 (11.4)	43 (41)	7(6.7)	12 (11.4)	21 (20)	1(1)	5(4.8)	105 (100)
Cultural Change	3(2.9)	6(5.7)	25 (23.8)	40 (38.1)	16 (15.2)	10 (9.5)	1(1)	4(3.8)	105 (100)
Economic Development	21 (20)	62 (59)	8(7.6)	12 (11.4)	2(1.9)	—	—	—	105 (100)
Urbanization	—	4(3.8)	6(5.7)	10 (9.5)	44 (41.9)	33 (31.4)	1(1)	7(6.7)	105 (100)
Political Power	25 (23.8)	10 (9.5)	13 (12.4)	16 (15.2)	9(8.6)	31 (29.5)	—	1(1)	105 (100)
Other*	2(1.9)	—	—	1(1)	—	—	5(4.8)	97(92.4)	105 (100)
Total	105 (100)	105 (100)	105 (100)	105 (100)	105 (100)	105 (100)	105 (100)	105 (100)	105 (100)

* Education as another model/strategy has been suggested by a few respondents.

2. Cultural change would facilitate appropriate usage of reservations as well.
3. Reservations' system is the first step with which awareness and economic status would improve, socialist revolution and economic development are prerequisites that effect overall development.
4. Reservations and economic development are the first steps for overall development.
5. Education is more important for realization of higher status for Dalits, next to it economic development is essential for progress, and then achieving cultural change would silence the criticisms against Dalits.
6. When the socialist revolution occurs, there is no need for reservations, an economy based on the model of China would ensure that there would be no caste system.
7. Reservations are necessary and subsequently economic development to capture political power.
8. Government must help Dalits to set up industries by providing them loans (without interest) so that they develop economically, the rest of the changes would follow automatically. There should be lower interest rates for Dalits so that it would be possible for them to repay loans without much burden.
9. Development is possible only with attitudinal change among Dalits, social change would lead to cultural change and ensure that Dalits do not lag behind.
10. Urbanization does not change caste discrimination.
11. Only social movements can lead to social transformation and the overall development of Dalits.
12. Education and reservations enable Dalits to access all fields. Proper utilization of reservations and government policies, combined with Ambedkar ideology, would give a sufficient push (education and employment wise), and lead to cultural change.
13. Socio-economic and cultural development is a pre-condition for overall development.

Views on Reservations Policy

In the wake of contestations regarding a suitable criterion for the provision of reservations, the very design of reservation system assumes importance. In the recent past, the Mandal Commission's recommendations for the extension of reservations related benefits to the 'Other Backward Classes' reiterated the rationale for such provision and justification for certain castes to be covered under the reservation system. The 'Mandal controversy' has thrown up issues that concern Dalits as well. It has often been articulated that the entire system of reservations needs to be rethought in the wake of success or failure of reservation system in uplifting the marginalized communities from their relative educational, social and economic backwardness. The 'success' theory articulates that, now, after the long presence of reservations in the fields of education and employment, a considerable number of individuals have benefited from it, hence, it can be withdrawn, not only for them but also to others. On the other hand, the 'ineffectiveness' attributed to the reservation system in its present form in terms of uplifting the 'real poor' and the 'most needy' also suggest the closure of the reservations policy. The underlying assumption in both the articulations is to prevent the 'ineligible' from benefiting through reservations.

Experiences related to their family's economic background and their own usage of reservations had made them develop their own opinions regarding the purpose and utility of reservations. While some found the role of reservations to be crucial in ensuring social and economic mobility for Dalits, others perceived it as having a negative impact on the degree of competitiveness or competence among them and thus earning the wrath of other communities, especially those who were envious of such 'favouritism' towards Dalits from the government. However, these impressions had been formed on the lines of the anti-reservationists' criticisms. During the anti-Mandal agitations, the 'upper-caste' Hindus often proffered such views against the entire policy of reservations. It has been widely observed that, in order to avoid such criticism, some Dalits subscribed to their detractors' very notions, thus giving scope for false assumptions that the 'mobile Dalits' were against reservations.

In order to elicit the views of the middle class Dalits on the policy of reservations, the following statements were presented to them:

1. Reservations must continue for the betterment of Dalits.
2. Reservations should be extended to the private sector.
3. The creamy layer should be covered under reservations.
4. The creamy layer should be kept out of reservations.
5. Reservations should be extended to Dalits converted into other religions (Islam, Christianity, etc.).

They chose one or more of the above statements. Based on their responses, the following classifications were evolved to group them into four categories, namely,

1. Proactive – those who chose 1, 2, 3 and 5 leaving out statement 4 suggesting that creamy layer Dalits should not avail reservations,
2. Status quo – those who chose 1, 2, 4 and 5 together in line with the spirit of social justice to keep only the marginalized under the gamut of reservations,
3. Positive – those who chose 1, 2 and 3 together suggesting that beneficiaries of reservations should be only those who are presently defined as Dalits and
4. Negative – of those who chose 1, 2 and 5 statements together.

The above statements aimed at understanding the views of a class, which had largely benefited from the reservation policy and continued to have a personal stake in it for the welfare of its future generations. Dalit middle class is seen as a product of the policy of reservations in the society and in their occupation or daily life. They are reminded of this fact – the reservations – in various ways by others (Table 4.24).

All of them, irrespective of occupation and gender, had a common view on the first two issues in terms of continuing with reservations and further extending it to the private sector in the changing scenario of shrinking opportunities in the public sector. The division of opinions was reflected only in the case of reservations for the creamy layer Dalits and extending them to Dalits who had converted to other religions such as Islam and Christianity.

Table 4.24 *Respondents' Opinions on Reservations*

Respondents' Occupation	*Respondents' Opinion on Reservations*					*Total*
	Proactive	*Status-Quo*	*Positive*	*Negative*	*No Response*	
Officer Cadre	3 (2.9)	10 (9.5)	1 (1)	1 (1)	—	15 (14.3)
Clerical Cadre	5 (4.8)	4 (3.8)	6 (5.7)	—	—	15 (14.3)
University Faculty	3 (2.7)	9 (8.6)	3 (2.7)	—	—	15 (14.3)
Bank Employee	3 (2.7)	10 (9.5)	2 (1.9)	—	—	15 (14.3)
NGO	2 (1.9)	7 (6.7)	5 (4.8)	—	1 (1)	15 (14.3)
Advocate	1 (1)	8 (7.6)	5 (4.8)	—	1 (1)	15 (14.3)
Doctor	1 (1)	5 (4.8)	4 (3.8)	—	—	10 (9.5)
Journalist	1 (1)	3 (2.7)	1 (1)	—	—	5 (4.8)
Total	19 (18.1)	56 (53.3)	27 (25.7)	1 (1)	2 (1.9)	105 (100)

Political Options before the Dalits to Achieve Equality

The Dalit movements and various political mobilizations of the Dalits have been in existence for a long time. On many occasions, they have worked in collaboration with other organizations and political movements (Table 4.25).

Table 4.25 *Political Options before the Dalits to Achieve Equality*

Possible Allies for Dalits	*Political Options before the Dalits to Achieve Equality*			*Total*
	Struggling Alone	*Aligning with Others*	*No Response*	
Tribals	—	1 (1)	—	1 (1)
OBCs	—	17 (16.2)	—	17 (16.2)
Left Parties	—	3 (2.9)	—	3 (2.9)
All Political Parties	—	56 (53.3)	—	56 (53.3)
All	—	9 (8.6)	—	9 (8.6)
No Response	—	8 (7.6)	—	8 (7.6)
Not Applicable	8 (7.6)	—	3 (2.9)	11 (10.5)
Total	8 (7.6)	94 (89.5)	3 (2.9)	105 (100)

An overwhelming majority of 94 have felt that it was essential to align with other like-minded communities and/or political parties in the pursuit of socio-economic and political equality. On the other hand, eight of them felt that other communities or the parties could not be relied upon completely to support the Dalits and, hence, the only option left before them was to fight alone for their rights. A further classification between social groups and political parties showed that a majority of 56 wanted alliances to be forged with all political parties, compared to the preference shown by only three other for left parties alone. Similarly, among the social groups, the numerically dominant OBCs were more preferable as political allies for 17 of them, compared to the tribals, who were preferable as allies for a sole respondent. Another nine have preferred alliances with all social groups and all political parties for the Dalits since they felt that the Dalits needed help from every quarter and relying solely on mobilizations by other weaker groups would not be of much assistance to them.

Awareness about Issues and Policies

Middle class Dalits have access to all kinds of media, and are constantly in touch with various social, economic and political issues, especially those concerning Dalits. They discuss and debate social and political issues within their own circles and with others. Their understandings about various socio-political issues in groups have shaped groups as the locus for the development of a collective consciousness (Table 4.26).

Table 4.26 *Awareness about Issues and Policies*

Issues/Measures Known	*Knowledge about Issues/ Measures Related to Dalits*			*Total*
	Yes	*No*	*No Response*	
Chundur/Karamchedu/ Vempenta Massacres	100 (95.2)	4 (3.8)	1 (1)	105 (100)
Reservations in Education, Employment & Political Spheres	103 (98.1)	1 (1)	1 (1)	105 (100)
National SC/ST Commission	91 (86.7)	13 (12.4)	1 (1)	105 (100)
Special Economic Measures	95 (90.5)	9 (8.6)	1 (1)	105 (100)
Ban on Untouchability	102 (97.1)	2 (1.9)	1 (1)	105 (100)

Except one respondent, all the others had high levels of awareness on many issues related to Dalits. The overall awareness about the various atrocities committed upon Dalits, the special economic measures provided to Dalits, reservations in various fields and the legal measures banning untouchability are an indication of their constant engagement with such issues. Further, many have also suggested a few necessary changes for the effective implementation of those measures.

Prioritization of Socio-economic and Political Issues

Many socio-economic and political issues are a cause for concern among all Dalits in the present times. Some of these issues are articulated by the Dalit middle class in response to the problems faced by the Dalits. Such issues usually evoke a lot of interest in the members of the Dalit middle class who engage with them extensively. In that process, the middle class Dalits also prioritize these issues. In this regard, an attempt has been made to understand their priorities in relation to such issues (Table 4.27).

For as many as 68.6 per cent of them, Dalit identity/self-respect is more important than the problem of economic inequality (for 9.5% of them). All those who accorded first rank to Dalit identity have given second rank to economic inequality and vice versa. The first ranks were given to social, economic and political equality by 17.1 per cent of them, caste discrimination by 3.8 per cent of them, problems such as unemployment, poverty, landlessness and illiteracy among Dalits by 1 per cent of them and not to issues related to conversions to Christianity, Buddhism, etc. This revealed that the majority of the Dalit middle class was engaged with the question of self-respect and identity rather than other social, economic and political issues. They were contemplating issues concerned with identity and ideology in a much more practical way.

Opinions on General Issues

Two sets of statements dealing with (1) globalization, reservations and corruption and (2) caste and Dalits were presented to them for their views and comments (Table 4.28).

Table 4.27 *Social, Economic and Political Issues in Order of Interest/Concern/Priority*

Issues	*Order of Preference*							*Total*
	Rank 1	*Rank 2*	*Rank 3*	*Rank 4*	*Rank 5*	*Rank 6*	*No Rank*	
Dalit Identity/Self-respect	72 (68.6)	10 (9.5)	3 (2.9)	3 (2.9)	16 (15.2)	—	1 (1.0)	105 (100.0)
Economic Inequality	10 (9.5)	71 (67.6)	16 (15.2)	—	5 (4.8)	2 (1.9)	1 (1.0)	105 (100.0)
Social, Economic & Political Equality	18 (17.1)	16 (15.2)	36 (34.3)	22 (21.0)	2 (1.9)	3 (2.9)	8 (7.6)	105 (100.0)
Unemployment/Poverty/Landlessness/ Illiteracy	1 (1.0)	6 (5.7)	9 (8.6)	44 (41.9)	24 (22.9)	7 (6.7)	14 (13.3)	105 (100.0)
Caste Discrimination	4 (3.8)	1 (1.0)	20 (19.0)	18 (17.1)	38 (36.2)	18 (17.1)	6 (5.7)	105 (100.0)
Conversions to Christianity/Buddhism	—	—	15 (14.3)	11 (10.5)	7 (6.7)	59 (56.2)	13 (12.4)	105 (100.0)
Total	105 (100.0)	104 (99.0)	99 (94.3)	98 (93.3)	92 (87.6)	89 (84.8)	43 (41.0)	105 (100.0)

Table 4.28 *Opinions on Globalization, Reservations and Corruption*

Opinions on	*Agree*	*Disagree*	*Cannot Say*	*No Response*	*Total*
Globalization Eradicates Caste System in India	5 (4.8)	92 (87.6)	1 (1)	7 (6.7)	105 (100)
Merit Should be the Criterion for Job Recruitment	7 (6.7)	91 (86.7)	—	7 (6.7)	105 (100)
Economic Growth with Social Justice is an Unachievable Idea	13 (12.4)	85 (81)	—	7 (6.7)	105 (100)
The Policy of Reservations Has Increased the Scope for Corruption in India	1 (1)	97 (92.4)	—	7 (6.7)	105 (100)

Though the priorities of the government were changing in favour of privatization and thereby reducing employment opportunities for Dalits, they largely felt that the principle of social justice could not be done away with at this point of time. Similarly, they contested other notions such as globalization leading to the eradication of the caste system, merit being the sole criterion in job selections and the notion that the reservation system had increased the scope for corruption. An overwhelming majority of them strongly disagreed with these notions. On the other hand, a few of them have agreed with these notions. The notion that 'globalization would eradicate the caste system in India' was agreeable only to five of them. Merit as the criterion for job recruitment found favour with seven of them. In the present times, the notion that economic growth with social justice was unachievable was shared by 13 others. The notion that the 'policy of reservations has increased the scope for corruption in India' found favour with only one respondent.

Perceptions on Issues Related to Caste and Dalits

The basic idea here was to assess the middle class Dalits' perceptions about the contemporary nature of caste and its consequences for the Dalits. Issues such as Brahminism, purity and pollution, casteism and communalism, achieving Dalit unity through intercommunity marriages among the Dalits and additional burdens that the Dalit women faced in comparison to Dalit men were presented to them for their opinions (Table 4.29).

Table 4.29 *Opinion on Brahminism, Purity and Pollution, Casteism-Communalism, Dalit Unity and Additional Burdens of Dalit Women*

Issues	*Opinions*					*Total*
	Strongly Agree	*Agree*	*Strongly Disagree*	*Disagree*	*No Response*	
Brahminism is All Pervasive	51 (48.6)	46 (43.8)	—	1 (1)	7 (6.7)	105 (100)
Questions of Purity and Pollution Are Unobservable in Urban Life	41 (39)	31 (29.5)	9 (8.6)	21 (20)	3 (2.9)	105 (100)
Casteism is Not the Bane of Indian Politics Like Communalism is	47 (44.8)	31 (29.5)	2 (1.9)	17 (16.2)	8 (7.6)	105 (100)
Intercommunity Marriages among Dalits Would Achieve Dalit Unity	40 (38.1)	53 (50.5)	3 (2.9)	4 (3.8)	5 (4.8)	105 (100)
Dalit Women Do Not Face Additional Burdens as Distinct from Dalit Men	42 (40)	7 (6.7)	9 (8.6)	44 (41.9)	3 (2.9)	105 (100)

Of these statements, only the notion that Brahminism was all-pervasive was agreed upon by almost all of them. In contrast, the other two general issues pertaining to caste were contested by them. Thirty have disagreed with the notion that purity and pollution were non-observable in urban life and another 19 disagreed with the notion that 'casteism is not the bane of Indian politics like communalism is'. The two perceptions related to the Dalits, namely, 'Dalit unity through intercommunity marriages' was agreed upon by 93 of them, and the issue of Dalit women facing additional burdens compared to the Dalit men was contested by another 51 of them.

The politics (pragmatic and ideological) of the Dalit middle class are analysed in terms of their membership in organizations/political parties, their preferences in effective models/strategy for overall development of Dalits, views on reservations, views related to political options before the Dalits for achieving equality, knowledge about issues/measure related to Dalits, prioritization of socio-economic and political issues and their views on some important socio-economic and political issues in understanding their identity and ideology.

Thus, this chapter attempted to comprehend the ideology and identity patterns of the middle class Dalits, specifically the respondents, through understanding their (1) life situation, (2) identity patterns, (3) ideology and (4) politics. Their life situation when contrasted to their socio-economic background and their middle class location, in terms of education and employment indicates a uniqueness that is specific to the Dalit middle class. Similarly, the identity patterns of the members of Dalit middle class are distinctive compared to others. Though the middle class Dalits have many identity options before them, their most preferred identity in most given social, economic and political contexts is a Dalit. At a personal level, they prefer a non-caste identity for them. Though they have experienced upward mobility in their education and employment statuses, they are not yet 'free' of caste biases and discrimination, the same was well outlined in the responses provided by them. They have definitive views on many social, economic and political issues affecting the Dalits today. Individually, not all of them are in a position to engage constantly with the Dalit politics, but each individual possesses strong political convictions with concern for the poor Dalits and the overall development of all Dalits in mind.

NOTES

1. On the lines of traditional *varna* order, namely, Dalit, OBC and other 'upper castes'.
2. Saavala's study (2001) suggests the religious observance among middle class Dalits has few takers from caste-Hindus.

3. Saavala (2001: 194) negating the sanskritization model observes that 'The "cultural identification" of urban low caste families who have managed to gain economic security remains contradictory. At face value they share their way of life with middle class families of higher caste background. Many, especially those of ex-Untouchable identity, nevertheless feel a need, at times desperate, to hide their social background and to avoid being exposed and recognised through their jaati'.
4. Sheth (1999: 2510) observes that 'Membership of today's middle class is associated with new lifestyles (modern consumption patterns), ownership of certain economic assets and the self consciousness of belonging to the middle class. As such, it is open to members of different castes – which have acquired modern education, taken to non-traditional occupations and/or command higher incomes and the political power – to enter this middle class'.
5. Its literal meaning is 'broken' or 'grounded down', see Zelliot (1992: 267).
6. See Sharma (2001: 98). In the case of Scheduled Castes, the terms 'untouchables', 'harijans', etc. have a derogatory meaning, which is contested by them. For similar reasons, the term 'shudra' has been replaced by Other Backward Classes in official parlance and the 'Bahujans' in political articulations, and in the case of Scheduled Tribes, the term 'tribal' has been replaced by 'Adivasi' mostly in the latter.
7. The respondents in Kulke's study (1976: 251) preferred Gandhi (58.5%) to Ambedkar (31.7%). Further, the educated showed allegiance to Ambedkar (70.8%) as against illiterates towards Gandhi (84.9%).

CHAPTER 5

Dalit Middle Class and Narratives of Self and Community

This chapter attempts to map the trajectory of Dalit middle class[1] in India and formulates a case for how community as a context and mobility as a factor lead to the formation of Dalit identity among the middle class Dalits in contemporary India.[2] At a different level, it also seeks to examine to what extent the individual Dalits recruited into this (middle) class, individually or as a group, contribute to the shaping of a radical Dalit ideology that could be considered as an example for emulation by the larger Dalit milieu elsewhere. Thus, eight case studies, one from each occupation/profession, have been included here. These case studies, which take the form of simple narratives, sometimes in the respondent's words, do not necessarily represent all the Dalits pursuing these occupations in general or even the respondents in particular; rather they are reflective or indicative of the life trajectories of the individuals in them and seek to represent the most outstanding individuals pursuing these occupations. A brief analysis and conclusion has also been presented at the close of each case study.

MR ESWAR, BANK EMPLOYEE

Family Profile

Mr Eswar is an Assistant Manager in the State Bank of India. Aged 49 years, he belongs to the Mala community and was born and brought up in Hyderabad city. His father, an illiterate, hailing from a small village in nearby Mahabubnagar district, migrated to Hyderabad in search of work and was employed as a Class-IV employee in Andhra Pradesh State Electricity Board (APSEB). His mother was also a Class-IV employee. He has two children, a daughter and a son, who are pursuing their Intermediate and X standards, respectively.

Eswar's childhood was spent in a prominent Dalit slum (*Basti*). All four of his siblings (two sisters and two brothers, all elder to him) are educated. While one sister and one brother are settled as Class-IV employees, one brother is an ex-serviceman and a bank clerk now. Another sister is a homemaker. The most memorable incident in his childhood, as he recounts is reading Ambedkar's life story (*Ambedkar Jeevitha Charithra* by Yendluri Chinnaiah), while he was in VII standard in 1968. In 1969, within a year, he translated it into English and spoke from a dais on the eve of Ambedkar Jayanthi in his Basti. In the history of Hyderabad, that was the first public celebration of Ambedkar Jayanthi in Hyderabad city. Prior to that, Ambedkar Jayanthi was usually celebrated in closed circles, within four walls.

The night school run by the Bhajana Mandali in the Basti encouraged school-going children to study under the supervision of volunteers. Eswar was thus able to do well in his studies. During his student days, he took an active part in all Dalit mobilizations and activities. Mr J.B. Raju, a Dalit IAS Officer, who was also an active and important leader of the Dalit movement, inspired the Dalit youths during those days with his speeches on Ambedkar. He was considered a promising youth with a strong Dalit orientation. At the same, he resolved to enter government service as most of the Dalit leaders of the time were government employees. In the period 1969–1971, he participated in the separate Telangana agitation and was jailed twice along with other activists.

Worldview and Political Participation

He was one among the few who formed Ambedkar Yuvajana Sangham (Ambedkar Youth Association) that became the first state-level organization, with a large membership base and was instrumental in spreading Ambedkar's ideology among the rural youths. It continuously engaged in many issues related to Dalits and actively contributed to the strengthening of the Dalit movement. However, soon after the completion of his graduation (B. Com) in 1973, he was appointed as a clerk in State Bank of India in Hyderabad. Since then, he has been organizing the employees and taking part in the activities of various other Dalit organizations. Now he holds the rank of Assistant Manager, with a posting at Hyderabad.

Continuing with his involvement in Dalit political activities, he became a committee member in the Andhra Pradesh Scheduled Castes Welfare Association (APSCWA) in March 1974. Then, the association was headed by Mr C. Ramulu (an assistant director in Social Welfare Department) and Dr K. Nagaiah (Postal Department), who were president and general secretary, respectively. Later on, he rose in rank in the organization and became its General Secretary in 1981.

One important issue the APSCWA took up under his leadership was protesting against the denial of entry of Mr Masala Eeranna, a Telugu Desam Party MLA, into Mantralayam temple in 1981. Both Ambedkar Yuvajana Sangham and APSCWA took out rallies protesting against the discrimination.

Recently, during the MRPS's Madiga Dandora Movement, he along with other Mala leaders, suggested an alternative to MRPS's demand of categorization of SCs into ABCD groups, namely, dividing Dalit groups into three groups, consisting of below poverty line (8% of SC population) middle class (5% of the population) and upper middle class (2% of the population) in order to provide reservations in proportion to their population. He felt that instead of dividing the SCs, reservations could be provided to the needy, based on their educational and economic backwardness. His view was to earmark a total budget of one 5-year plan period for the development of only the below poverty line population without allocating budget for any other social groups, so that the poorest sections would be benefited by it.

He strongly feels that 'a social tax should be imposed (5% or 10% of their salary) on all employees or only the reserved category employees who had availed reservations, which should be spent on the development of Below Poverty Level (BPL) families'. He observes, 'Nowadays, there are many changes in Dalits' lifestyle and politics. In Hyderabad city, many Dalit youths drop out from schools or colleges and as they are unemployed, their political allegiance develops more in conformity to the present day politics. Instead of developing their own political symbols, the Dalits are becoming followers in mainstream political parties'. With regard to the growing number of Dalit organizations, he feels, 'unlike in the past, where few organizations existed and everybody worked for one or the other organization, with a view to strengthen the already existing Dalit organizations, these days, many Dalits prefer to form new organizations for the sake of their own individual identity'.

With reservations policy, three significant changes have taken place, according to him, namely, economic development, social awareness and improvement in the numbers of educated Dalits. According to him, 20 years ago, revealing caste identity was out of the question for many economically and socially successful Dalits. Now, with the increasing awareness and politicization with newer caste movements, asserting caste identity has become easier. In his personal experience, 'urbanization had not had much influence in reducing caste discrimination'. During his childhood, he had lived in a slum along with other Dalits and faced the same kind of discrimination that was prevalent in the rural areas. Only after entering into his present job, involving a predominantly middle class lifestyle, had he found that the degree of caste discrimination at place of residence and work had reduced. Since he lives in a bank employees' colony, he interacted with both Dalits and non-Dalits at the family level as well.

He advocates, 'What is needed today is activism concentrating on legal aid to victims of caste atrocities and the assertion of a Buddhist identity for Dalits. This alone could help Dalits face the increasing atrocities and prevent such atrocities from occurring in the future'. As at present Dalit politics was heading towards disunity, witnessing the breaking up of organizations due to individuals' selfish egoistic nature, the future of the Dalit politics seemed very grim, in his opinion. He further adds, 'at this rate, there is no hope in the near future that all the Dalit leaders and organizations would come together to forge a broader Dalit platform that would work towards claiming political power'. However, he is not going to 'give up in despair'. He wants to make his best efforts to change the present situation, to bring in unity among all Dalits, in order to resume the aborted struggle for Dalit emancipation.

Analysis and Conclusion

Mr Eswar is a typical Dalit leader actively involved in the Dalit movement in Andhra Pradesh. His life trajectory mainly reflects the life circumstances of Dalits living in Hyderabad city 30 years back. He is also a typical example of an individual recruited into the Dalit movement early in life who eventually grew into a Dalit leader. His views on politics were all shaped in a collective process. His contribution to the Dalit movement is very significant compared to many of his contemporaries. He is a state-level Dalit leader representing Dalit employees as well as other Dalits' interests. He had risen early in leadership and enjoys the privilege of being one among the prominent Dalit leaders. So far, he had not diverged from his original enthusiasm and was still planning many activities for Dalit development.

VEERAIAH, UNIVERSITY TEACHER

Family Profile

Veeraiah is a lecturer in a state university having 9 years of service. He is 42 years old and belongs to the Madiga sub-caste. For a brief period of 6 months, he worked as a Trainee Manager in the Railway Recruitment Board. Later on, he worked in the SC Corporation for 2 years on deputation. He hails from a village in Rangareddy district and migrated to the city in 1980 for his studies. He is a third-generation literate. His grandfather had been a bonded labourer in his youth. Unable to bear the workload and ill-treatment, Veeraiah's grandfather ran away from his employers. He was sheltered by Christian missionaries who taught him to read and write. Later on, his grandfather was brought back to the family and was made to continue with bonded labour. Veeraiah's father was also literate. Unlike his grandfather, his father was an agriculturist. The family had four acres of land and sold two acres in 1973 towards Veeraiah's educational expenses. In turn, after obtaining a job, he had invested ₹ 40,000 for sinking a bore well in his ancestral land.

He has two siblings, a brother and a sister. The brother is less educated and, hence, is looking after the agricultural activities of the family. Since Veeraiah is economically well off compared to his brother, he does not want to claim his share in the ancestral family property. Now, Veeraiah is not contributing towards the family's agricultural activities. Instead, he intends to take up the responsibility for performing the marriages of the children of his siblings. Recently, his wife contested in the municipal elections in Hyderabad, as a ward councillor on the basis of reservations for SCs. That could be the first time, he thinks, that people in his locality had found out his caste background. Prior to that, there had been no other situation where he had had to reveal his caste identity.

Worldview and Political Participation

Personally, as an educated Dalit he claimed that he had never faced caste discrimination. He reflects, 'in those days caste discrimination was widely prevalent in villages'. One incident of caste discrimination he remembers in this context relates to his school days. While rehearsing for a school play, his role was changed to suit the prevailing caste sentiments. Originally, he had been selected for a role which required the touching of his feet by a co-actor, a caste-Hindu boy. But the village elders did not permit this to occur. When he was young and still residing in his native place, he protested against the bonded labour, contract annual labour system and *Uronthu* (traditional village services the Dalits have to do on a nominal payment such as removing the dead cattle, assisting in cremation of the deceased and advertising important news to the villagers by beating a drum) in his village as he felt that these systems were oppressive and exploitative.

In 1982, in the context of Meenakshipuram (in Tamil Nadu) religious conversions, the local Bharatiya Janata Party (BJP) unit (at his native place in Rangareddy district) held a meeting against religious conversions. He opposed the BJP in the meeting who, he felt, had tried to make it a political issue in his village when it had no basis. Instead, he demanded that the BJP take a clear stand on the 'system of using two glasses' in the hotels, one for caste-Hindus and the other for Dalits, which he felt was a clear example of discrimination against Dalits. Later on, he was instrumental in the formation of an 'SC, ST, BC, Minority Welfare Association' at the Mandal level to fight against Reddy's domination.

He has a strong commitment towards the overall development of all the Dalits in his village. Similarly, he has been contributing to the development of his native village. He was instrumental in getting a 'Community Hall' sanctioned for Dalits. He has an active role in his native village development programmes. He helps village youths to organize sports and cultural events in the village. He encouraged an NGO to adopt his village for development. While he was in SC Corporation on deputation, he recommended land allotments to few landless Dalits. Throughout his studies and career, he had received help from caste-Hindus. A Brahmin teacher as well as his childhood friends from OBC and upper-caste backgrounds had helped him financially and by way of providing career-related advice. Similarly, he had helped others, when he had attained economic stability. He sheltered a Mala youth who was pursuing studies for 8 years and two OBCs for a year.

Analysis and Conclusion

Veeraiah is a typical example of a successful Dalit, who has achieved social and economic mobility. He has strong family ties and community consciousness and, thereby, involves himself in various development activities. Due to his offers of financial and other assistance and participation in development-related activities in his native village, he is respected by all the villagers. In his present location, Hyderabad, he is respected in his social milieu for his compassionate nature and commitment to the cause of Dalits.

RAMASWAMY, ADVOCATE

Family Profile

Ramaswamy is an advocate. He is 37 years old. He has done MA, LLB, and has been working as an advocate for the last 4 years. He got married at the age of 35 and has a child. His wife, who is a graduate, works as a clerk in a private concern. He hails from Guntur district, where he has pursued most of his studies. He belongs to a large family of three brothers and three sisters. His father was a teacher who was interested in providing education to all his children. All his brothers and sisters are qualified teachers. He too worked as a teacher for a brief period.

During his intermediate course, he was attracted to Left politics. After getting through his intermediate examination in 1983, he came under the influence of the local people's war squad (*Dalam*). When he joined BA in 1987 at a college in Guntur, he was made the in-charge to organize the students of that college by the People's War Group (PWG). He joined an MA Course in 1988 at Nagarjuna University; however, due to his involvement in party activities, he could not complete the course. In 1989, when he became a full-time member of the party, he was asked to work with the villages near Tenali town. He also served as the town cell member – in-charge of students' mobilizations. In 1986, he was arrested by the police and was freed after 3 days. In 1987, when he was arrested for the second time, his identity was known to the police and he subsequently spent a week in jail. A 'bind over' case was booked against him; however, he managed to get off with a warning, forbidding him to engage in party-related activities. He worked in the party for 2 more years before quitting it in 1992.

Later on, he studied LLB during 1995–1998 and has stayed away from party politics since then. After completion of his LLB, with a view to begin his professional career in Hyderabad, he took a crop loan of ₹ 20,000 from a bank to come to Hyderabad city in 1999 and began his apprenticeship to a legal practitioner in 2001. From July 2001 to May 2003, he worked as a legal assistant to a well-known advocate at the High Court. Prior to that, in the initial days of his career in the city, as he had no contacts, he had to join under an advocate much younger to him. Ramaswamy was 'ill-treated' by this advocate and, hence, had to look out for apprenticeship under another senior advocate. He did not perceive any caste discrimination by seniors or clients all through his career. However, in spite of his best efforts, he found that he was 'unable to work with any senior advocate on a sustained basis'. He feels that 'interpersonal relations are indeed formed on caste basis' at his workplace, though he adds 'it is very difficult to prove it'. Such discrimination, he says, is 'a mental perception one always feels', at the same time, it is an 'unseen feeling'.

While he was working as a legal assistant, he was paid a monthly salary of ₹ 2,000. After quitting the last senior advocate, he received a contract from a reputed cement company to represent their case. The mode of payment was on a case-to-case basis. As the company lawyer, he has to deal with recovery and check bounce cases in the lower court at Secunderabad. Even after 2 years of legal practice, he has not fixed his nameplate in front of his residence. He wishes to learn law 'adequately' and only then display his nameplate. At present, he finds no use for a nameplate as most of his cases come from his native place, mostly recommended by his friends and relatives.

In between, he tried becoming a pastor (priest) in a Church and tried his hands at Dalit politics. He brought out a collection of Dalit poetry in 1998. He is 'always ready to work for his community', but at present, his 'economic conditions do not permit it'. However, he wants to help the Dalits, within the purview of his profession, by providing legal aid. His views regarding the Dalit movement and Dalit politics are firmly based on his exposure to few important Dalit leaders. He is most appreciative of the movement led by Madiga Reservation Porata Samithi for sub-categorization of reservations in favour of Madigas and other Dalit communities who underutilized them.

Worldview and Political Participation

He finds himself 'lost in this world', for he is still struggling to make a career for himself. As of now, his wife, who is working as a clerk in private company with her earnings of ₹ 5,000 a month, is managing the household. Though he sometimes earns ₹ 5,000 to ₹ 7,000 a month, his income is mostly 'irregular and uncertain'. He prefers to work on contract basis with companies or obtain an assistant government pleader post in order to earn a regular income and to survive in this profession. He feels that establishing himself independently, solely on the basis of individual cases, is non-affordable.

He finds the legal profession increasingly competitive and ruthless, 'which does not care much for the well-being of others'. So far, he had faced problems in terms of improving his skills, increasing his practice, earning more money and coping with the system. He is very critical of the profession, but at the same time, finds it fascinating and engaging. If not for his interest in the legal profession, as such, he would not have stayed back in Hyderabad, he feels. If he is unable to make a future in this profession, he is 'ready to migrate abroad, even to work as a casual labourer' and has been making attempts in that direction. He grew up in the protected environment of a well-educated family. In his childhood, his family enjoyed a lot of respect, as his father was a school teacher. In his youth, he got drawn into the radical Left movement, hence missed out on a regular work career. After quitting politics, he studied law and has been trying to make a career for himself. He is still struggling.

Analysis and Conclusion

Ramaswamy is a struggling middle class Dalit. Belonging to a lower middle class background, he had witnessed economic insecurity, mainly due to his involvement in the Left movement for nearly 5 years. He now considers those years, during which he was unemployed, as an unproductive period in his life. However, he quickly got back to his studies, graduated with an LLB degree and tried to settle down as an advocate. However, his struggles in the pursuit of economic stability are not over as yet. However, despite all these uncertainties, his political understanding had developed under the influence of both Dalit ideology and Marxism. Thus, he could easily assume a Dalit activist role, soon after coming out of the Left movement. His problems are more to do with the 'elusive stability' in work career rather than related to identity and ideology. His problems from the beginning are related to his social location in those sites that are characterized by anxiety and uncertainty.

KOTESWAR RAO, EMPLOYEE, CLERICAL CADRE

Family Profile

Koteswar Rao is a Junior Office Assistant, aged 39 years and hails from a very poor family in the East Godavari district. He has two daughters and one son. He wants his three children to study MBBS and become doctors, a profession he likes the most. He likes to teach children and consequently teaches many of them who reside in his neighbourhood. He values education so much that he spends most of his free time in teaching subjects such as mental aptitude, general knowledge and mathematics to young children. He also lectures on memory skills and preparation for examinations in schools and colleges on the invitation. He believes that 'one should cultivate one's mental abilities on one's own'.

Worldview and Political Participation

So far he has admitted 50 boys and girls in hostels and helped them with some kind of financial assistance. During Sundays and holidays, he conducts special classes for village children on mental ability and memory skills. He is also providing guidance to a few uneducated youths on how to prepare for competitive examinations and encouraging some of them to learn shorthand and typewriting. He likes to conduct games and quiz competitions for village children. Since he accords a lot of value to education, he sometimes spends his own money towards stationary-related expenditure and prizes, when he conducts special classes and summer camps. He describes himself as a 'self-motivated' person. He tries to instil joy and hope in others. Rao, who migrated to Hyderabad in 1990, plays a very active role in the Dalit employees' association. He is the President of SC, ST employees' association in his office. He interacts closely with many Dalit leaders. In his view, any Dalit who gets into a government job or is pursuing a profitable profession is 'successful'. He sees success in relative terms. He considers 'an improvement in the original social and economic status as success'. In his opinion, he is also a 'successful' Dalit.

At his workplace, he discovered that Dalits were not being recruited as per reservations quota. Currently, he is mobilizing a few Dalit employees to represent this issue to the government. Similarly, he is also playing a lead role in representing the employees' problems for the officials. Koteswar Rao keeps in touch with all his Dalit colleagues even after office hours and also maintains relations with their families. He feels, as non-Dalit colleagues do not interact at family level with Dalits, 'all Dalit employees have to maintain close family based interactions, even if they reside in places which are located far away from each other'.

With regard to the development of Dalits, he feels, 'donations could be collected from all Dalit employees and used for financing education and employment related training programmes for Dalit children and youth'. He feels, 'to achieve equality in the society, firstly, Dalits have to aim at achieving unity among themselves and also address their differences. Education and awareness regarding the changes that are taking place worldwide are needed to guide the Dalits towards social and economic equality, on par with others. Education is very important for the realization of such equal status'.

Analysis and Conclusion

Koteswar Rao is hard working by nature. He has built his life all by himself. He had neither family support nor the guidance of friends and well wishers in his struggle to achieve educational and economic mobility. His mobility was aided by the utilization of reservations in education and employment. He is aware of the importance of education and hard work in a Dalit's life. Thus, he motivates youths to give their best in their pursuit of education and employment. His interest and contribution in the development of the Dalit community has been primarily in the form of educational development. He believes that development in education would lead to economic development. Though he is adequately motivated and has a strong commitment towards the development of all Dalits, he knows his limitations and thus focuses only on one activity, that of providing education to Dalit children and career guidance to the youths.

RAMAIAH, JOURNALIST

Family Profile

Ramaiah is aged 41 years and belongs to Manyam caste from the Telangana region. He got married at the age of 16 and 'recently celebrated the Silver Jubilee of (his) wedding anniversary'. He is one of the very few Dalit journalists who work in Hyderabad city. His forefathers were employed as Sunkari (tax collectors). Two of his brothers and one sister work in the coal mines in Kothagudem in Karimnagar district. Initially, he was selected as a rural/mofussil contributor/reporter in the newspaper *Andhra Patrika*. He worked until 1989 as a rural contributor and moved to Hyderabad in 1990 as a reporter in the head office. After arriving here, he realized that, except him, there was not a single Dalit journalist in the city. In the next 5 years, he tried to actively encourage many Dalit youths to enter the field of journalism. As a result, now, there are a few Dalit journalists in Hyderabad city, along with a number of rural/mofussil contributors/reporters all over the state. In his career as a journalist, he learnt 'how difficult it is to survive in a field like journalism'. Whenever he raised the issue of absence of Dalit journalists, he was 'mocked at and faced hostility from (his non-Dalit) colleagues and the management'. He says that since the last 13 years, he has continued to carry out his agenda and is unmindful of its consequences to his career.

As a journalist, Ramaiah always tried to focus on new and emerging issues. His professional performance could not further his career prospects since his social background was not conducive to it, he feels. He maintains that caste is very crucial in the profession of journalism. He has worked in *Andhra Patrika, Samayam, Suprabhatam, Vaartha* and *Think Soft*. He opines that 'like in any other field, journalism is full of caste bias, nepotism and is prejudiced against assertive Dalits. Dalits are not encouraged to work in this profession. Many of the superiors in the journalism field possess a mentality of harassing talented people, especially if one is a talented Dalit'. Ramaiah had to face harassment, discrimination from superiors and the management and also had to frequently shift from one newspaper to another.

Worldview and Political Participation

He is highly active in Dalit politics. He works closely with several Dalit organizations. He is an active member of the National Campaign on Dalit Human Rights (NCDHR). He was one of the founding members of the Centre for Dalit Studies, which was formed by 20 like-minded Dalits and non-Dalits to address research, documentation and policy-related issues. He was also the founder of *Janapada Kala Parishodhana Vedika* (Folklore Research Centre). He is also a member of the Andhra Pradesh Union of Working Journalists (APUWJ).

Analysis and Conclusion

Ramaiah belongs to a numerically small Dalit community. He is a professional, who was the pioneer among the existing few Dalit journalists in Hyderabad and was well established in his field. He is also one of the few Dalit intellectuals to have arisen from among Dalit professionals. At present, he is diversifying into research on Dalit issues. His success in the profession of journalism has fetched him repute and recognition as an intellectual. He is very proficient in many contemporary Dalit issues and of late has evinced interest in developmental issues. He has formulated strategies for the Dalit movement and the socio-economic development of Dalits. His involvement in research would further enable him to hone his skills as an individual and the same would result in comprehensive articulations by an intellectual of his repute. It certainly helps his profession and the Dalit movement as well.

RAMESH, NGO PROFESSIONAL

Family Profile

Ramesh, aged 40 years, is an NGO professional who belongs to the Mala community. He has done MA, LLB, and is presently pursuing a PhD at Osmania University. His father is a supervisor in a spinning mill in Bombay. He has a brother who works in a private company. In his native place, in Nizamabad district, his family owns a small piece of agricultural land, which is not being cultivated as his father resides in Bombay and he and his brother are living in Hyderabad.

Ramesh got married 4 years ago and has a 1-year-old daughter. His wife is a graduate and presently a housewife. He is the sole breadwinner of the family. He used to pay his brother's expenses while he (the brother) was pursuing his studies. His brother was dependent on him until last year.

He is the first-generation educated in his family who migrated to Hyderabad for purposes of education. Even as a student, he began working on projects and financed his studies himself. For nearly 6 years, he has worked in various government projects and small NGOs in and around Hyderabad. During his student days, he was an active member of student organizations and was instrumental in mobilizing Dalit students. After entering the NGO sector, he had acquired membership in Dalit NGOs and Volunteers' Network and is actively pursuing the Dalit cause through NGO sector.

Worldview and Political Participation

Ramesh believes in collective actions and mass mobilizations to solve the problems faced by rural Dalits, hence, he chose the profession. His experience of working at grass-roots level had helped him in formulating a suitable development model for Dalits. Ever since he entered the NGO sector, he has been attempting to sensitize it to be receptive to the needs of the Dalits in designing and implementing projects for development.

He has built a house recently with loans taken from his office and finance companies. Even though his family does not own much property in his native place and he had begun earning only recently, it has not prevented him from realizing his dream of owning a house in the city.

In spite of resource constraints, he somehow manages to be part of informal collective efforts towards providing financial help to poor Dalit students and occasionally engages in such activities on his own. He is actively involved in many Dalit organizations. He is a member in *Kula Vivaksha Vyatirekha Porata Samithi* (Struggle Forum Against Caste Discrimination). He, along with a few of his friends, extends legal and financial help to persons who wish to enter into intercaste marriages. So far they have conducted half a dozen intercaste marriages in which either the groom or the bride was a Dalit. Besides conducting the marriage, they provide protection and legal assistance to the couple until the problems with their respective families are resolved. In these issues, the group seeks police assistance in providing protection for the couple. In cases where legal complaints are lodged against the Dalit groom or bride, the group provides legal assistance to them.

Along with individual and collective efforts, he feels Dalit employees and professionals should symbolically participate in the activities of larger organizations. Further, it is a social responsibility of all those who avail the reservations to take part in meetings and Ambedkar birthday celebrations.

Analysis and Conclusion

Ramesh has a strong Dalit consciousness. Having lived in Hyderabad city as a student, he was exposed to the most sophisticated Dalit ideology early in life. Moreover, his rural background made him stand apart from the others in his urban setting. Since his student days, he has had wide exposure to the problems of untouchability and caste discrimination at personal and community levels. Such experiences drew him nearer to the other Dalit students, who had similar backgrounds and experiences, to foster a group identity as a Dalit. Thus, he grew in the articulations of the problems of the Dalit students and thereby emerged as a student leader.

The same objectives set the agenda for his career. Thus, he chose to work in the NGO sector. As part of his work, he is focusing on developmental issues related to Dalits. His participation in Dalit politics is more pragmatic and result oriented. He believes that a sustained contribution to the Dalit cause is essential by all the members of the community in their individual capacity and through their vocation. Every Dalit, he feels, should think and act, taking into consideration the welfare of poor Dalits from their respective locations, to realize the overall objective of Dalit development.

DR VENKATAGIRI, DOCTOR

Family Profile

Dr Venkatagiri works as a medical officer in a Public Limited Company. He has an MD and has put in 15 years of service in his profession. He belongs to the Madiga community and hails from a village in Warangal district. His father was a mason, the first literate person in the family. Having understood the importance of education and the opening up of many opportunities for educated Dalit youths in those days, his father educated all his children. He has two sisters and two brothers, all of them are married and well settled. His parents live independently at his native place. All the brothers and sisters reside at different places. Dr Venkatagiri is the second son in the family. He had developed a fascination for the medical field in his childhood and was determined to pursue medicine. His parents encouraged him and his elder male sibling in their studies and had borne all expenses from their meagre earnings. He and his elder brother were very hardworking and through their success, they could influence many other youths from among their relatives to take up professional courses and become well settled. During his pursuit of a medical degree, he fell in love with a girl who belonged to the Reddy community and married her. The marriage had occurred 17 years ago. Now, he has a son and a daughter aged 16 and 14 respectively, who are pursuing intermediate and IX class respectively. He wants to provide all the requisite educational facilities for his children and leave the choice of career options for them.

He lives in the company allotted quarters and bought a site for constructing a house in the city in 1996, having taken a loan of ₹ 4 lakh from his office. He intends to build a house and settle down in Hyderabad after retirement. He has all the consumer goods that an average upper middle class family possesses and has adapted to a middle class lifestyle. Before joining the present job, he ran his own clinic in his native place for 3 years. After being selected for the present job, 14 years ago, he shifted to Hyderabad. Two persons from his native place helped him with economic assistance and career guidance. He still maintains close relations with them. Having realized the importance of such assistance to him during his studies, he extends financial help to the Dalit youths pursuing their studies and provides them with career counselling. In terms of his individual contribution to the Dalit community, he has developed a few health projects for rural Dalits. He intends to provide medical help and health education to the poor Dalits.

Worldview and Political Participation

As part of his professional interaction with other colleagues, he came under the influence of Osho's teachings and took to meditation. Now, he actively works towards spreading awareness on the importance of Yoga, which he prescribes for his patients. His free time is dedicated to the cause of advocating the importance of meditation as an aid in medical treatment. He has a strong sub-caste consciousness and feels that asserting sub-caste identity is necessary for the development of his community. He had contributed financially to the MRPS's movement for SC reservations categorization. He finds reservations an effective tool for the upliftment of the Dalits. He is not a member of any organization or political party, but believes in individual contributions for the development of the Dalits.

Analysis and Conclusion

Dr Venkatagiri is the second-generation educated, who had the support of parents and elder siblings to pursue higher education and settle well professionally. In a way, his paternal family background facilitated his upward economic mobility. After completion of his studies, he forged an entry into the medical profession. Since then, he has been much focused and career oriented. He has not been exposed to Dalit ideology, but has a strong community identity. However, his involvement is limited to supporting the most important issues pertaining to their economic development. His financial contribution to the SC reservations categorization movement, he feels, is his responsibility towards his own community. At the same time, he believes in contributing in an individual capacity to the well-being of Dalits.

NARSINGA RAO, EMPLOYEE, OFFICER CADRE

Family Profile

Narsinga Rao, BA, aged 46 years is a Superintendent in a university. He belongs to the Mala community. He had completed his graduation in 1984. He has one brother, elder to him, who works as an agricultural labourer-cum-sharecropper at his native place in Amalapuram in East Godavari district. Narsinga Rao's brother's income is uncertain. His father and mother were landless agricultural labourers. His father expired when he was 4 years old. His mother brought up, both he and his brother, by working as a daily wage labourer. As his mother's income was insufficient to support both their education, his brother discontinued his studies after V standard and started working as a labourer, while Narsinga Rao continued with his studies. His brother and mother, who were working as labourers, supported his studies till he completed his BA.

Soon after completing his studies, he obtained a clerk's job in his present office. Since the economic condition of his family was not stable, he immediately took up the job. He is the first person from his family to migrate to Hyderabad. Since his brother is unable to earn enough money to support his family on his own, Narsinga Rao extends financial assistance to him very often.

Rao got married 4 years after he first began working. His wife hails from the same community and is a matriculate. She is a housewife. He has one daughter and one son. His daughter is pursuing a MSc Degree and his son is pursuing a B Tech. (Computers). His brother's daughter came to Hyderabad to pursue her studies and she stays with his family. He is supporting his niece financially with regard to tuition fees, etc. as his brother cannot afford it. Narsinga Rao feels it is his obligation to sponsor her studies, as his brother supported his studies. He lives in the house of a Dalit, in a predominantly Dalit colony in the city. Initially, when he was searching for rental accommodation, he experienced some form of caste discrimination. The present house, owned by a Dalit, is very small in size and inconvenient for residential purposes. However, he has never tried to change his residence since he cannot afford the rent in other areas of the city. Recently, he took a housing loan from his office and bought a site near his rented house. As of now, he is not in a position, financially, to build a house on the site.

He owns a very minimum number of consumer goods. The necessity never arose earlier because his family lives in a lower middle class locality, moreover, the children were very young and did not demand such comforts then. Recently, he had purchased a motor bike and a colour TV on the insistence of his children. He does not find any sudden changes in his lifestyle. Throughout, he has tried to resist imitating other people who could afford luxuries, but also kept with the changes that are required for the new 'income group'. The changes that have occurred in his lifestyle over a period of time have been mainly due to his improved economic status. His perceptions of these lifestyle changes are reflected in the comment that 'arriving into the middle class is like entering a totally different class. This class has a lifestyle similar to the rich'. He devotes a lot of time in his office. Hence, family outings are also very rare. His two children have studied in private educational institutions, since he wished to give them the best possible education. Though he wanted his son to pursue an MSc Degree like his daughter, his son preferred to pursue a B Tech Degree. With regard to their career options, he prefers to leave the choice to them. He feels that they would have to make their decision based on the opportunities available to them.

Worldview and Political Participation

Caste discrimination, he feels, is a community question, not one concerning the individual. It is always community oriented, though it affects individuals too. Personally, he had never faced caste discrimination. He feels that 'it is not directly visible, but when an opportunity arises, caste discrimination would be there'. The situation according to him was that 'caste discrimination is experienced by individuals, but it is always below the level that can be made public. It might not be individually oriented, but, when it comes to the community, certainly, favouritism towards own and discrimination against the others exists'. Even in the case of social relations, he feels, 'interaction between two individuals is always along expected lines. Caste is invariably involved'.

He has great admiration for B.R. Ambedkar as the one person who had proved to the world that 'a Dalit can attain high standards, despite the hurdles encountered'. He acknowledges the contribution of other nationalist leaders to the development of the nation and Dalits in particular. In his view, the Dalit movement has been divided due to the SC reservations sub-categorization issue brought up by the Dalits. Despite, which, he feels that the Dalit movement has been able to get some benefits from the government. He believes that all the progress the Dalits have made is mainly due to reservations, the jobs in the public sector and the evolution of Dalit representatives of political parties could be mainly attributed to reservation system. With regard to reservations, he feels society in general would only benefit if the government helped the weaker sections. In his opinion, reservations are very essential for Dalit development. He concerns himself more with issues related to social, economic and political equality than Dalit identity/self-respect issues. His view is that for achieving real progress from the present status, the Dalits have to develop economically first. Then only, will they be in a position to address their other requirements.

Analysis and Conclusion

Narsinga Rao is a typical example of a product of the reservation system. His present level of economic upward mobility would not have been possible for him without the reservation system. Though he had ascended in employment and consequently in economic ranks, his upward mobility had been gradual and phased in manner. It limited his 'psychological mobility' to a great extent. Compared to many other Dalits in his present occupational position, he had begun his career in a low cadre and made slow progress. He had to focus a lot on his career in order to progress to the current level. His level of engagement with Dalit politics is limited. However, he is appreciative of many Dalit leaders and interacts with many 'economically successful' Dalits, thus he gets to know all the current issues concerning the Dalits. He feels, his present location does not allow him to engage in the Dalit movement or community development activities in a direct and constant manner.

NOTES

1. The socially and economically upwardly mobile section among the Dalits, especially those who have joined 'white-collar' jobs and as independent practitioners of other professions such as law, medicine and journalism are considered as the Dalit middle class. See Kulke (1976), Ram (1988), Guru (2002) and Omvedt (2002) for a description of this new class within the Indian middle classes that has a Dalit origin.
2. Dalit middle class is unique in terms of its class composition, disposition, lifestyle and political opinions. Dalit middle class, as is identified and defined by various scholars, is distinct from the global as well as the 'general' Indian middle class. Studies by Kulke (1976), Ram (1988) and Omvedt (2002) emphasize this aspect of Dalit middle class.

CHAPTER 6

Conclusion

Towards a Sociology of Dalit Middle Class

The emergence of Dalit middle class is distinctly unique from the general middle class that is largely constituted by the 'upper castes' or the ruling classes or the traditionally propertied. It was largely based on ascription for the upper castes, which could easily translate their access to resources to form/enter the middle class. Whereas given the discriminated social status and lack of resources and opportunities, Dalits and other 'lower castes' could not enter the middle class until the enabling social environment was created by the policies of the government in post-independence period. The provision of access to education and occupations in the modern spheres to the Dalits enabled them to aspire for the middle class position. The emergence of middle class in India is generally attributed to the British who created a section of the educated from among the natives to be employed in middle-level bureaucracy to run the administration. In that process, the literate 'upper castes' were recruited into these 'new' occupations during the initial stages itself and thereby they have continued to hold their dominance in those occupations ever since. However, the aspirations of the lower castes to get into such positions made them improve their educational level and in the process a few of them have succeeded to enter.

In the direction of enabling more numbers of marginal social groups to have access to modern education and employment, in the post-independence period, the Indian state provided reservations for them. Thus, for the first time the Dalits and other marginalized sections who took the benefits of reservations entered modern occupations at all levels. As the social background and orientations of these new entrants are different compared to the 'upper castes' who dominated the middle class, the former are generally considered as 'new middle class' in India. In the case of Dalits, who traversed from untouchable status to 'attaining middle class positions', it seems to possess a distinctive identity and ideology that is necessitated by issues such as self-respect, dignity and underdevelopment of the Dalits in general. Theoretically, the middle class is a non-caste phenomenon, emerging contrary to the traditional ranking of communities. The middle class as a new phenomenon attracts individuals from various caste groups and provides them with a privileged economic status and lifestyle, akin to the economic status and lifestyle thus far enjoyed only by the 'upper castes'.

Here, emerges the question of the discontentment of upper castes towards the new recruits who are 'unduly' enjoying the privileges of upper castes. It often results in caste discrimination in a new non-caste location – the middle class. As a result, the new recruits from the lower sections revive their community identity in self-defence. Such continued intolerance on the part of 'upper castes' towards the upwardly mobile individuals from the lower castes forces the latter to fall back on their own community identity. Thus, the lower castes and the Dalits articulate their traditional (community) identity in a modern context (middle class). They articulate it as a reaction to the attitudes of the upper castes. Given the caste system, which is being in place, it has continued to play a discriminative role in the modern context. This has been clearly brought out by the study wherein Dalits are facing problems in the workplace, social relations and in neighbourhoods.

It is in this context that the need for looking at the economic mobility as well as political ideological formations among the Dalits arises even if it is in the form and level of an individual, and which is apparently unconnected. The process of induction of individuals from non-middle class families into a class that is considered to have achieved much that is otherwise not possible for many other Dalits. In this connection, it is important to understand the transformation and progress among the Dalits. It is very useful to analyse the ideology and identity formation processes among the middle class Dalits who reportedly had been removed from the Dalit reality of suffering, subjugation and thereby are also not eligible to represent the Dalit masses, a view that is held by both Dalits and the caste-Hindus, is significant in more ways than one. While the Dalit masses observe (to some extent from their experience) that the middle class Dalits have been separated from their roots and do not feel for their community any longer, the caste-Hindus, on the other hand, perceive a threat in the mobility of Dalits in general and the existence of the Dalit middle class in particular. The Dalit middle class, thus, faces opposition from the caste-Hindus for closely networking among them and growing independent, advantaged and well placed unlike the poor Dalits. This animosity gets further aggravated when the Dalit middle class organizes itself, for their own cause or for Dalits in general.

Studies that focused on the mobility, class formation, identity patterns or political articulations among the Dalits have indicated that there is a visible intergenerational upward mobility and at the same time, their paternal family's low socio-economic status had a bearing on the level of upward mobility among them. The other socio-economic indicators such as education, occupation and income levels of the middle class Dalits are higher than their paternal families. The Dalits who experienced educational and employment upward mobility were largely concentrated in government service, autonomous institutions, government teaching and research institutions, public sector units, independent professions and private sector. Compared to Dalit men very few Dalit women have entered into the modern professions and occupations. A large number of middle class Dalits today are second-generation employed, nearly half of them having come from agricultural families.

Education is the source of social and economic mobility and a means for joining the middle class. Given that a large number of middle class Dalits are urban and employed in white-collar occupations, education played a deciding role in their entry into the middle class. In certain occupations, technical educational credentials are a prerequisite to obtain/achieve it. The Dalits are provided with concessions (relaxation) in minimum qualification for eligibility as part of reservations in employment in the government sector, nowadays, with the increased internal competition among the Dalits, they possess not only the minimum qualifications but also additional educational qualifications while competing for government jobs.

Middle class Dalits predominantly come from few Scheduled Castes. In correspondence with the general pattern of Dalit population in Andhra Pradesh, the Dalit middle class in the state, especially in Hyderabad, was largely constituted of the two numerically dominant castes, namely, Madiga and Mala. As numerically dominant, these two major communities accessed all mobility options and formed more than 85 per cent of the Dalit middle class. Among these upwardly mobile Dalits, marriages were arranged with partners, not only within but also outside their community, with friends and acquaintances acting as mediators. In a considerable number of love marriages, a partner from outside the community was the norm rather than partners from within the community. The pattern of marriage among the middle class Dalits illustrated that while arranged marriages were the norm, love marriages were also widely prevalent among the upwardly mobile Dalits.

The economic status of middle class Dalits' paternal family played a major role in shaping up their future. This was evident in many respects, their educational level, career options and the current economic status. In all instances, there was upward mobility among the middle class Dalits compared to their paternal and maternal families. The educational profile of parents and grandparents suggests that the majority of the middle class Dalits were first-generation educated. In a few instances, wherein either the parents or the grandparents were educated, they had benefited in terms of resources and guidance with respect to their education and career. Second- or third-generation educated middle class Dalits were highly educated than the first-generation educated. This indicated that Dalits had access to education only in recent times. Apart from that, Dalit men had the privilege of being highly educated than Dalit women. The educational profile of the middle class Dalits' fathers, mothers and grandparents shows that the majority among all the three categories were predominantly illiterate. The pattern of occupation too corresponded with that of education, placing fathers over mothers and grandparents. Similarly, Dalit men were better placed in modern occupations than Dalit women. The economic status of middle class Dalits is mainly dependent on their income they earn from the occupation or profession. Also it is influenced by the dependence of their parents, siblings, relatives, friends and acquaintances for needs such as shelter, economic support, career advice and recommendation. These dependency patterns show that the higher the economic status of middle class Dalits, higher the dependence, and it has a bearing on their lifestyle and further upward mobility chances.

Reservations in education and employment have played a major role in the occupational and economic mobility among Dalits, without reservations almost none of the present members of the Dalit middle class would have made it into the middle class at all. Even in the case of those middle class Dalits who had not availed reservations, utilization of reservations by their earlier generations might have initiated the process of economic mobility. In the present study, almost all middle class Dalits had availed reservations at various stages of their life, namely, education and employment.

Dalits both in rural and urban areas are prone to caste discrimination of various kinds and levels. Middle class Dalits, who hail from a rural background, have experience of varied forms and intensity of caste discrimination. After being removed from a social and economic setting where severe caste restrictions are enforced on Dalits, the middle class Dalits may or may not perceive similar caste discrimination in their present setting. Those who perceive some form or level of caste discrimination might be having a sufficient basis for the same or it could be because of their experience that they perceive it larger than its original proportion. Thus, their present social setting prompts them either to act against it or tolerate it. In the context of middle class Dalits, two possible contexts of caste discrimination, that is the workplace from their superiors and colleagues (discrimination experienced in career growth) and in the neighbourhood has a bearing on their work and personal life, thus limiting their mobility. This leads the middle class Dalits towards ethnocentrism, mobilization on caste lines and collective action (through the formation of SC/ST Welfare Associations to fight such problems).

Unlike the general middle class, the middle class Dalits have become part of that class due to the achieved (economic) mobility. Most of the middle class Dalits are solely dependent on the income they earn from their present occupation or profession. Their income and expenditure patterns suggest that their economic status is not in congruence with their income levels. In most cases, middle class Dalits are the sole earning members of the family and the main source of income is their occupation or profession. Considering the fact that many of the middle class Dalits were first generation of economically upward mobile in their families, they have financial and other responsibilities to support their paternal family, and often their expenses exceed their income. Comparatively, employees have larger incomes than the majority of professionals. Notwithstanding the practice among the middle class in general, a major chunk of middle class Dalits' expenditure is towards household expenses, on the other hand, assets creation, children's education and other needs formed a negligible percentage.

Though the middle class Dalits have a middle class income and lifestyle, the second-generation Dalits are often living in poorer localities than the middle class localities as the middle class, posh localities are predominantly occupied by other communities. However, unlike in the past, the first-generation migrants to the city are educated and employed in modern occupations. In the case of predominantly second- or third-generation migrants, their families have migrated long back and witnessed economic mobility; therefore, they are now placed in middle class localities. Increasingly, middle class Dalits are acquiring own houses or living in rented houses in either non-Dalit localities or a locality with mixed population compared to exclusive Dalit localities. A vast majority of them still live in rented houses and only one-third of them have own houses. Except few, the majority of the middle class Dalits do not have stakes in agricultural lands at their native place as they are the most economically well off in their families and have given up their share for their siblings' or parents' subsistence needs. A few others showed interest in family-related agricultural activities by providing financial inputs sporadically, but also expected returns from such investments.

Few lifestyle aspects of middle class Dalits, namely, consumption pattern, religious practices, interpersonal relations and so on, reveal that there is a change in their lifestyle, especially among those who come from a poor economic background. However, most of the middle class Dalits are not alien to these lifestyle practices of middle class, even those who come from rural and poor backgrounds too experienced or witnessed them during their education, well in advance to make themselves acquainted with the middle class lifestyle. There was a noticeable surge in terms of qualitative changes in the middle class Dalits' lifestyle after entering into their present occupation/profession; these were largely related to food habits and dressing among the middle class Dalits and language among middle class Dalits. Interestingly, these two aspects either witnessed an increase in terms of quantity and quality or remained the same.

Interpersonal relationships at the workplace are ideally caste, class and ethnicity neutral, in the case of middle class Dalits forging of alliances other than friendship, camaraderie or acquaintance in various occupations and professions are generally formed on caste lines. In some instances, they were direct and openly visible and in others, they were discreet and hard to prove. In personal friendships, the Dalits have no particular preference for their own community; like others, they too have friends from all castes. However, proximity of such friendships varies significantly between friends from own and other communities. In such friendships, occupation and age facilitate them in forming friendships across various gender, class, caste and age groups. This is mainly due to the commonality they had with middle class members from other communities. However, these social interactions were individual in nature, did not involve their families and were not an indication of the assimilation of different communities. On the other hand, interpersonal relations in the neighbourhood are still marked with the limitations of caste. Forming friendships on mutually agreeable terms in the neighbourhood, suiting all their interests was difficult compared to an office or the workplace. As family-level interactions involved social and religious occasions, their preferences lay towards their own community rather than other communities. However, gradually there is a change towards increased interaction, even at family levels.

The middle class Dalits retain close community connections with other Dalits, namely, family, colleagues and acquaintances either living in the city or in native places. As their assimilation into the general middle class is incomplete, many middle class Dalits give priority to their social relations within their own community. Other Dalits, they interact with include those who have political leadership, high-rank bureaucratic positions and economically successful business/enterprise ventures. Often, such individuals are non-relatives, outside their professional acquaintances and are role models to many Dalits. Taking inspiration from each other, middle class Dalits either initiate or participate in individual and collective activities for development of Dalits.

The identity patterns of middle class Dalits indicate their social milieu, economic roles, status identification and aspirations. The constant exposure to circumstances that evoke community consciousness and identity assertion, the middle class Dalits identity revolves around the community. However, the self-identification is often marked with identity preferences away from the community centric. The same becomes evident in their perceptions of ascribed identity that other Dalits perceiving them as essentially Dalits and non-Dalits as middle class. Thus, the Dalit identity is an in-group identity and identification with the profession or being middle class is a new identity, they present to non-Dalits. Further, the status differentiation between Dalits and non-Dalits reflects on their own acquisition or lack of cultural capital, middle class lifestyle and social integration.

The middle class Dalits are members of various Dalit organizations and political parties or SC/ST employees' associations. This is more prevalent among the officer cadre employees of various public sector organizations than among the professionals. This is in accordance with their participation in various movements and political mobilizations. On many occasions, they work in collaboration with other organizations and political movements as they feel that it is essential to align with other like-minded social groups and/or political organizations in the pursuit of socio-economic and political equality for Dalits.

The Dalit middle class engages with Dalit identity and economic inequality like it does grapple with group identity and self-respect. They see an intrinsic relationship between Dalit identity and economic inequality. Thus, they are considering a consolidated identity and cohesive ideology as a solution to address the economic inequality. They make a distinction between Dalits and others in Indian society and advocate for specific development model for Dalits, especially in the context of privatization and globalization. Their perceptions about the contemporary nature of caste and its impact on Dalits indicate that they are wary of the pervasiveness of caste, the influence of Brahminism even today. Thus, their worldview is largely shaped by their life experiences and expectations pre- and post-mobility. Their articulations of self- and community identity are pointing in the direction of a direct political action and their willingness to be in the centre of it.

Middle class Dalits articulate their Dalit identity more clearly than the poor Dalits in villages and city slums. Deprivation, discrimination and atrocities might not be part of their daily life, but the sense of alienation, rejection and difference certainly are. Their daily life does not necessitate them to feel 'untouchables' but their interaction with non-Dalits, especially individuals from 'upper castes' – who consider themselves superior to Dalits – prompts them to fall back on Dalit identity. For Dalits, gaining entry into the middle class is a lot easier than becoming acceptable to other members of that class. Many invisible barriers restrict the middle class Dalits from acquiring a middle class attitude, behaviour and disposition.

The very process of emergence of Dalit middle class necessitates uniqueness in its location, characteristics and politics. Unlike the general middle class, which is formed on the lines of the hierarchical structure of the society with asymmetry based on ascription as its central character, the Dalit middle class is constituted largely through competition among individuals characteristically based on achievement. In the formation of Dalit middle class, a vivid upward mobility of the very best and often more talented among the Dalits takes place. The commonality of shared traits, similar background and a collective future propels the individual recruits of the Dalit middle class to hover together. Similarly, the external environment, particularly their interaction with the caste-Hindus, has a bearing on their integration into the middle class.

The very emergence of Dalit middle class is attributed to the reservations policy. It runs contrary to the expectations of the independent Indian state that prioritized the goal of achieving integration in society over quicker development of disadvantaged groups, thereby choosing reservation system over community-based 'special development packages'. Thus, reservations policy was originally aimed at individual-based upward mobility among the Dalits, with an intention to integrate them into the 'mainstream'. The very emergence of a Dalit middle class suggests that it is distinctively separate from the general middle class, in its own identity and politics. Often, it is opposed to the ideals, values of the general middle class; the same is manifested in its own priorities and politics. As its social composition, formation process and shared values and beliefs indicate that the Dalit middle class is ordained to be distinct from the general middle class.

The ideals, values and goals nurtured and developed by the Dalit middle class suggest that it is developing a grand vision of achieving socio-heconomic and political equality for the Dalits on par with others. The very fostering of a separate identity away from the general middle class is a product of a protest ideology that has been shaping up through the centuries. The protest ideology that was articulated by Ambedkar is now being received by the middle class Dalits. Thus, Dalit middle class is interpreting, reshaping and developing a more comprehensive Dalit ideology. It is being shaped by the common experiences and collective beliefs as Dalits belonging to the middle class.

References

Abbasayulu, Y.B., 1978, *Scheduled Caste Elite: Study of Scheduled Caste Elite in Andhra Pradesh*, Book Links Corporation, Hyderabad.

Aggarwal, P.C., 1983, *Halfway to Equality*, Manohar, New Delhi.

Ahmed, L.N. and H. Ahmed, 1964, The Politics of Social Mobility in India: A Hypothesis, *Indian Journal of Social Research*, 5 (3), pp. 236–244.

Aiyappan, A., 1965, *Social Revolution in a Kerala Village: A Study in Cultural Change*, Asia Publishing House, Bombay.

Ambedkar, B.R., 1946, *Annihilation of Caste*, The Bharat Bhushan Press, Bombay.

Aron, Raymond, 1950, Social Structure and the Ruling Class: Part 1, *Journal of British Sociology*, Vol. 1, No. 1 (March, 1950), pp. 1–16.

Augustine, P.A., 1991, *Social Equality in Indian Society: The Elusive Goal*, Concept Publications, New Delhi.

Bell, Daniel, 1974, *The Coming of Post Industrial Society*, Arnold-Heinemann Publishers (India) Pvt. Ltd., Delhi.

Bendix, Reinhard and Seymour Martin Lipset, 1966, *Class, Status and Power: Social Stratification in Contemporary Perspective*, Routledge & Kegan Paul, London.

Bendix, Reinhard, 1956, *Work and Authority in Industry: Ideologies of Management in the Course of Industrialization*, Wiley, New York and London.

Bottomore, T.B., 1964, *Elites and Society*, C.A. Watts, London.

Braverman, Harry, 1979, *Labour and Monopoly Capital*, Social Scientist Press, Trivandrum.

Broom, L. and P. Selznick, 1970, *Principles of Sociology*, 4th Ed., Harper and Row, New York.

Charsley, S.R. and G.K. Karanth (Eds), 1998, *Challenging Untouchability: Dalit Initiative and Experience from Karnataka*, Sage, New Delhi.

Charsley, S.R., 1996, 'Untouchable': What is in a Name?, *Journal of Royal Anthropological Institute*, (N.S.) 2, pp. 1–23.

Chibbar, Y.P., 1968, *From Caste to Class: A Study of Indian Middle Class*, Associated Publishing House, New Delhi.

Cole, G.D.H., 1955, *Studies in Class Structure*, Routledge & Kegan Paul, London.

Crompton, R. and J. Gubbay, 1977, *Economy and Class Structure*, St. Martin's Press, New York.

Croner, Fritz, 1954, *Die Angestellten in der modernen Gesellschaft*, Frankfurt am Main, Wien and Humboldt-Verlag, Vienna.

Dahrendorf, R., 1959, *Class and Class Conflict in Industrial Society*, Routledge & Kegan Paul, London.

Damle, Y.B. and K.S. Nair, 1982, Protective Discrimination: A Sociological Perspective, *Social Change*, December, 12 (4), pp. 6–12.

Damodaran, H., 2008, *India's New Capitalists: Caste, Business, and Industry in a Modern Nation*, Palgrave Macmillan, New York.

Desai, A.R., 2000 (1948), *Social Background of Indian Nationalism*, Popular Prakashan, Bombay.

Deshpande, S., 2003, *Contemporary India: A Sociological View*, Penguin Books, Delhi.

Dube, S.C., 1988, Foreword, in Nandu Ram's *The Mobile Scheduled Castes: Rise of a New Middle Class*, Hindustan Publishing Corporation, New Delhi.

Dubey, S.M., 1972, *Social Mobility among the Professions: Study of the Professions in a Transitional Indian City*, Popular Prakashan, Bombay.

——. 1975 (1971), *Modernization and Elites in Arunachal Pradesh*, Census of India, Delhi.

Dushkin, L., 1972, Scheduled Caste Politics, in J.M. Mahar (Ed.), *The Untouchables in Contemporary India*, University of Arizona Press, Tucson.

Friedman, J., 1992, The Past in the Future: History and the Politics of Identity, *American Anthropologist*, New Series, December, 94 (4), pp. 837–859.

Ghurye, G.S., 1969, *Caste and Race in India*, Popular Prakashan, Bombay.

Glass, D.V. and J.R. Hall, 1967 (1954), Social Mobility in Great Britain: A Study of Inter-Generational Changes in Status, in D.V. Glass (Ed.), *Social Mobility in Britain*, Routledge & Kegan Paul, London.

Gokhale, J.B., 1990, The Evolution of a Counter Ideology: Dalit Consciousness in Maharashtra, in F. Frankel and M.S.A. Rao (Eds), *Dominance and State Power in Modern India*, Vol. II, Oxford University Press, Delhi.

——. 1993, *From Concessions to Confrontation: The Politics of an Indian Untouchable Community*, Popular Prakashan, Bombay.

Goldthorpe, L. et al., 1968, *The Affluent Worker: Political Attitudes and Behaviour*, Cambridge University Press, London.

Gore, M.S., 1993, *The Social Context of an Ideology: Ambedkar's Political and Social Thought*, Sage, New Delhi.

Guru, G., 1984, Reservations and the Sanskritization of Scheduled Castes: Some Theoretical Aspects, *Sociological Bulletin*, 33 (1/2), pp. 29–38.

——. 1993, Dalit Movement in Mainstream Sociology, *Economic and Political Weekly*, 3 April.

——. 2002, Dalit Middle Class Hangs in the Air, in Ahmad Imtiaz and Helmut Reifeld (Eds), *Middle Class Values in India and Western Europe*, Social Science Press, New Delhi.

Heimsath, C.H., 1964, *Indian Nationalism and Hindu Social Reform*, Princeton University Press, Princeton.

Issacs, H., 1965 (1964), *India's Ex-Untouchables*, Asia Publishing House, Bombay.

Jain, P.C., S. Jain and S. Bhatnagar, 1997, *Scheduled Caste Women*, Rawat Publications, Jaipur.

Jain, Sagar C., 1971, *Indian Manager: His Social Origin and Career*, Somaiya Publications Pvt. Ltd., Bombay.

Jayaram, N., 1977, Higher Education as Status Stabilizer: Students in Bangalore, *Contributions to Indian Sociology*, 11 (1), pp. 169–191.

Jeffrey, R., 2001, [Not] Being There: Dalits and India's Newspapers, *South Asia*, XXIV (2), pp. 225–238.

Jesudason, Victor, 1977, Some Correlates in the Process of Recruitment into Elite Status through Higher Education Abroad, *Social Change*, 7 (2).

Jodhka, S.S., 2010, Engaging with Caste: Academic Discourses, Identity Politics and State Policy, Working Paper Series, Indian Institute of Dalit Studies and UNICEF, 2 (2).

Jogdand, P.G., 1999, Reservation Policy and Empowerment of Dalits, in S.M. Michael (Ed.), *Dalits in Modern India: Vision and Values*, Vistaar Publications, New Delhi.

Kananaikil, J., 1983, *Scheduled Castes and the Struggle against Inequality: Strategies to Empower the Marginalized*, Indian Social Institute, New Delhi.

——. 1993, The Emerging Dalit Identity, *Social Action*, October–December, 43, pp. 401–411.

Kerr, Clark, John T. Dunlop, Frederick Harbison and Charles A. Myers, 1960, The Logic of Industrialism, in *Industrialism and Industrial Man: The Problems of Labor and Management in Economic Growth*, Harvard University Press, Cambridge.

Khan, M.A., 1994, *Identity Formation and Self Identity among Harijan Elite*, Uppal Publishing House, New Delhi.

Khare, R.S., 1984, *The Untouchable as Himself: Ideology, Identity and Pragmatism among the Lucknow Chamars*, Cambridge University Press, Cambridge.

King, A.D., 1970, Elite Education and the Economy - IIT Entrance: 1965–70, *Economic and Political Weekly*, 5 (35), pp. 1463–1472.

Knowles, L.C.A., 2006 (1921), *The Industrial and Commercial Revolutions in Great Britain during the Nineteenth Century*, Routledge & Kegan Paul, London.

Krausz, E., 1969, *Sociology in Modern Britain: A Survey of Research*, Batsford, London.

Kulke, E., 1976, Integration, Alienation and Rejection: The Status of Untouchables, in S. Devadas Pillai (Ed.), *Aspects of Changing India*, Popular Prakashan, Bombay.

——. 1983, The Problems of the Educated Middle Class Harijans, in John P. Neelsen (Ed.), *Social Inequality and Political Structures*, Manohar, New Delhi.

Lal, S.K., 1974, *The Urban Elite*, Thomson Press, Delhi.

——. 1995, Approaches to the Identification of Elites in Social Inequality, in K.L. Sharma (Ed.), *India: Profiles of Caste, Class, Power and Social Mobility*, Rawat Publications, Jaipur.

Lasswell, H.D., 1952, *The Comparative Study of Elites: An Introduction and Bibliography*, Stanford University Press, Stanford.

Lederer, Emil and Jakob Marschak, 1926, Der neue Mittelstand, in *Grundriss der Sozialökonomik*, Section IX, Part I, Tübingen.

Malik, S., 1979, *Social Integration of Scheduled Castes*, Abhinav, New Delhi.

Mannheim, Karl, 1940 (1935), *Man and Society in an Age of Reconstruction: Studies in Modern Social Structure*, Harcourt, New York.

Mathew, J., 1986, *Ideology, Protest and Social Mobility: Case Study of Mahars and Pulayas*, Inter-India Publications, New Delhi.

Matto, A., 1991, *Reform Movement and Social Transformation in India*, Reliance Publishing House, New Delhi.

Mayer, K.B., 1963, The Changing Shape of the American Class Structure, *Social Research*, Winter, 30 (4), pp. 458–468.

Mendelsohn, O. and M. Vicziany, 2000, *The Untouchables: Subordination, Poverty and the State in Modern India*, Cambridge University Press (Foundation Books), New Delhi.

Mendelsohn, O., 1986, A 'Harijan Elite'? The Lives of Some Untouchable Politicians, *Economic and Political Weekly*, 22 March, 21 (12), pp. 501–509.

Mills, C. Wright, 1946, The Middle Classes in Middle Sized Cities, *The American Sociological Review*, December, 11, pp. 520–529.

——. 1956 (1951), *White Collar: The American Middle Classes*, Oxford University Press, New York.

Misra, B.B., 1961, *The Indian Middle Classes: Their Growth in Modern Times*, Oxford University Press, London.

Mosca, G., 1933, *The Ruling Class*, McGraw Hill, New York.

Mukherjee, P., 1988, *Beyond the Four Varnas: The Untouchables in India*, Indian Institute of Advanced Study, Shimla and Motilal Banarsidass, Delhi.

Nadel, S.F., 1956, The Concept of Social Elites, *The International Social Science Bulletin*, Vol. 8 (413–24).

Nagaraj D.R., 1993, *The Flaming Feet: A Study of the Dalit Movement in India*, South Forum Press, Bangalore.

Navlakha, S., 1989, *Elite and Social Change: A Study of Elite Formation in India*, Sage, Delhi.

Omvedt, G., 1994, *Dalits and Democratic Revolution: Dr Ambedkar and the Dalit Movement in Colonial India*, Sage, New Delhi.

——. 2001, The Dalits: Dynamic Upsurge, *The Week*, 30 December.

——. 2004, *Untouchables in the World of IT, Panos Features*, February, http://www.indiasocial.org/cgi/news.asp?id=3048&sel=1.

Oommen, T.K., 1968, Strategy for Social Change: A Study of Untouchability, *Economic and Political Weekly*, 22 June, 3 (25).

——. 1977, Sociological Issues in the Analysis of Social Movements in Independent India, *Sociological Bulletin*, 26 (1), pp. 14–37.

——. 1994, Panchamas to Dalits: The Context and Content of Identity, *Times of India*, 11 May.

Pandey, G., 2009, Can There be a Subaltern Middle Class? Notes on African American and Dalit History, *Public Culture*, 21 (2), pp. 321–342.

Patwardhan, S., 1973, *Change among India's Harijans*, Orient Longman, Delhi.

Philips, W.S.K., 1990, *Social Stratification and Mobility in Urban India*, Rawat Publications, Jaipur.

Pimpley, P.N., 1990, Social Reform for the Untouchables: Some Issues for Examination, in Rajeshwar Prasad (Ed.), *Social Reforms: An Analysis of Indian Society*, Y.K. Publications, Agra.

Pinkney, A., 1984, *The Myth of Black Progress*, Cambridge University Press, Cambridge.

Prakash, N., 1989, *Scheduled Castes: Socio-Economic Change*, Chuge Publications, Allahabad.

Prasad, B., 1968, *Socio-economic Study of Urban Middle Classes*, Sterling Publishers Pvt. Ltd., Delhi.

Prasad, N., 1970, *Change Strategy in a Developing Society in India*, Meenakshi Prakashan, Meerut.

Pushpendra, 1999, Dalit Assertion through Electoral Politics, *Economic and Political Weekly*, 34 (36), pp. 2609–2618.

Raj, M.C., 1998, *From Periphery to Centre: Analysis of the Paradigm of Globalization, Casteism and Dalitism*, Ambedkar Resource Centre, REDS, Tumkur.

Rajora, S.C., 1987, *Social Structure and Tribal Elites*, Himanshu Publications, New Delhi.

Ram, N., 1988, *The Mobile Scheduled Castes: Rise of a New Middle Class*, Hindustan Publishing Corporation, New Delhi.

——. 1995, *Beyond Ambedkar: Essays on Dalits in India*, Har-Anand Publications, New Delhi.

Ramaswamy, U., 1974, Scheduled Castes in Andhra: Some Aspects of Social Change, *Economic and Political Weekly*, 9 (29), pp. 1153–1158.

Rao, M.S.A., 1967, Educational Social Stratification and Mobility, in M.S. Gore, I.P. Desai and S. Chitins (Eds), *Papers in Sociology of Education in India*, NCERT, New Delhi.

——. 1972, *Tradition, Rationality and Change: Essays in Sociology of Economic Development and Social Change*, Popular Prakashan, Bombay.

Reddy, G.N., 1984, Scheduled Castes Movement, *Voluntary Action*, November.

Renner, Karl, 1924, *Die Wirtschaft als Gesamtproxess und die Soxialisierung*, Berlin.

——. 1952, *Mensch und Gesellschaft: Grundriss einer Soziologie*, Verlag der Wiener Volksbuchhandlung, Wien.

Richardson, C.J., 1977, *Contemporary Social Mobility*, Nichols Publishing Company, New Delhi.

Roy, R. and V.B. Singh, 1987, *Between Two Worlds: A Study of Harijan Elites*, Discovery Publishing House, Delhi.

Ruben, Walter, 1957, Die Lage der Sklaven in der altindischen Gesellschaft, Akademie-Verlag, Berlin as quoted in Prabhati Mukherjee, 1988, *Beyond the Four Varnas: The Untouchables in India*, Indian Institute of Advanced Study, Shimla.

Saavala, M., 2001, Low Caste but Middle Class: Some Religious Strategies for Middle Class Identification in Hyderabad, *Contributions to Indian Sociology*, 35 (3), pp. 295–318.

Saberwal, S., 1972, Status, Mobility, and Networks in a Punjabi Industrial Town, in S. Saberwal (Ed.), *Beyond the Village: Sociological Explorations*, Indian Institute of Advanced Study, Shimla.

——. 1976, *Mobile Men: Limits to Social Change in Urban Punjab*, Vikas, Delhi.

Sachidananda, 1974, *The Harijan Elite*, Thomson, New Delhi.

Sau, R., 1986, *Economy, Class, Society*, University Press, Madras.

Selvanathan, S., 1989, *Status of Scheduled Castes*, Ashish Publishing House, New Delhi.

Shah, G., 1985, Anti-Untouchability Movements, in I.P. Desai et al. (Eds), *Caste Conflict and Reservations*, Ajantha Publications, New Delhi.

——. 1990, *Social Movements in India: A Review of Literature*, Sage, New Delhi.

——. 1994, Identity, Communal Consciousness and Politics, *Economic and Political Weekly*, 7 May, pp. 1133–1140.

Shah, G. (Ed.), 2002a, *Dalits and the State*, Concept Publishing Company, New Delhi.

——. 2002b, *Caste and Democratic Politics in India*, Permanent Black, Delhi.

Sharma, B.R., 1976, Professionals in the Making: Their Social Origin, Review of Management, *Economic and Political Weekly*, 11 (9), pp. M5-M10.

Sharma, K.L., 1986, *Caste, Class and Social Movements*, Rawat Publications, Jaipur.

——. 2001, *Reconceptualising Caste, Class and Tribe*, Rawat Publications, Jaipur.

——. 2006 (1994), *Social Stratification & Mobility*, Rawat Publications, Jaipur.

Sharma, K.N., 1986, Dynamics of Structuration: A Note, in S.C. Malik (Ed.), *Determinants of Social Status in India*, Indian Institute of Advanced Study, Shimla.

Sheth, D.L., 1999, Secularization of Caste and Making of New Middle Class, *Economic and Political Weekly*, 21–28 August, 34 (34–35), pp. 2502–2510.

Singh, G., 1985, *The New Middle Class in India: A Sociological Analysis*, Rawat Publications, Jaipur.

Singh, S., 1987, *Scheduled Castes of India: Dimensions of Social Change*, Gian Publishing House, Delhi.

Singh, Y., 1986, *Modernisation of Indian Tradition*, Rawat Publications, Jaipur.

——. 1995, Integration of Marginalized Groups into Indian Society: The Case of the Scheduled Castes, Scheduled Tribes and Backward Classes, in Muchkund Dubey (Ed.), *Indian Society Today: Challenges of Equality, Integration and Empowerment*, Har-Anand Publications, New Delhi.

Sinha, Surjeet, 1974, Caste in India: A Trend Report, in ICSSR (Ed.), *Survey Research in Sociology and Social Anthropology*, Vol. III, Popular Prakashan, Bombay, pp. 233–275.

Sorokin, P.A., 1959 (1927), *Social and Cultural Mobility*, The Free Press, New York.

Srinivas, G., 1996, *Intersecting Identities: A Study of the Dalit Middle Class in Hyderabad*, M. Phil. Dissertation, Mimeo, University of Hyderabad.

Srinivas, M.N., 1966, *Social Change in Modern India*, Orient Longman, Delhi.

——. 1989, *The Cohesive Role of Sanskritization and Other Essays*, Oxford University Press, Delhi.

Srinivas, M.N. (Ed.), 1996, *Caste: Its Twentieth Century Avatar*, Penguin Books, New Delhi.

Stub, Holger R., 1972, The Concept of Status Community, in Holger R. Stub (Ed.), *Status Communities in Modern Society*, Dryden Press, Hinsdale.

Tewari, B.N., 1998, Semiology of Dalit Consciousness: A North Indian Experience, *Eastern Anthropologist*, 51 (2), pp. 170–184.

Tripathy, R.B., 1994, *Dalits: A Sub-human Society*, Ashish Publishing House, New Delhi.

Vakil, A.K., 1985, *Reservation Policy and Scheduled Castes in India*, Ashish Publishing House, New Delhi.

van Dijk, T.A., 1998, *Ideology: A Multidisciplinary Approach*, Sage, London.

Venkateswarlu, D., 1987, Psychological Conflict between Harijans and Upper Castes/Middle Class Caste Hindus: A Study in Andhra Pradesh, *Sociological Bulletin*, 36 (1), pp. 77–98.

Vishwanathan, G. and K. Narasimha Reddy, 1985, *Scheduled Castes: A Study in Educational Achievement*, Scientific Services, Hyderabad.

Warner, W.L., 1957 (1949), *Social Class in America*, Chicago.

Weber, M., 1953 (1946), *From Max Weber: Essays in Sociology*, H.H. Gerth and C.W. Mills (Eds and Trans), New York: Oxford University Press.

Webster, J.C.B., 1992, *The Dalit Christians: A History*, ISPCK, Delhi.

——. 1999, Who is a Dalit?, in S.M. Michael (Ed.), *Dalits in Modern India: Vision and Values*, Vistaar Publications, Delhi.

Whyte, W.H., Jr., 1956, *The Organization Man*, Doubleday Anchor Books, New York.

Zelliot, E., 1992, *From Untouchable to Dalit: Essays on the Ambedkar Movement*, Manohar, New Delhi.

Index